# CROSSFIRE HURRICANE

# CROSSFIRE HURRICANE

## INSIDE DONALD TRUMP'S WAR ON THE FBI

## JOSH CAMPBELL

ALGONQUIN BOOKS OF CHAPEL HILL   2019

Published by

ALGONQUIN BOOKS OF CHAPEL HILL
Post Office Box 2225
Chapel Hill, North Carolina 27515-2225

a division of
WORKMAN PUBLISHING
225 Varick Street
New York, New York 10014

A Cataloging-in-Publication record for this title is on file with the Library of Congress.

10 9 8 7 6 5 4 3 2 1
First Edition

*To the men and women of the FBI,*
*both past and present,*
*whose professionalism remains unparalleled.*

There are some things you learn best in calm, and some in storm.
—WILLA CATHER, *The Song of the Lark*


When you're attacking FBI agents because you're under criminal investigation, you're losing.
—SARAH SANDERS, *spokesperson for Donald Trump*

# CONTENTS

# CROSSFIRE HURRICANE

# PROLOGUE

---

As THE DOOR of the Gulfstream sprang open, a frigid blast of winter air filled the cabin of the jet. The hissing of its engines soon spooled down to a faded hum, and the security agents on board began making their final preparations for our arrival. They checked weapons, tested radio communications, and ran through the schedule one last time to ensure that every movement was scripted, down to the smallest detail. During this flurry of activity, our main passenger sat calmly in front of me, nodding in rhythm to a John Legend song playing over his wireless headphones.

"No turning back now," FBI director James Comey told me with a half smile, a nod to the unprecedented meeting that awaited him.

Two dark SUVs, flanked by police cruisers with flashing lights, pulled up to the stairs of the aircraft, and the lead security agent gave me the thumbs-up. It was only when I hit the doorway that I realized we had pulled directly alongside a Boeing 757 emblazoned with the word TRUMP on the fuselage. I had seen this impressive machine before, during trips that brought me through New York's LaGuardia Airport, and on one occasion I'd even caught a glimpse of Donald Trump himself, barreling out of a Chevrolet Suburban driven by Secret Service agents, his phone pressed to his ear as he climbed the jet's stairs, no doubt on his way to yet another campaign stop as he attempted to overcome long odds in a vitriolic election cycle. But now, as I stood there staring at a gigantic airplane with the Trump name painted in gold, I couldn't help but marvel at the showmanship and branding skills of the man who had just been elected leader of the free world. For Comey, it was now time to meet the new boss.

It was January 6, 2017, two weeks before Donald J. Trump would take the oath of office and assume the role of commander in chief, responsible for protecting the United States against all enemies, foreign and domestic. Comey had flown to New York to join his counterparts in the national security community to brief the president-elect and his transition team on their findings on actions the Kremlin had taken to interfere in the 2016 US presidential election.

Whether countering terrorists seeking to kill innocent Americans, identifying cybercriminals probing our critical national infrastructure, or uncovering foreign spies working to undermine our sacred electoral process, the mission of the men and women of the US intelligence community is a deadly serious one. The four men who traveled to New York that morning had spent nearly their entire adult lives working to protect the United States from foreign adversaries. They would now channel their expertise into a briefing intended to equip the incoming chief executive with the knowledge and tools necessary to counter an ongoing—and serious—threat to the nation.

But the director of the Federal Bureau of Investigation had one additional duty that day, something the chiefs of the Central Intelligence Agency, the National Security Agency, and the Office of the Director of National Intelligence would get a pass on. For months, a series of memos had been privately circulating among members of the media and across government that contained unverified but explosive charges against then candidate Trump. As the world now knows, Christopher Steele, a former officer with the United Kingdom's Secret Intelligence Service (MI6), had been contracted by a private investigative firm to look into Trump's background. Steele, a veteran operative, drafted a series of memos describing information about compromising material that Russian intelligence services had purportedly obtained on Trump. In addition to outlining allegations of illegal business practices that might result in Russia having leverage over Trump, the "Steele dossier," as it would become known, also included tawdry alleged details of Trump's sexual proclivities and illicit acts conducted while in Moscow. At one point, Steele thought the information so potentially damning that he approached the FBI and provided it with his reporting.

In fact, Steele was not the only one concerned that Trump might be in a compromising position with the Russians. Two powerful Republican senators had already separately approached the FBI director expressing their dismay at the revelations the former British spy had possibly unearthed. In November 2016, when Comey was speaking with legislators on Capitol Hill, Senate Intelligence Committee Chair Richard Burr (R-NC) pulled Comey aside to warn him of something very troubling. Their conversation had gone unreported until now.

"There is some material circulating," Burr whispered cryptically. "It has some disturbing things in it. I just want to make sure you're tracking."

"We are," Comey said.

"I don't need to know any more about it," Burr said, expressing his respect for the FBI's independence in addressing possible counterintelligence threats. "I just felt like I needed to make sure you were aware."

Then, in December 2016, Senator John McCain called our office and indicated that he needed to come see Comey. He brought with him a single envelope, the contents of which were a mystery to us as the senior statesman slowly walked past me and down the long walkway into Comey's office.

"He had returned from the annual Halifax defense conference in Nova Scotia," Comey later told me, "and someone he knew had given him Christopher Steele's material. He had read it enough to realize he needed to give it to me."

"I don't know what to make of this," McCain had told him, "but I know enough to know you should have it. You don't need to talk to me about it ever again."

"Thank you," Comey responded. He did not acknowledge that the FBI already had the same material.

The four intelligence chiefs decided Comey should brief the incoming president on the salacious material one-on-one, both because the FBI had originally received the information and because Comey was the only one in the group who was guaranteed to remain on the job when the new administration came in. (Unlike the heads of the other intelligence agencies, the director of the FBI serves a statutorily mandated ten-year term, and Comey was in year three.) Conscious of the personal embarrassment this sensitive brief might cause the president-elect, the FBI director opted to discuss it with Trump separately at the end of the larger briefing on Russian interference.

As our two dark Suburbans neared Trump Tower, we faced a predicament: we were early. Director of National Intelligence James Clapper, CIA director John Brennan, and NSA director Michael Rogers had all flown into Newark Liberty International Airport and were still fighting Midtown Manhattan traffic, even with marked units from the NYPD clearing their path. There was no way Comey wanted to arrive ahead of the others and break the united front the agency heads had agreed upon, and he also didn't want to find himself sitting in some reception room—with Trump transition staffers engaging him in chitchat—something he loathed to his core.

I had learned this about him early on in my tenure as his special assistant, when Comey was set to join an elected politician at an event and I'd assumed that I should carve out time for the two men to meet privately beforehand to catch up. "You assumed wrong," Comey had said dryly, taking a blue felt-tip pen out of his jacket pocket and crossing that part off the draft schedule before him in an overly dramatic fashion. It wasn't that he disliked the person; he just had little patience for politics. "I also see you've seated the two of us together," he'd said, striking through the seating chart with another stroke of the pen. "You sit next to him!"

On our drive to Trump Tower, I asked the agent seated up front to slow our roll, and he eventually found an open space a few blocks away where we could pull over and wait for the others to catch up.

"Do you have the laptop?" Comey inquired, the third time he had asked me that day.

"Check," I replied, pointing to the vehicle behind us, where an FBI communications specialist sat with a secure bag containing a laptop computer that was certified for the transmission of information classified as Top Secret.

Although the FBI director travels with an array of specialized equipment that keeps him connected 24/7 to the White House and the rest of the nation's command authority, this was the first time in my nine months working directly for him that Comey had ever asked me to make a laptop available to him immediately following a meeting. This may sound like a menial task, but Comey wanted me to understand that it was a vitally important one. Aware of the unprecedented nature of an FBI director confronting a newly elected president with explosive material about his personal life, coupled with the fact that the president's campaign was secretly under investigation for its possible ties to Russia, Comey wanted to make certain that he fully documented the interaction in writing. He would later tell me he knew it was possible the president-elect might one day lie about the exchange if it ever came to light.

It would be the first of many meetings he would feel the need to memorialize.

"They're two minutes out," the lead security agent said over his shoulder, whispering a series of instructions to his team into the microphone clipped to the shirtsleeve at his wrist. He advised us that our vehicles and the three others carrying the national intelligence chiefs were about to converge into one long motorcade and, in a preorchestrated fashion, make the short drive through the concentric rings of Secret Service protective checkpoints. As a sea of tourists, spectators, and protesters watched from behind barricades erected along the sidewalk, the armored battlewagons moved in unison along Madison Avenue, turned left onto closed-off East Fifty-Sixth Street, and pulled up to a side entrance of Trump Tower.

Before stepping out, I handed Comey his black leather binder, which on that day carried the document that would eventually play an instrumental role in his firing.

In the lobby, Secret Service agents held two elevators that would take the delegation part of the way up along the residential side of the building. There they crossed over to the nonresidential part and took another set of elevators to meet the Trump team. The group then entered a small, basic conference room. The only incongruous item was a giant, heavy gold curtain that had been draped along the glass wall facing the hallway. Puzzled by drapery that seemed out of place for such a drab setting, the officials were told by the Secret Service that blocking the window would permit the room to be certified for the discussion of classified information. They milled about waiting for the transition team, and were soon joined by President-Elect Donald Trump; Vice President Elect Mike Pence; incoming chief of staff Reince Priebus; National Security Adviser Designate Michael Flynn; Flynn's deputy, K. T. McFarland; then congressman Michael Pompeo; and a CIA briefer.

Director of National Intelligence James Clapper kicked off the meeting, walking the incoming administration through the same intelligence community assessment on Russian interference that President Barack Obama and his team had been briefed on the day before. It was also the same briefing the intelligence chiefs had provided that morning to the "Gang of Eight"—a bipartisan group of leaders and intelligence committee chairs and ranking members from both houses of Congress—before we had departed Washington. As Comey told me, and as Clapper has since said publicly, what struck the intelligence chiefs that day was how focused the Trump team was on demanding to know whether any votes had been manipulated—which might thereby delegitimize Trump's victory—rather than on demonstrating concern over the news that the Russians had brazenly attempted to subvert a US election.

At the end of this discussion, Clapper spoke up and told Trump there was one last piece of information they would like to present, but that Comey would prefer to do it alone. Priebus asked Trump if he would like him to remain behind, and Trump dismissively waved him off.

After the large group filed out, Comey began his prepared remarks. James Comey is not someone who typically walks into a setting having rehearsed in advance his precise wording, but this was no ordinary occasion. When Comey got to the tawdry details contained in the dossier, Trump became defensive, cutting him off and denying the allegations. "Do I look like the kind of guy who needs prostitutes?" Trump asked. He then went on to recount, unprompted, a number of allegations against him by various women, which he claimed were all false. Comey indicated that the intelligence community was aware that the claims in the dossier were unsubstantiated, but that he nevertheless wanted Trump to be aware the information was circulating through government and media circles. Trump thanked Comey for the information, signaling the end of the short one-on-one meeting.

While Comey was still in with President-Elect Trump, it occurred to me that we might not have the luxury of making a clandestine escape. In the weeks since the election, media outlets had set up camp near the elevator bank on the first floor of Trump Tower in an attempt to catch glimpses of the dignitaries paying visits to the transition team, frequently being treated to impromptu press availabilities with Trump and whatever luminary he was meeting that day. I realized that we had not actually inquired of Trump's staff whether he would expect the intelligence officials to join him to address the media. Would the president-elect, with Comey solo at his side, try to preempt the classified document's leaking by taking it head-on and describing it to members of the press gathered on the first floor? A president is permitted to declassify anything he wants, but what about a president-elect? Would Trump be violating the law if he disclosed secret information? It was a very real possibility that Trump would then hand the floor over to Comey to describe what he had just been briefed on. Although usually calm, I was suddenly nearing panic.

I grabbed one of the Trump staff members nearby and asked whether the president-elect was planning a press availability after the meeting. He shrugged, barely looking up before returning to his phone. Assuming the Secret Service would be aware of any scripted moments for the day, I walked over to three agents who were huddled over what looked like a printed schedule.

"Excuse me," I interrupted, identifying myself as a special agent on the FBI director's staff. "Do you know if the president-elect is planning to hold a press conference after this meeting?"

"Not that I'm aware," one of the agents replied.

"Is it possible that may change?" I asked, attempting to gauge the likelihood of Trump running an audible.

The three agents looked at each other and erupted in laughter. Seeing my quizzical look, one of the agents said, "I'm sorry, man. This guy's schedule changes every two minutes. But, yes, as of this second, we are not expecting him to do any press conferences today."

Once safely back in the car, I immediately handed Comey the secure laptop. He didn't say a thing—the first time we had ever climbed into a vehicle without exchanging words—but began typing. He paused every so often to stare out the window as we navigated the city, and then went back to his writing. After about twenty minutes, and following a thorough proof-read, he handed me the computer, pointing to the place on the screen where I should begin reading. I was now learning Comey's version of a meeting that would spell the beginning of the end of his career, and one that would mark the start of a veritable hurricane—a torrent of attacks on the rule of law that would risk threatening the viability of our national institutions of justice.

"One of the most bizarre meetings of my life," James Comey said woefully before resuming his gaze out the window at the passing cityscape.

ON FEBRUARY 2, 2018, I resigned from a career I loved and walked out the doors of the FBI field office in Los Angeles for the last time. The cardboard box I carried contained the pictures and mementos I had collected during more than a decade of service in the preeminent law enforcement agency in the United States. After starting as an intern in 2004, I had been assigned to FBI offices coast-to-coast, handled years-long international assignments hunting terrorists and rescuing kidnapping victims in places like Pakistan and Southeast Asia, and found myself near the center of power in Washington, DC, as a special assistant on the FBI director's staff. During those years, I had served under Presidents George W. Bush, Barack Obama, and Donald Trump.

My journey to the FBI began in earnest on September 11, 2001, just over one week into my freshman year of college at the University of Texas at Austin, as I sat in a hallway waiting for class to begin, huddled around a television with fellow students, watching an endless loop of a commercial airplane slamming into a Lower Manhattan skyscraper. Its sister tower stood engulfed in smoke. Over the following hours, I thought constantly about the first responders who had rushed to the scene, ignoring their own safety as they worked to help others. It was then that I set my sights on the FBI. In my extremely close family, my parents—my mom a nurse, my dad a proud former soldier in the Army—had preached the nobility of serving others, and I had always known that some form of public service would be in my future. After 9/11, I oriented nearly every course and decision throughout college with the ultimate goal of serving in the bureau.

To put it simply, I grew up in the FBI. It is not hyperbole to say that my work there shaped me into the person I am today. Although I am as flawed as the next human being, one does not spend years in an organization dedicated to truth, justice, and ethics, to protecting the American people and upholding the Constitution, without having one's own character benefit as a result. Often when people leave a job, they reflect on how much they gave to the organization. The FBI is different. Although the hours were brutal and the work taxing, those who leave the bureau—myself included—instead dwell on all the organization did for them. From cherished experiences to lifelong bonds forged with some of the most honorable people on earth, I believe that I became a better person having set foot inside the FBI.

So why leave?

The short answer: to speak out.

After the hits the organization took during the Hillary Clinton email investigation and the Trump election, and over a year of systematic attacks on the FBI by the president of the United States, I could no longer stand by silently. The president and his allies were engaged in a coordinated campaign to undermine the institution, which would help discredit whatever investigative conclusion Special Counsel Robert Mueller might reach.

I wasn't the only person at the bureau who felt this way. It didn't inhibit our work—we were not going to give our critics the benefit of rendering us ineffectual—but the attacks frequently consumed many of us on the inside. Our bewilderment at Trump's antics quickly morphed into anger once we realized that the organization's reputation was being threatened by politicians in survival mode.

These feelings of frustration transcended personal political views. Although I consider myself middle-of-the-road politically—I've supported both Republicans and Democrats—it was fascinating to hear friends who skewed more conservative than I often expressing the most outrage. How, they wondered, did the "party of law and order" find itself at the forefront of efforts to undermine it? For most of us, love for our organization far surpassed party loyalty. We felt increasingly under siege.

For me, the last straw was an incident that occurred on the South Lawn of the White House on December 15, 2017. With the blades of Marine One spinning under a low ceiling of gray clouds, President Trump, about to depart to give a speech to law enforcement officers participating in a training program at the FBI Academy in Quantico, Virginia, walked over to the waiting press corps—and laid into the bureau, in comments broadcast around the world. "It's a shame what's happened to the FBI," the president exclaimed. He then insisted that there was widespread public outrage and anger at the bureau's investigation into his campaign, calling it "disgraceful" and "very sad."

I had finally had enough. I had been on the inside during the investigation and knew so many of his attacks were untrue. Over the following weekend, I debated whether to remain in the organization and hope the storm would pass, or conjure the courage to step out into the unknown and find a way to join those sounding the alarm. Leaving would mean giving up not only a rewarding job but also a secure one. There would be no retirement pension or long-term financial security, but I balanced all of that against how I would feel looking back, knowing I could have helped defend our precious institutions of justice against unfair attack but had instead decided to keep my head down just to draw a paycheck. On Monday, I decided it was time to leave and look for a public position that would allow me to explain the real FBI to the American people.

I'm a regular guy, a former rank-and-file agent, lucky enough now to have a platform as a television analyst and author. I never imagined writing a book. However, faced with a stream of lies from the White House, I became convinced of the need to tell the real story about these career public servants, whose integrity the president and his allies have repeatedly maligned. To be clear, this book is neither an impulsive nor emotional response to the whims of Donald Trump—or to the firing of my boss, James Comey. Nor is it intended to be a "tell-all" about my time working in the corridors of power. I have no ax to grind. I was not fired; I left the agency voluntarily because I felt the public was being manipulated by politicians. My only goal here is to tell the truth. Using my inside knowledge of the FBI and what has happened over the last several extraordinary years, I simply hope to illuminate for US citizens the current and lasting consequences of Trump's attacks on law enforcement.

I'm under no illusion that I alone can succeed in convincing readers that this campaign of attack has been dangerous for the United States, but I can at least try.

CROSSFIRE HURRICANE, TAKEN from the Rolling Stones song "Jumpin' Jack Flash," was the FBI's official code name for the counterintelligence investigation into the Trump campaign's potential connection to Russian interference in the 2016 election, as reported by the *New York Times*. This book will show how that name became an apt metaphor for the FBI itself.

Although the FBI is a household name, much of the public does not have a solid understanding of how the bureau works or of its unique role in ferreting out public corruption and national security threats. Many have only a passing familiarity with its history, the good and the bad, but it is important to delve into the past in order to understand how far we have departed from established norms. It is important for readers to understand that this book is not a blind endorsement of every action taken by the FBI. Far from it. In illuminating the corrosive nature of the attacks on the institution, it is imperative also to highlight the organization's own missteps—which warrant close scrutiny—but then distinguish them from the purely political lies told about the agency. This book seeks to provide important context crucial to understanding the truth about a case that engulfed the national news cycle for over two solid years.

To write *Crossfire Hurricane*, I interviewed dozens of current and former government officials and experts, with personal beliefs ranging across the political spectrum. In most cases, especially those involving currently serving officials at the FBI and inside the intelligence community, people have asked not to be named in order to be able to speak freely. Their insights are intended to help ensure that the story you are about to read isn't simply the recitation of the experience of one person who lived it. While most of the quotes used in the book came from direct interviews, some were also drawn from my own recollection, which was aided by the willingness of many of my colleagues to revisit past events. In some areas these officials disagreed vehemently with decisions made by law enforcement, but most were united in their disdain for the overt attempts by a sitting president to permanently damage the FBI's credibility—attacks that only intensified after I quit, enabled by leaders in the legislative branch.

I wish this book weren't necessary. But the success of the FBI rests squarely on the confidence and support of the public it serves. In order for the FBI to be effective, it must be believed. When an FBI special agent knocks on someone's door seeking help in solving a crime, the willingness of that person to assist is directly correlated to his or her view of the agency as honest and trustworthy. When an FBI special agent rises in a courtroom to testify, the success of the case often hinges on the jury's belief that the agent is telling the truth. If unscrupulous politicians succeed in convincing the American people that the FBI is corrupt, dishonest, and political, they will also succeed in making the nation less safe.

Never did I imagine a day when the greatest threats to our institutions would come from within our own government. But here we are.

# CHAPTER 1

# More Than a Motto

THE SOURCE WOULD have less than an hour to meet us and tell us what he knew. Any longer, and friends and associates might notice his absence. Also, the weather was looking dire: it was monsoon season, and the robust foliage surrounding our camp in the Philippines was starting to shake more violently by the minute as a gathering storm slowly pushed our way. As our convoy of Toyota Land Cruisers rumbled out onto the main thoroughfare, our windshield wipers struggled to keep up with the blinding rain slamming down. There wouldn't be much time to meet the source before the system came ashore.

Although we had not yet been able to assess his credibility, the source claimed to be in a position to lead authorities to a high-value terrorist responsible for death and destruction across a wide swath of Southeast Asia. The wanted subject had spent years on the run, miraculously escaping violent brushes with a cavalry of special operations teams hot on his trail. He existed in the shadows, with support from a vast network that frequently moved him across islands, by car or boat, to new safe houses—sometimes nightly.

Because this man had been implicated in the murder of US citizens, it was the job of my FBI counterterrorism team to work with foreign partners to find him, prosecute him, and get him where we believed he belonged: behind bars for the rest of his life. It mattered little to us whether the prison he would call home was overseas or back in the United States, but getting him off the streets and out of the business of killing was our mission. This latest tip—from an actual human source—might prove to be the linchpin in neutralizing a dangerous threat to US national security. There was a real possibility he would opt to go down fighting rather than be taken alive. But that was a second-order issue—our first goal was to find him. The thousands of miles my partner and I had traveled and the incalculable amount of money spent and resources expended by the US government would be worth it if this one tip proved fruitful.

Our convoy turned off the road and toward a clearing, where we used bright-orange tape to mark a makeshift landing zone for our next mode of transportation. A half dozen US Marines from our security detail encircled us, looking outward, their index fingers extended above the triggers of their semiautomatic rifles as they scanned the horizon for threats. As we stood in the sweltering mixture of heat and stinging rain, we began to sense the pulsating reverberations of an approaching aircraft, which turned into a crackle as a Bell 412 helicopter crested the tree canopy above us and set down in the field.

This would be the last chance to mentally review our operational order one more time before the mission began in earnest. I pulled out my steno pad and flipped through several pages of questions we would ask the source during our meeting. I then reached into a pocket in my cargo pants and read from a laminated card I had kept in my wallet since graduating from the FBI Academy. FBI DEADLY FORCE POLICY was printed at the top in bold block letters. Although every FBI agent knows this mantra by heart, it is standard procedure to review it, solo or as a team, before any action that might involve danger:

> FBI special agents may use deadly force only when necessary—when the agent has a reasonable belief that the subject of such force poses an imminent danger of death or serious physical injury to the agent or others.

Although we were in a foreign country, an agreement between the United States and the Philippines permitted us to carry weapons there, in a part of the world our government still considered a war zone.

Once airborne, we would fly to a nearby island, where the source had traveled by boat, connect with a host-nation intelligence service team, and then meet and debrief the source, allowing him enough time to return home before his absence was noticed. The mood among the team was calm and cautious optimism. Although we could be plenty riotous in our down-time, we were now mission-focused. Confident we were ready, we climbed aboard the helo—rotors still spinning—and were skids-up on our way to the rendezvous point.

After navigating across the southern Philippines archipelago, we landed on an island and linked up with our intelligence counterparts. We were soon speeding along a bumpy road, desperately trying to make up time we had lost in the air due to high winds. As we neared the outskirts of a village, we looped behind a ramshackle hotel and into an empty parking lot, where the stranger stood. I knew from experience that an agent's first instinct when meeting someone who has risked his own safety to provide critical intelligence is to rush and greet him, quickly working to establish rapport. However, since December 2009, when seven brave CIA personnel were killed in Afghanistan by a suicide bomber pretending to be a source, US intelligence officers operating abroad have been admonished to remain vigilant when dealing with unknown human assets. For the moment, our personal safety would have to override standard human courtesy. We were trained to start any meeting with someone whose allegiances were unknown with a set of commands that would allow the source to be searched for weapons before being permitted into our proximity.

Once deemed safe, the source was brought to our vehicle, and he climbed inside. I sat in the rear seat next to him, offering my hand and a warm greeting, expressing my admiration for his willingness to come forward. Up front, my partner sat next to a local police official, each resting a hand on the grip of the 9-millimeter pistol holstered in his waistband. The source walked us through the information he had, periodically pausing long enough for me to take notes and ask more questions. His English was better than I'd expected, making it unnecessary to use our foreign police counterpart as a translator. At one point, I handed the source a blank sheet of paper, and we all sat in silence as he carefully sketched out the terrain where he believed the high-value terrorist was located. There was much more I wanted to ask, but realizing we were already pushing the limits of his time, we moved the discussion toward setting up a follow-up meeting after we had confirmed some of the information he had provided.

"I have to ask you one more question," I said with genuine curiosity as he reached for the door handle. "I don't get it. We came all this way, traveling through the pouring rain in cars, boats, airplanes, and helicopters, just to meet and hear you out. Why didn't you just walk into a local village police station and tell them what you know?"

"Trust," he replied after a moment, turning his gaze from me to his hands, which he was slowly wringing in his lap. "You are the FBI. Everyone knows you can trust the FBI."

I HAVE PLAYED that conversation over in my mind a hundred times in the years since, particularly when the organization I worked for found itself facing various reputational challenges. The trust this one man—and other sources like him—placed in the bureau helped us to understand aspects of the wanted terrorist's network, and to eventually apprehend the dangerous fugitive. It is the same trust that was vital in solving countless other cases in the past, and will—I want to believe—be relied upon in investigations yet to come. These successes in making the world safer serve as reminders that the FBI's brand is more than a nicety, that its motto, "Fidelity, Bravery, and Integrity," means something: it serves as the foundation of its effectiveness in stopping crime, fighting terrorism, countering foreign spies, and enlisting the support of human sources around the world.

That motto can be traced back to 1935, when FBI inspector W. H. Drane Lester explained in a publication for law enforcement professionals that, after years of being called the Bureau of Investigation, the official name for the crime-fighting agency would henceforth be the Federal Bureau of Investigation, with the acronym FBI. As Lester wrote, "Those initials also represent the three things for which the Bureau and its representatives always stand: Fidelity - Bravery - Integrity." As Robert Mueller would note during his time as FBI director, "Fidelity, Bravery, and Integrity set the expectations for behavior; they set a standard for our work. More than just a motto, for the men and women of the FBI, Fidelity, Bravery, and Integrity is a way of life."

This way of life starts the moment a new recruit sets foot on the grounds of the FBI Academy in Quantico. I vividly recall my first official day, on March 16, 2008, when my class of forty-nine young professionals from coast to coast and all walks of life gathered in a drab auditorium on a plot of land inside a military base and raised our right hands to take our oaths. By the time we arrived, we had been told that we'd already achieved something remarkable, as fewer than 1 percent of applicants actually make it through the battery of exams and interviews required to be considered for the next phase of training. Each step of the selection process is geared not only to identify those who excel in their respective fields of expertise but also to weed out those whose ethics and judgment are less than solid.

Throughout the next twenty-one weeks of intense training, we recruits were constantly watched and tested by instructors and by each other. At the completion of each training simulation—mock arrest scenarios, deadly-force encounters, felony traffic stops, and the like—we were asked to explain the actions we had taken. The goal was not to see if someone would make a mistake (we made them often) but to see if we would own up to our mistakes, such as the accidental discharge of a Simunition paint gun used in training (unlike real weapons, these fired so quietly one could do so undetected) or the failure to adequately search a criminal who then turned violent. During moot court sessions, we would sit on the stand testifying and get grilled by an instructor playing the role of defense counsel. Were we *sure* the subject being prosecuted was the person who committed the crime? Did we fail in the investigative process to collect a vital piece of evidence that might suggest that a person was innocent? Had we cut any corners? By testing our responses, we were constantly reminded of the agency's zero tolerance for malfeasance.

Apart from being required to conduct themselves with integrity, new recruits at the FBI Academy are also sensitized to the fact that even the smallest misstep in their career might prove fatal. This is because when FBI special agents testify in a court of law, they are serving as witnesses on behalf of the government. According to the US Supreme Court's 1972 ruling in *Giglio v. United States*, prosecutors must turn over to the defense any information about a witness's past that may serve to impeach their credibility. In layman's terms, this means that everything about an agent's past is potentially fair game—every administrative personnel action and every time an investigator may have run afoul of the law—and can be used by defendants to question the credibility of an agent serving as a witness. For practical purposes, this means that an agent caught lying or otherwise breaking the law is no longer of use to the FBI. If a particular case rests on what an agent saw or heard and it turns out that agent has in the past not been truthful, the agent risks jeopardizing the entire investigation.

The tests of character that happen daily at the FBI Academy vary in their level of intensity. At the simple end of the spectrum are things like written and physical tests. Did you cheat on your legal exam? Did you do fifty push-ups or forty-nine? These are easy to measure, because the FBI sees everything. One doesn't sit as a new recruit inside the United States' premiere law enforcement and intelligence agency and not expect every action to be scrutinized. As recruits are told from day one: "You are always being watched." Fortunately, we never had a single instance in my class of someone being disciplined for integrity issues.

Other issues are a little murkier. For example, during one training scenario, I sat in a vehicle far away from a simulated apartment building; I was conducting surveillance on a criminal subject. The goal was to practice collecting information that would be presented to a federal judge, who would make the determination about whether a lawful arrest was warranted. The man I was surveilling stood outside talking to two associates, and was soon joined by another associate, this one wearing blue jeans and a white T-shirt. These were all role players we would get to know well by the end of our training. I took down notes about the surroundings and everything happening in front of me. Once the exercise was over, it was time to explain what I saw.

"So, what happened?" asked the lead instructor as we all gathered around inside a nearby classroom.

I ticked through the day's events, reading from my surveillance log and explaining what the group of men had been doing.

"This guy over here walked up and handed our subject an envelope," I said, pointing to the role player in blue jeans.

"This guy?" asked the instructor.

I sensed the beginning of an inquisition.

"Yeah, someone who looked just like this guy," I said, suddenly questioning whether this was actually the person I had seen from afar.

"Okay, wait a second," said the instructor. "Was it this guy, or was it someone dressed like this guy?"

A long pause ensued.

"I can't say for certain it was this guy," I continued. "But someone resembling him."

"Right answer," said the instructor, turning the exchange into a teachable moment for everyone gathered. "When you get out in the field, the things you see and hear might literally ruin lives. 'I think' and 'I know' are two very different things with very different consequences. You must have the personal integrity to admit when you don't know something for certain."

There are moments in an FBI career we never forget. The first is day one, when new employees are overwhelmed by the realization that they have now made it inside one of the most prestigious institutions on the planet. For special agents, another momentous occasion is the day of graduation from the FBI Academy, when we walk across the stage to receive our badge and credentials. On my graduation day in 2008, I'd been elected class speaker, and I had the responsibility of providing remarks on behalf of my esteemed crew before turning over the floor to then director Robert Mueller.

Before I was old enough to become an agent, I had worked at FBI headquarters in a nonagent role and had heard him speak dozens of times about the special nature of the institution. As I searched for what to say at graduation, it occurred to me that there was no way I would be able to describe the organization's mission better than Mueller had in the past. Because he was someone I greatly admired, I decided to quote him.

The part I hadn't fully thought through was the fact that the quotes I'd decided to use were some of Mueller's greatest hits—comments he had used many times before and had planned to use again that day. About mid-speech, I turned to face him and was welcomed by an icy glare as he sat scratching out portions of the prepared remarks in his lap. Oops.

When I had finished, Mueller stepped up to the lectern and decided to have a little fun. He had taken on (and embraced) mythical status inside the organization as a no-nonsense tyrant. "Many of you may not know that Josh used to work for me in the director's office," he said. Leaning into his reputation for insanely high standards for his employees, he continued. "I told him that if he screwed up his class speech, his first assignment would not be to California, but to Yemen," he said, and the crowd roared. "But relax, Josh. I've decided you're not going to Yemen."

AFTER GRADUATING AND being sent out into the field, the life of an FBI agent is marked by an endless stream of opportunities to seize and challenges to overcome. No two agents will ever find themselves on the exact same path; the sheer multitude of threats the FBI is responsible for countering requires a workforce with skill sets as diverse as the agency's broad mission. For instance, when I entered the FBI, my passion centered on countering terrorist threats from abroad, and I was able to use my degree in government to join teams working with foreign nations and bringing extremists to justice. Other men and women rely on backgrounds in business and the private sector to target white-collar crime. Walk the halls of any FBI field office, and you're just as likely to run into a cyber expert working to disrupt threats in the digital space as you are a tactical agent preparing to launch an operation aimed at arresting a fugitive.

Despite their differences, one thing unites each of those fortunate enough to identify themselves as one of the approximately thirty-six thousand employees of the FBI: an understanding that "Fidelity, Bravery, and

Integrity" is, as Mueller often said, more than a motto. It is an internalized orientation toward excellence that makes any misstep by any one employee so incredibly damning. Those who fail, or stray from the organization's values, do so at a very real cost to the entire institution. Indeed, I fully acknowledge that the bureau's history is replete with examples of those who have embarrassed the FBI through either intentional or unintentional personal failings.

Among the most extreme instances of disgracing the badge is the case of Robert Hanssen, a former FBI special agent who continues to rot in federal prison after being prosecuted for spying for Russia. Less extreme, but no less damaging to the organization's core values, are the many others who have been reprimanded or punished for lying, stealing, and abusing their law enforcement powers. Their stories are routinely studied internally when the FBI's Office of Professional Responsibility—the bureau's internal affairs division—sends out its quarterly all-employee message highlighting recently adjudicated cases of wrongdoing by bureau employees. These messages help serve as a constant reminder of the organization's strict handling of those whose actions risk threatening public confidence in the FBI.

The importance of a strong, trustworthy brand is made evident to all employees the first time they display their credentials. Not only does the badge open doors, as I learned my first month out in the field, the name can also elicit instant cooperation from suspected criminals.

Late one night shortly after graduating from the academy, I pulled out of the FBI parking garage in Los Angeles and headed down Wilshire Boulevard. I noticed a police cruiser with its lights on, off to my left in front of a convenience store. While most people who see a cop while driving reflexively look down at their speedometer, new-agent training taught me that the first thing you do when passing a patrol car executing a traffic stop is to look and make sure the officer doesn't need help. Everyone is a force multiplier, the thinking goes, and contrary to what they show on TV, law enforcement officers constantly look out for one another regardless of which agency they happen to work for. There is actually a nonverbal exchange you might notice if you look closely when one law enforcement officer slows to check on a colleague. If everything is fine, they'll flash four fingers to the passing officer, signaling the situation is "Code 4"—copspeak for "under control."

But everything wasn't under control that night in LA. As I got closer to the stopped patrol car, I noticed an officer trying to restrain two kids he had placed under arrest. One of them was flailing about and resisting as the officer tried to keep them both pinned down on the trunk of his car. I instantly hit the lights on my FBI car and busted a U-turn, coming to a screeching halt next to him. I was in civilian clothes, but the strobe lights popping on my dash and the flashing headlights told him he was no longer alone.

"One of you, two of them," I said as I ran up to his car. In two quick motions, I pulled a set of handcuffs from my belt and snapped them onto the wrist of the resisting subject.

"Thanks, man," the officer said after he caught his breath. "These kids just robbed someone here outside the store, and my partner went to chase after one of their friends."

As he described what was happening, the kid I was holding down—who had to be all of seventeen years of age—was hurling all kinds of nasty insults our way about cops. I just calmly stood there waiting for others to arrive.

Suddenly, the intersection lit up with the brightest light I have ever seen; an LAPD helicopter banked low and switched on its powerful spotlight, instantly turning night into day. Sirens approached from all directions, and when backup arrived, the two subjects finally relaxed.

"Who are you with, by the way?" asked the officer next me.

"Oh, I'm with the FBI," I said.

With a look I will never forget, the punk whose arm I was holding swiveled around in disbelief.

"FB . . . ," he said, trailing off. "Um, sir," he continued. "I have some weed in my bag, and a couple of syringes."

He was starting to confess to crimes before being asked a single question.

"What the hell?" said the cop as others walked over and took custody of the two subjects. "These idiots try to fight us and yell all kinds of terrible things, but the second you say you're with the FBI, he starts singing like a canary!"

I experienced many moments like this during my career wearing the badge. Having such a strong brand helps agents do the job. So when politicians attempt to smear the FBI and label the men and women wearing the badge as part of some "deep state" conspiracy of rogue criminals, such disgraceful accusations cut to the core. All FBI employees understand the requirement that they remain apolitical in their work and resist outside influences that might threaten their independence. Although in the United States, institutions of justice are led by political appointees and report to civilian leadership, one key aspect of law enforcement in this nation that separates us from authoritarian regimes has been the norm that politicians do not interfere in the work of the FBI. This critical norm has been tested many times throughout our history; conflict between the White House and our institutions of justice is nothing new. What is unprecedented, however, is Donald Trump's method of dealing with such conflict.

# CHAPTER 2

# Hands Off

JUDGING BY HIS past performances, the FBI director was gearing up to execute a covert campaign of total manipulation. His arrival in New York that fall day would shake the newly elected president to his core. The director had controlled many politicians in his lifetime, and this time would be no different. Although the president of the United States was widely regarded as the most powerful person in the world, the head of the nation's mighty federal law enforcement agency wielded unusual influence over those who technically held the levers of power.

As he sat across from the president-elect at the Pierre hotel on the edge of Midtown Manhattan, the director's first goal was to win over the new chief executive by letting him in on some secrets. Doing so would not only serve to ingratiate him with his new boss but would also help shape their power dynamic by subtly signaling that the FBI could be either his friend or his foe. This had been his modus operandi for many years: doling out tidbits of information that would impress the listener while also demonstrating the bureau's seeming omniscience.

"When you get into the White House," the director said, "don't make any calls through the switchboard." The telephone lines were monitored. "Little men you don't know will be listening."

The director then dropped another bombshell. The FBI had bugged the cabin of the president-elect's campaign plane at the direction of the outgoing commander in chief. The stunning claim rattled the characteristically paranoid politician. He would later fume that "every damn thing" he had discussed on his flights was in the possession of his political enemies. As the new president's chief of staff would later describe it, the FBI director's tactics in sharing sensitive information served "to create an impression of how useful the Bureau could be to the President."

For his part, the new president was all too willing to forge this alliance. The FBI's power was something he might be able to exploit for personal political gain. "You are one of the few people who is to have direct access to me at all times," the president said.

As J. Edgar Hoover stood and left the Pierre that day in 1968, President-Elect Richard Nixon turned to an aide and said, "We'll get that Goddamn bugging crap out of the White House in a hurry."

NEARLY FIFTY YEARS after the Nixon-Hoover meeting, a future FBI director would find himself in a very similar position only three blocks away—briefing an incoming president on potentially damning material. However, as James Comey sat across from Donald Trump inside Trump Tower, his motivation could not have been more different from Hoover's. In sharing details of the Steele dossier, Comey was merely seeking to make the new president aware of potentially embarrassing information that had been swirling throughout official Washington. He was not there to impress the president, nor had he come to blackmail him. But Trump saw that initial conversation much differently.

"In my opinion, he shared it so that I would think he had it out there," Trump later said, suggesting that Comey was purposefully lording embarrassing material over him. Asked if he believed Comey was attempting to gain leverage over the president by claiming he knew things that might be damaging if made public, Trump said, "Yeah, I think so. In retrospect."

J. Edgar Hoover, unlike Comey, was almost certainly attempting to exert some form of psychological control over the president. When Nixon arrived in Washington as a freshman congressman in the late 1940s, he and Hoover struck up a close personal relationship based in part on their shared hatred of communism. During his time in Congress, Nixon served as a staunch ally of Hoover's, regularly advocating for increased appropriations for the FBI and acting as defender when conversations arose about whether Hoover may have been in his job for much longer than appropriate. However, although they had once been friends, Nixon's assuming the presidency meant he was now Hoover's boss. True to form, Hoover would work to ensure his own professional survival. He had equities to protect.

As the first formal director of the Federal Bureau of Investigation, Hoover built an empire; he created from scratch the preeminent law enforcement agency he would lead for almost five decades. He dedicated his entire professional life to government service, working to craft a bold crime-fighting image for both himself and the organization he led. Elected leaders feared him and the secret files he accumulated about their transgressions. He was famous for doing what Trump was accusing Comey of: letting officials know that the FBI had damaging personal information on them under the guise of a "heads-up," but in reality causing many to wonder whether Hoover was trying to blackmail them.

"This was a way of putting congressmen on notice that we had something on them and therefore they would be more disposed to meeting the bureau's needs and keeping Hoover in power," said former FBI deputy associate director John McDermott.

As historian Stephen Ambrose explained of Hoover, "He did not have to threaten; his control of the raw files was in itself a sufficient threat."

The FBI had amassed so much power throughout Hoover's lengthy career that even the most reticent chief executive was loath to get rid of him. Hoover simply knew too much. "I would rather have him inside the tent pissing out than outside the tent pissing in," President Lyndon Johnson once said.

Although the modern-day FBI would not be what it is today without Hoover's ambition, he is also responsible in part for the profound distrust some Americans have felt toward law enforcement. As Pulitzer Prize–winning journalist Tim Weiner said about Hoover, "He was not a monster. He was an American Machiavelli . . . He practiced political warfare and secret statecraft in pursuit of national security, often at the expense of morality." And in the name of national security, for decades he violated the civil liberties of countless US citizens. As the Senate's "Church

Committee"—the body later charged with investigating allegations of abuse by the US intelligence community—outlined in its scathing 1976 report, government agencies, including the FBI, had engaged in "tactics unworthy of a democracy, and occasionally reminiscent of the tactics of totalitarian regimes."

Under Hoover, the bureau accumulated some five hundred thousand domestic intelligence files as it worked to root out communists, spies, and fascists. There is little doubt that Hoover truly believed radical causes had to be stopped—and his continued directorship appeared to be a means to that end—but many of his tactics were unsavory. And while his ultimate aim had been to build, and then protect, the FBI as an institution, he did so at great expense to the organization's reputation for honesty and independence once his misdeeds became public. After his death, the public would learn he had conspired with presidents and other politicians to share political dirt and gossip. In some cases, he would placate his bosses in the White House by handing over investigative files containing damning information about their political opponents. He helped bug their political enemies and shared some of the most private information one could imagine.

Near the end of his life, something changed. The decade in which Nixon came to power was a tumultuous one marked by widespread riots ignited by the civil rights movement and Vietnam War protests. Antigovernment sentiment was unlike anything Hoover had experienced in his lifetime. He sensed an evolution in public opinion as it related to the powers of the government. So by the time Nixon became president, in 1969, Hoover was beginning to scale back his penchant for testing the limits of the law. As Tim Weiner noted, "Hoover changed course—he refused to do Nixon's dirty work—because he felt the slowly rolling earthquake of the 1960s. The geotectonic plates of American politics were shifting under his feet. If the FBI had been caught burglarizing Democratic Party headquarters, as Nixon's men were, shortly after Hoover's death, it would have destroyed everything he had worked to build for five decades."

This isn't to say that Hoover didn't continue the role of inveterate manipulator. He continued to play to Nixon's ego and ambition, serving as a sounding board while the president privately unloaded on his ever-increasing list of enemies, the media first among them.

In one late-night exchange captured on Nixon's now-famous recordings—as it turned out, he had installed his own "Goddamn bugging" system—the director played into Nixon's obsessions, with a highly inappropriate conversation about Katharine Graham, the publisher of the *Washington Post*.

"I would have thought she's about eighty-five years old," said Hoover. "She's only about, I think, something like fifty-seven."

"Oh, no, I know that," said Nixon.

"And I had an idea she was a great deal older when I looked at her last night," continued Hoover, adding, "she's aged terribly."

"She's a terrible old bag," said the president.

"Oh, she's an old bitch in my estimation," said the director of the FBI.

WHEN PEOPLE TALK about the trampling of modern institutional norms by Donald Trump and his efforts to undermine federal law enforcement, some may wonder how the FBI's independent reputation came to be in the first place. How did society come to accept the existence of an agency so strong that even its bosses inside the White House would—usually—pause before entertaining the notion of interfering with its work?

The congressional investigators who unearthed FBI and intelligence community abuses after Hoover's death deserve the most credit. After publicizing their shocking revelations, they set out to reform the national security state and established permanent oversight committees that would watch over the intelligence community. With the support of President Jimmy Carter, they passed legislation reining in the powers of the FBI, CIA, and other intelligence agencies. They also passed a law limiting future FBI directors to a single ten-year term. There would be no more J. Edgar Hoovers. Gone were the days of law enforcement and intelligence services operating on their own without checks and balances from the legislative branch and the courts. And future administrations would be on notice that any attempt to inappropriately use the powers of law enforcement for extralegal purposes—regardless of what ends might justify extraordinary means—would face scrutiny from these coequal branches of government.

Although Hoover had been at the forefront of widespread abuses, his decision to buck President Nixon and refuse his requests to continue using FBI resources for political purposes—even if it was done only to prevent public embarrassment—ultimately led to Nixon's downfall. Faced with an FBI director who would no longer play ball, Nixon set out to form "the plumbers," a secret group of malcontents initially focused on stopping White House leaks, who then moved on to committing other crimes. This was the group that executed the botched break-in of the Democratic National Committee's headquarters on June 17, 1972, which soon became known as the Watergate scandal.

"Nixon was a criminal president from the beginning of his presidency to the end," said Watergate journalist Carl Bernstein in an interview with me for this book. "Because Hoover would no longer conduct break-ins or do other dirty business under the guise of national security, Nixon had to do it himself. He basically took Hoover's tactics and moved them into the White House."

Ironically, rather than engaging in unlawful activity on behalf of the president, the FBI would find itself leading the charge, along with the press, to unearth massive corruption and illegality among Nixon's inner circle. Dozens of people would be charged with crimes relating to the burglary and other acts of political espionage. After firing the special prosecutor investigating the case, and after the revelation of the "smoking gun" tape containing audio of the president ordering CIA to block the FBI's investigation, Nixon resigned in disgrace.

There are FBI veterans to this day who continue to defend Hoover as a product of his time. It is difficult to judge someone today through the standards of the past, they argue. This might appear to be rationalizing the behavior of someone who knew he was operating outside the bounds of the Constitution, but it remains a deeply held belief among some current and former employees. "Director Hoover, like most of us mortals, did some things he's probably not proud of," said current FBI director Christopher

Wray at a congressional hearing in December 2017, "and some things we should all be very grateful for in terms of building the FBI into the organization it is today. So, like most people, he's complicated."

WHEN WE SURVEY Donald Trump's assault on the rule of law, it is striking to observe the way in which it contrasts with how most other presidents have handled themselves when facing FBI scrutiny in the post-Watergate era. (Of every president since Watergate, only Barack Obama made it through his full tenure without someone senior in his White House either tainted by, or becoming the direct subject of, a major investigation by the US Department of Justice.)

President Gerald Ford spent much of his time in the White House dealing with the aftermath of Watergate—pardoning his predecessor and watching several members of the Nixon team prosecuted for their role in the affair. For Jimmy Carter, there was the special counsel assigned to investigate his family's peanut business. Although investigators cited irregularities with certain financial transactions, they ultimately determined no criminal charges were warranted. With President Ronald Reagan, there was first "Debategate"—the investigation into how briefing papers belonging to Carter had made their way to Reagan's team before a debate—and then the probe into the secret sale of arms to Iran. In that scandal, known as the Iran-Contra affair, investigations by Congress and an independent counsel resulted in a slew of indictments, ranging from charges of perjury to obstruction of justice. (The issue of the missing campaign binder remains a mystery to this day.) For Reagan's successor, President George H. W. Bush, a banking scandal dubbed "Iraqgate" led to an investigation into whether billions of dollars in loans were funneled from the US government to arm Baghdad. And President Bill Clinton faced "Filegate," "Travelgate," "Whitewater," and a scandal over his sexual involvement with a White House intern. He was impeached by the House of Representatives and subsequently acquitted by the Senate.

Although the targets of these cases, and their allies, would blast the perceived politicization of the investigations—Hillary Clinton's claim of a "vast right-wing conspiracy" out to get her husband was among the most famous—one unwritten rule was that criticizing career agents and prosecutors was off-limits. (One major departure from this norm was the campaign launched by President Clinton and his allies to destroy the credibility of Independent Counsel Kenneth Starr, who they believed was on a political fishing expedition aimed at bringing down the president. In the process, they angered many career FBI officials I know, who still believe Clinton thought he was above the law.)

Even during the intense political trench warfare that characterized the Clinton era, you rarely saw the president of the United States himself using the bully pulpit to undermine entire agencies. As one confidant of former president Clinton told me, "He would regularly seethe and vent at what he considered to be unfair treatment. But what sets him apart from Donald Trump is that his venting would take place privately. You would frequently get a late-night call from the president, fuming over something that had happened that day in the investigation. Then he would hang up and go back to work."

One aspect of the Clinton situation that made his reluctance to attack the FBI even more fascinating is the fact that the president and the FBI director at the time, Louis Freeh, absolutely loathed each other. When talking about the importance of independence from politicians, folks inside the bureau still tell the story of how Freeh decided to turn in his White House badge after learning the president was under investigation. Doing so, in his mind, would further distance the FBI from the appearance of politics. As Freeh told *60 Minutes* several years later, "The implications of a White House pass would mean I could come and go in and out of the building any time I wanted without really being recorded as a visitor. I wanted all my visits to be official." This act would infuriate Clinton.

President George W. Bush's administration also had its share of high-profile run-ins with federal law enforcement. In one now-famous showdown between the White House and the Justice Department, then deputy attorney general James Comey and then FBI director Robert Mueller threatened to resign after the White House decided to continue with the warrantless wiretapping of US citizens in the wake of the September 11 attacks. In a dramatic scene inside a Washington hospital in March 2004, two White House officials sought approval from Attorney General John Ashcroft—hospitalized for acute pancreatitis—to continue the top-secret surveillance program that Comey and others at DOJ believed to be unlawful. Ashcroft refused, and the program was reauthorized without the approval of the nation's chief legal authorities. Bush soon relented, however, and rather than continuing the intelligence collection program in its current form, which would have resulted in the resignation of top DOJ officials, he ordered the department to get it on proper legal footing. And when the episode became public, Bush did not opt to publicly blast DOJ or the FBI in order to defend himself.

Bush's respect for our law enforcement institutions would continue even when a member of his own administration ran afoul of investigators. In 2007, Scooter Libby, chief of staff to Vice President Dick Cheney, was convicted of lying to federal agents investigating the unauthorized public disclosure of the identity of CIA officer Valerie Plame. Although this period was fraught with peril for the Bush administration, with new headlines daily documenting the twists and turns of the growing scandal, the president did not attack the Justice Department and the career investigators working to unearth criminal activity. Rather, he acted presidential—respecting the line of demarcation between politics and justice.

To be sure, Bush angered many inside DOJ and the FBI by deciding to commute Libby's sentence, but his approach was far different from the destructive way Trump has dealt with federal investigators. (As if to further underscore his "power" over law enforcement, Trump pardoned Libby in 2018, criticizing the investigators he believed had treated Cheney's aide "unfairly.")

PUT SIMPLY, THE manner in which most presidents have handled the Justice Department historically stands in stark contrast with the age of Donald Trump, a president who has frequently trashed the rule of law. And Trump hasn't done this alone; he has benefited from the assistance of other administration officials, legal professionals, and friendly right-wing media outlets in his full-throated assault on investigators, calling them criminals and even Nazis.

I'm afraid to say that there are signs that their collective approach is working to chip away at public confidence in our vital national institutions. In one 2018 poll, only 51 percent of respondents expressed confidence in the FBI, a twelve-point drop from 2015. Among Republicans, the "party of law enforcement," trust in the agency dropped an astonishing twenty-two points over the same time period.

Trump's war on the FBI has no true ideological or philosophical under-pinnings; he has not spoken out as a civil libertarian genuinely concerned with government overreach. Instead, his approach has been personal and transactional. When law enforcement has targeted his political opponents, like candidate Hillary Clinton, or has otherwise been perceived as acting in a manner advantageous to him, as in the investigation into Supreme Court nominee Brett Kavanaugh, he has applauded their efforts. But since the Justice Department turned its sights on the multiple examples of cor-ruption and malfeasance by those operating in the president's inner circle, he has lashed out, claimed victim status, and attempted to manipulate the public into believing our institutions of justice have gone rogue. For many experts, this appears to come straight from the authoritarian playbook. We are now in a completely new age. To understand exactly how we got here, it is important to revisit the election that would not end.

## CHAPTER 3

# The Never-Ending Election

ONE DAY DURING the summer of 2018, I found myself in an unusual position: heading to lunch with someone I expected would almost certainly see me—a representative of a law enforcement agency many believe helped decide the 2016 presidential election in favor of Donald Trump—as a villain. Although no longer in the FBI, I had been an aide to the person who led the high-profile investigation into Democratic nominee Hillary Clinton. My lunch date had been campaign manager for the subject of that investigation.

As I strolled down Melrose Avenue in Los Angeles toward our intended destination, I wondered if the reception that awaited me would be marked by tension and resentment, or if the distance of time would allow for productive reflections on one of the most tumultuous periods in recent national memory. Did the Clinton camp continue to harbor a deep animus toward the FBI? Did they understand the series of tough decisions law enforcement had been forced to make amid a highly charged political climate? Whatever the answers to these questions might be, I wanted to know.

Although only thirty-five when he assumed a leadership role at the Clinton campaign, Robby Mook was already an election veteran, having worked for the Democratic Congressional Campaign Committee, Clinton's 2008 presidential campaign team, and Terry McAuliffe's successful gubernatorial run in Virginia. His reputation was that of an affable yet aggressive strategist, data-driven to his core. These traits became instantly obvious within seconds of sitting down with him. His easy and sincere laugh quickly faded, however, once the conversation shifted from small talk to the serious consequences of electoral politics. As we ate our chopped salads, we began by talking about our shared experience serving in the military and our similar civilian roles as contributors for CNN. Finally, we moved to discuss the elephant in the room.

Mook's woes began in the summer of 2015. Unbeknownst to the Clinton campaign, on the seventh floor of FBI headquarters in the suite of executive offices known as Mahogany Row, FBI deputy director Mark Giuliano made the short walk past a set of doors outside his office and into the ornate director's suite, complete with its glossy wood fixtures and thick, plush carpet. He took a seat opposite his boss—James Comey—who was busy on his desktop computer. Embossed in gray on the ceiling above their heads was a large FBI seal adorned with the agency's motto: "Fidelity, Bravery, and Integrity." The conversation Giuliano was about to initiate would require strict adherence to those three core values in a way neither man likely could have imagined at the time.

Comey told me he listened intently as Giuliano outlined an investigation the FBI had just opened into former secretary of state Hillary Clinton's handling of classified information during her tenure at the US Department of State. The FBI had received a "referral" to conduct this criminal investigation from the US intelligence community and the State Department inspectors general, who were jointly working to identify whether Clinton had acted inappropriately in sending and receiving classified material on a private email server set up at Clinton's residence.

Giuliano walked Comey through how the investigation would be worked. The Counterintelligence Division at FBI headquarters, using personnel already in the building and experts nearby at the bureau's Washington field office, would serve as program manager. It would have a joint supervisory structure that included both agents and intelligence analysts.

"Look," Comey recalled telling Giuliano, "I want to stay close to this investigation to make sure that I can protect it, both in reality and so I can credibly say that there was no political influence whatsoever." Comey also insisted that he wanted frequent briefings on the case. "You decide whatever cadence makes sense for providing me with updates and decision points," he said, "but I want it to be unlike anything we've done. I want to be kept up on it regularly."

The email server scandal had its roots in Clinton's early days as secretary of state. During confirmation hearings in January 2009, a Clinton aide registered the website domain clintonemail.com, setting up email accounts for Clinton, her husband and daughter, and a number of assistants. Rather than using a government email address on the state.gov domain, Clinton instead opted to use her personal domain for both private correspondence and official business. The public would begin to learn the extent of the issue five years later, when Clinton eventually found herself facing a barrage of criticism from Republicans regarding the administration's response to a terrorist attack in Libya.

At 9:42 p.m. on September 11, 2012, Islamic militants from the group Ansar al-Sharia raided a US diplomatic compound in Benghazi, Libya, tossing grenades over its walls and entering the facility under heavy gunfire. Militants spread and ignited diesel fuel, turning the compound into an inferno. The smoke would ultimately result in the deaths of US Ambassador Christopher Stevens and State Department officer Sean Smith. Around midnight, a nearby CIA annex also came under fire from militants launching mortars and rounds from heavy machine guns. After hours of fighting, the attack would claim the lives of Tyrone Woods and Glen Doherty, two decorated former Navy SEALs working as contractors for the CIA.

Almost immediately after the attack, Republicans in Congress clashed with the Obama administration, first over the language being used to describe the incident and then over whether government officials had done enough to secure both diplomatic facilities from harm. Underlying the debate over semantics was whether the attack was a spontaneous response to an anti-Muslim video by a US-based film producer that had been posted to YouTube or, instead, a premeditated terrorist act. No fewer than seven congressional committees began investigating the matter in order to ensure that there was no dereliction on the part of the government. Clinton herself faced days of grilling.

In the summer of 2014, a committee chaired by South Carolina Republican representative Trey Gowdy requested a number of documents from the State Department as part of its efforts to scrutinize communications between State Department and White House officials during the Benghazi attack. While reviewing the material they would soon hand over to Congress, State Department officials made two revelations: there were not that many messages available from Secretary Clinton herself, and the emails they did find came not from an official state.gov email account but from Clinton's private clintonemail.com address. State Department officials began a series of negotiations with Clinton's attorneys in order to gain access to material that pertained to her tenure as secretary of state. On December 5, the Clinton team ultimately handed over more than thirty thousand emails they claimed were work related, while withholding about the same number of emails they deemed personal in nature.

After news of the private server became public, the Clinton presidential campaign went into full crisis-response mode, fending off accusations of intentional wrongdoing by the former secretary and any notion that Clinton thought she was above the law. Her use of private email was merely a matter of convenience, they argued, not part of some devious plan to circumvent federal records laws. Even before she'd formally announced her candidacy, she sought to defuse the story by asking the State Department to release her emails so that Americans could see for themselves how the issue had been overblown. Members of her team also pointed out that other former secretaries of state had also used private email accounts for official business, even if the comparison was imperfect due to the establishment of a home server.

In public, the fight turned vicious. And behind the scenes, State Department personnel reviewing her private emails were growing increasingly concerned with what they were discovering. Officials soon realized they had a major problem on their hands: some of the communications contained information that appeared to be sensitive in nature, and at least a handful were classified.

WHAT HAD BEGUN as an unforced error morphed overnight into a full-fledged political scandal on July 23, 2015, when the *New York Times* first revealed that the inspectors general conducting a review of the Clinton emails had referred the matter to the Justice Department for investigation. Although DOJ had not yet determined whether the issue warranted formal investigation, the notion that officials in the US intelligence community were concerned enough by what they had found to refer the matter to prosecutors sent shock waves throughout official Washington.

At FBI headquarters, we started to get bombarded by media and congressional inquiries from people wanting to know whether Clinton truly was being investigated. We adhered to our time-honored tradition of neither confirming nor denying the existence of the investigation. There are three primary reasons why the FBI typically refuses to comment on investigations. The first is the most obvious: a subject who knows he or she is being scrutinized may destroy evidence, subvert witnesses, or otherwise alter their behavior in a way that could make it difficult to catch them in the act. The second reason for remaining tight-lipped is more altruistic: not everyone who is investigated is guilty, and a person eventually cleared of an allegation would certainly face an uphill battle in rehabilitating his or her reputation if the bureau habitually confirmed investigations that later turned out to be closed with no recommendation for charges. The final reason is more strategic: if the FBI made a practice of formally denying the existence of investigations where none existed, but offered a "no comment" when a case was indeed open, it would serve as an implicit confirmation of current investigative activity.

Despite the fact that the FBI was formally declining to comment on the investigation, there were leaks to the media from inside government, which fueled an endless storm of critical press reports. As Robby Mook explained to me, these leaks drove the Clinton campaign up the wall. "You have to remember this context," he said. "We knew nothing about the ongoing

FBI investigation but were constantly being asked to comment publicly on leaked information."

As someone inside the FBI, I was equally perplexed by what was driving people in the know to divulge sensitive information to reporters. We were regularly receiving calls from the press asking us for a formal response to some tidbit of information they had been given by a source. It was infuriating, and caused me to worry that there might be an anti-Clinton faction working to take her down. There were certainly mixed feelings about the email issue and, indeed, about the Clintons altogether. From Travelgate to Whitewater to the Kenneth Starr special counsel investigation—which had led to the FBI actually visiting the White House to obtain a DNA sample, physically drawing blood from the president of the United States—the Clintons and the bureau had crossed swords. I cannot remember meeting many older agents who had favorable views of the couple.

That was much different with the newer generation. Although, like many law enforcement agencies, the bureau tends to skew conservative politically, employees around my age hadn't been in the bureau during the Clinton presidency, so we tended to judge Hillary Clinton on her own merits rather than through the lens of past baggage involving her husband. Secretary Clinton was a dedicated public servant who had worked her way from US senator to the nation's chief diplomat, and who now stood a very real chance of becoming its next chief executive. We would rarely discuss politics in the office as it related to personal policy preferences, but we had opinions about, and frequently discussed the triumphs and blunders of, the candidates now running for office. And as Campaign 2016 wore on, there were plenty of both.

THE REVVING ELECTRIC guitars of Neil Young's "Rockin' in the Free World" pierced the lobby of Donald Trump's skyscraper on Fifth Avenue as the real estate mogul and reality-television personality walked alongside his wife to the roars of a crowd of supporters. Trump flashed a smile and his signature two-thumbs-up pose for the cameras before stepping onto an escalator that would take him down to the stage where he would announce his candidacy for president of the United States. It was June 16, 2015, a mere three months since Trump had formed an exploratory committee in an effort to test the political waters. On this day, Trump was one of many in a crowded field of Republicans hoping for a shot at the White House, but clearly the candidate had no lack of name recognition. His campaign's primary theme—that the average American was being taken advantage of by elitists—would square nicely with his repeated attacks on Clinton as someone who believed she played by a different set of rules when it came to her private email server.

"But her emails" has become an anguished catchphrase among those watching the scandals plaguing the Trump administration, but during the 2016 presidential campaign, the investigation was a political gift to Trump. He never missed an opportunity to invoke the scandal when stumping across the country. As he strolled through the crowd at the Iowa State Fair on August 15, 2015, flanked by heavy security protection and stopping periodically to shake hands and take pictures, Trump made his way over to a group of reporters. "It's a criminal problem," he said, referring to candidate Clinton's use of private email to discuss sensitive government secrets. Asked by CNN's Jeff Zeleny whether Republicans risked overplaying their hand on the issue, Trump was noncommittal. "It is what it is. It was a terrible thing she did."

Despite much speculation in the media about the existence of an FBI criminal investigation, the bureau did not formally acknowledge the pending case until October 1, during a quarterly roundtable with journalists covering the justice beat. These "pen and pads," as we call them, were routine affairs that provided journalists with an opportunity to question Comey on any topic of their choosing. Mike Kortan, the FBI's assistant director for public affairs, who had served as a mentor of mine since my early days as a bureau intern, would open up each meeting with a brief welcome and then lay down his only ground rule: no live tweeting. He wanted the briefings to serve as conversations during which reporters could delve deeply into important topics, ask probing questions, and circle back with follow-ups. Before each media availability, our press team would scan the headlines and compile a list of topics they expected would come up during the meeting.

Often, the briefing list was drawn from queries our press shop was regularly receiving in its day-to-day engagement with journalists. However, on this particular day, it did not take a public relations maven to predict what topic would be front-of-mind for journalists covering the Justice Department: Was Hillary Clinton under FBI investigation?

In deciding how to answer this question, Comey and our other colleagues in senior leadership had wrestled with two important aspects, both unique to this investigation. First, was public interest in the case enough to warrant disclosing that the FBI was indeed involved? Although standard practice is to decline comment, there are instances where the bureau can acknowledge investigations, should transparency with the American people be judged to outweigh secrecy. The decision was made easier by a second aspect: Everybody else involved was publicly talking about the FBI's work. The inspectors general who had originally referred the matter to the Justice Department had done so publicly. Even Clinton's own lawyers were publicly talking about their interactions with the FBI. In Comey's mind, by this point, it would have simply seemed foolish to continue playing coy with something the subject of the investigation had openly acknowledged.

The FBI director decided it was time to confront the question head-on, confirmed that the bureau was indeed investigating the Clinton server issue, and then declined to give any more details. Much of the remainder of the press gaggle was spent discussing the increase in murder rates in certain communities across the nation as well as the bureau's work to counter homegrown violent extremists.

In public appearances that fall and winter, Comey continued to get asked about the investigation—internally code-named Midyear Exam.

As a brief aside, many of us now in public life often get asked how FBI case code names are assigned and where they originate. The truth is, most of us don't have a clue. Naming a case is not a decision that makes its way to senior management but is instead typically something agents and analysts opening the case get to pick. Unless they were specifically there on the investigative team when the case started, the actual genesis of the code name remains a mystery to them. The main purpose in using a code name,

apart from brevity, is so you can easily reference a matter while still maintaining some operational security. For example, when Comey received
operational briefings on cases, we could simply list the code name on his
schedule without going into further detail. If you passed someone in the
hall and wondered where they were headed, they could say, "I'm going
to this Midyear Exam meeting," without telling everyone in earshot, "I'm
going to this meeting about Secretary Hillary Clinton's alleged mishandling
of highly sensitive classified information." Finally, inside the FBI there is
a mythical computer program that spits out random words to form code
names for those who find themselves lacking the creative capacity to come
up with their own. I say "mythical," because everyone has heard of this
program, but no one I've met has ever used it.

Each time Comey was asked about the Midyear Exam case in public,
he would run the same play: decline specifics and assure the person asking the question that the investigation was being conducted professionally.
A congressional hearing in February 2016 was one of many occasions
Comey was asked about the case. As I sat behind him waiting for the Clinton
question, I pondered how long it would take for a member of Congress on
the committee charged with overseeing the FBI's budget to somehow manage to twist an appropriations-related question into a dig for information
about the Clinton investigation. Then, Rep. John Carter (R-TX) asked the
question that was on the mind of every US citizen with even a passing
interest in politics: When was this thing going to end? Comey responded
he could not provide a timeline, but assured the committee that he was
getting regular updates on the case, and promised it was being done both
promptly and correctly.

WHILE COUNTERINTELLIGENCE INVESTIGATORS and analysts at FBI
headquarters were working to obtain and review emails that had passed
through Clinton's private server, agents were also busy interviewing those
in Clinton's orbit who might have had insight into why the secretary
chose to use a private server. Agents interviewed the staffer who set it
up, Clinton's personal attorney, and her personal assistant, among many

others. After poring over thousands of documents and spending untold hours sitting across from witnesses, investigators could not say with certainty that there was criminal intent behind Clinton's decision to communicate government business over private email.

By the end of May, absent some new revelation, it was becoming increasingly clear the investigation was in its final stages. On a trip to Nashville to meet with law enforcement officers, Comey and I spent our time before an event kicking around his possible options for closing the case. "Here's the dilemma," Comey told me. "There is such intense public interest in this case I feel like the American people need to know more than just what we ultimately decide to recommend, but how we arrived at that conclusion. There are pros and cons to maximum transparency. What do you think?"

I had privately pondered for months about the various ways the investigation might end, but now, finding myself being asked point-blank for my opinion, I thought again for a moment before responding. "Whatever you ultimately decide," I said, "whether to close the case or recommend she be prosecuted, your hallmark has always been transparency. That is what you are known for. What you have to do is put yourself in the shoes of the public and ask whether they deserve to know what happened in one of the highest-profile cases in FBI history. I don't think you can do a Joaquin Phoenix in *Gladiator* and simply give a thumbs-up or -down."

I don't want to overstate my role in Comey's decision-making—he was hearing from a number of colleagues more senior than I—but I believed then as I do now that the FBI must never forget that public confidence in the organization is what aids its effectiveness. It isn't enough to simply ask for the public's blind trust. When circumstances warrant, especially at the end of an investigation when a case is about to be either closed or handed over to attorneys for possible prosecution, the organization must weigh what is actually in the public interest. If the FBI had recommended prosecution, the bureau could have simply let the case speak for itself in court; the American people would have been privy to all supporting evidence and testimony that had guided the recommendation. If the decision were not to prosecute, however, there would be no trial. Without any sort of public explanation, the bureau would have been in essence saying: *Trust us.* Given the intense national partisan polarization at that moment, *Trust us* would have been untenable.

Comey began drafting remarks for a possible statement advising the public of the FBI's final decision. Although the case was not over, it was clear where it was headed: The investigative team was troubled by Clinton's slipshod manner of communicating, but they had not yet found any evidence that she was deliberately breaking the law. Comey wanted as much lead time as possible to write, edit, and circulate his recommendation among members of the investigative team for input. Realizing the election was fast approaching, he pushed hard for investigators to finish their work as quickly as humanly possible. "We are going to do this as professionally and promptly as we can," he recalled explaining to the investigative team. "I want this over as much as the next person, but we are not going to sacrifice thoroughness for speed."

While the Midyear Exam team plugged away, a key question remained: Would the FBI director make the announcement by himself or do so alongside the attorney general? The answer to the second question became much easier following a misstep at an airport in Arizona.

On June 27, as Attorney General Loretta Lynch's airplane sat on the tarmac of Phoenix Sky Harbor International Airport, former president Bill Clinton walked onto the plane to say hello. According to Lynch, the two talked about golf and their grandchildren, but the optics could not have been worse. Here we had the nation's chief law enforcement officer in private conversation with the spouse of the subject of a high-profile criminal investigation.

Trump pounced. "It was really a sneak," he said while appearing on a conservative radio show. Conspiracy theories abounded, with Republicans convinced that surely the topic of Hillary Clinton's emails had come up.

Inside the FBI, leadership started getting wind of a line building in media circles theorizing that somehow the bureau was at fault for having allowed the meeting to occur at all. The attorney general's security detail is staffed and managed by career FBI agents, and this new conjecture included the preposterous notion that these agents should have predicted the public relations nightmare such a meeting would cause and should have taken steps to prevent it. One FBI official vented to me at the time, "Are they out of their minds? The FBI's job is to prevent harm and embarrassment, but that doesn't include putting a hand up in front of a former president of the United States and blocking him from a meeting a protectee has agreed to take."

For James Comey, the Lynch-Clinton tarmac meeting dictated his eventual decision to distance the FBI from the Department of Justice when the time came to announce the FBI's recommendation in the Clinton email case. In his view, assuming there was nothing new gleaned from an actual interview of Clinton, the decision would almost certainly be to decline prosecution. He had studied years of case law involving espionage investigations and those pertaining to the mishandling of classified information and could not find a similar instance of someone being prosecuted on the facts presented during the Clinton investigation. But now, how could he decline prosecution without explanation after the meeting in Arizona had cast a cloud of doubt over the department's independence? To be sure, there was no evidence Lynch ever acted inappropriately—to this day, she is widely believed to be an honorable person—but in such a polarized and toxic climate, perception mattered.

EACH INDEPENDENCE DAY, tourists from around the world flock to our nation's capital to take in the historic landmarks and watch the famous fireworks display on the national mall. For government employees, the holiday is usually a nice break that allows an opportunity to enjoy aspects of the city often taken for granted by those with monuments and landmarks outside their doors.

Inside the bureau that holiday weekend in 2016, however, our FBI team was bracing for a political firestorm. While the Midyear Exam investigators made final preparations for the interview of Hillary Clinton, a small number of us on the director's staff were quietly working to arrange the logistics for Comey's planned press conference announcing the results.

Hosting a press conference that would likely be broadcast live around the world is not like flipping a switch. The logistics involved are complex. But the sensitivities surrounding this particular investigation meant the operation would have to be done by a very small group. Rather than calling all hands on deck for assistance, we had two hands on deck—FBI assistant director Mike Kortan and me. On Friday afternoon, Mike and I scoped out the room on the first floor of FBI headquarters where the announcement would be made. We moved lecterns, lined up chairs for reporters, dragged flags in from around the building, adjusted lighting, and tested the sound system. We also set up a giant screen at the back of the room, where I would run a teleprompter that would allow Comey to read his prepared remarks.

Once things were set, we brought Comey down to familiarize him with the room and allow him to run through his speech a couple of times. I pulled aside Jim Rybicki, Comey's chief of staff and longtime confidant, so I could ask something that had been nagging at me all afternoon.

"I don't get it," I said, pointing to the podium. "What if she lies during her interview tomorrow?"

"Simple," Jim replied. "If she lies, this is all off. If agents learn something new they need to run down, this is all off. If they walk out of the interview with even more questions or a hint of suspicion, this is all off."

ON SATURDAY, JULY 2, the armored Suburban driven by Hillary Clinton's Secret Service detail arrived at the J. Edgar Hoover Building, where an elevator was waiting to whisk the former secretary of state to a conference room in the building's emergency operations center on the fifth floor. Clinton and her lawyers sat for nearly three and a half hours of questioning. One thing that struck the team was how little Clinton actually appeared to know about technology. They concluded that the most basic of explanations—that Clinton truly seemed to be a digital neophyte—may have been the reason for her carelessness.

Much has been made by critics of the FBI's investigation regarding the dynamics of the Clinton interview. Why wasn't she placed under oath? Why was there no recording? How could the FBI permit her lawyer Cheryl Mills to take part in the interview when she herself was a witness in the case?

For those who may not be familiar with the bureau's work, FBI agents don't make a practice of placing people under oath. It's unnecessary: if someone lies to an agent about a material fact during the course of an FBI interview, they can be prosecuted regardless of whether they were placed under oath. Additionally, recordings are made when interviewing a subject who is in custody. In this case, however, Clinton was there voluntarily. For this same reason, the FBI had no way to dictate which lawyer she decided to bring to represent her. If Clinton had been under arrest, the FBI would have had greater latitude in limiting who could be present.

The next day, we rallied back at headquarters to discuss next steps. I joined Rybicki, Kortan, and then associate deputy director David Bowdich, as we milled about waiting for the director. Comey soon arrived, casually dressed in khaki pants and a light-blue shirt. We were all dressed down, and I laughed at the realization that all five of us were too exhausted to even put on a suit. The FBI is an extremely buttoned-down institution, and few walk the hallways of headquarters without wearing business attire. But on that Sunday morning, we all assumed we would be forgiven for breaking protocol.

Comey updated us on the final conclusions of the investigative team and their determination that the Clinton interview had not changed the recommendation against prosecution. We were to proceed as planned with the press conference and then brace for impact.

TUESDAY, JULY 5, started just like any other day at the bureau. As employees filed in and chatted about their holiday weekend, Mike Kortan and I were busy meeting with the public affairs specialists who would play an instrumental role in executing the press conference. They rapidly went to work calling reporters and advising them that the FBI director would soon hold a press conference. Given how rare it was for the FBI to hold a press conference at headquarters, much less one involving the director, journalists scrambled to get to the room. They knew that the fact that the FBI was keeping the topic secret likely meant only one thing.

Up in the director's suite, Comey picked up the phone and called his boss across the street. "Madam Attorney General," he said. "I just wanted to let you know I am about to hold a press conference announcing the FBI's conclusion in the Hillary Clinton investigation. For reasons I hope you'll realize, I'm not going to tell you what that decision is."

Loretta Lynch asked Comey for an indication of what exactly was about to transpire, to which Comey replied, "I'm sorry, Madam Attorney General. I just can't discuss it. I hope one day you'll understand why."

With that, Comey prepared to walk downstairs and to the microphones. He thanked the team for all their hard work amid such intense outside pressure. He then asked Kortan to press SEND on an all-employee email, disseminating his remarks bureau-wide and allowing FBI personnel a brief heads-up on what he would soon tell the world.

When all of the reporters in attendance had been seated, Comey stepped out to the cameras and began his remarks.

"What I would like to do today is tell you three things: what we did; what we found; and what we are recommending to the Department of Justice," he said, and for the next fifteen minutes he detailed the FBI's findings, outlining Clinton's sloppiness in using an unsecured email server and describing the State Department's culture of lax information-security practices, before finally announcing the case would be closed and his recommendation that Clinton not be prosecuted.

He then offered a parting shot at all of the partisan critics who had engaged in endless armchair analysis, as well as a note of appreciation to the investigators and analysts who had dedicated nearly a year of their lives to one of the most high-stakes cases in recent memory.

"I know there were many opinions expressed by people who were not part of the investigation—including people in government—but none of that mattered to us. Opinions are irrelevant, and they were all uninformed by insight into our investigation, because we did the investigation the right way," Comey said. "Only facts matter, and the FBI found them here in an entirely apolitical and professional way. I couldn't be prouder to be part of this organization."

Officials in the Department of Justice were furious. In their view, the FBI director—a subordinate official—had violated Justice Department protocol by unilaterally announcing the case was now closed. And Donald Trump was seething. In a popular refrain he would sing time and again, he said that the system was "rigged," that the FBI was clearly in the tank for Clinton and had ended its investigation in order to save her from prosecution.

Clinton allies were understandably aghast. Comey had just bloodied their candidate, criticizing her behavior even though he was recommending against charging. As Robby Mook told me, the campaign team watched the press conference in silence. "It was highly climactic," he said. "We just literally had no idea what was going to happen. I think that's an important piece. I think sometimes the press almost assumes that we had the backstory and we knew what was going on. We knew less than they did about what was happening."

"What were you thinking after hearing Comey criticize her behavior?" I asked him.

"What do you do?" he replied. "He's just said I didn't find anything wrong, I'm not referring it for prosecution, but she's a terrible person. We just wanted to move on. We thought that it would close the book on this. Because we falsely assumed that it was over. But it wasn't, unbeknownst to us."

"I'M TOTALLY SCREWED," Comey remarked nearly four months later as our fully armored SUV lurched from the basement garage of FBI headquarters and rounded the corner onto Pennsylvania Avenue. We were headed for the CIA. It was a chilly autumn morning in the nation's capital, and as the motorcade slowed to allow a throng of tourists in overcoats to shuffle through the intersection in front of us, Comey stared at them through the vehicle's bulletproof windows, no doubt wishing he could trade places with any one of them.

Minutes earlier, he had given the green light to his senior leadership team to send a letter to congressional leaders advising them that the bureau had reopened its investigation into Hillary Clinton. The night before, members of his senior leadership team had called an impromptu meeting to brief him on something they never saw coming. During the course of an unrelated FBI investigation of Anthony Weiner, a disgraced former Democratic congressman from New York, investigators had found thousands of emails between Clinton and Huma Abedin, Weiner's estranged wife, who for years had been one of the former secretary of state's closest confidants. Originally puzzled by their discovery, investigators quickly realized that Abedin had utilized her husband's laptop to back up her own communications, which now served as a possible investigative gold mine. They had turned to Comey for authorization to obtain a search warrant in order to lawfully seize the records, which might reveal a different motivation for Clinton's establishing the personal server.

These revelations presented Comey with two difficult decision points, which he sat studying with clasped hands. First, should he authorize the reopening of the case so investigators could proceed with obtaining a search warrant? To him, this was a no-brainer. Career FBI agents and analysts who had overseen the Clinton investigation had just told him new evidence of possible criminal activity was sitting on a seized laptop in Manhattan. "Go!" he instructed.

The next decision was more difficult: What, if anything, should he say to Congress about the new investigative action he had just authorized?

During a tough congressional hearing called by irate Republicans after the initial investigation, Comey had promised that he would advise the members if any new information came to light warranting additional investigation. That had just occurred. Now, however, it was mere days before a national election for president of the United States, and the Department of Justice operated under a long-held norm that agents and prosecutors should refrain from doing anything that might impact an election. On the other hand, if it came to light after the election that the FBI had once again started investigating Clinton and had kept it a secret, the bureau might be accused of a cover-up.

Should he speak, or should he conceal? In Comey's mind, either option was an action, and he once again found himself in the position of erring on the side of radical transparency.

Comey's October 28 letter to Congress announcing that there was new material that may or may not be "significant" leaked almost immediately. Rep. Jason Chaffetz (R-UT), apparently arresting any inclination to adhere to standard protocol and not discuss sensitive investigative matters, was the first to proudly tweet: "'The FBI has learned of the existence of emails that appear to be pertinent to the investigation.' Case reopened."

The letter was like lobbing a mortar into the campaign for the highest office in the United States.

For his part, Trump was filled with glee. This was just the shot of energy his campaign needed. Suddenly, he loved the FBI and he loved James Comey. After repeatedly slamming the FBI and accusing it of being rigged in favor of Hillary Clinton, Trump was now saying Comey had redeemed himself. "Hillary Clinton is guilty," Trump said at a campaign rally in Michigan. "She knows it, the FBI knows it, the people know it, and now it's up to the American people to deliver justice at the ballot box on November 8."

AT FBI HEADQUARTERS, Comey was once again imploring the team investigating the Weiner laptop to operate in the same manner as they had conducted the original Clinton case: do it fast, but do it well. It was just over a week until the presidential election, and if it were humanly possible for the bureau to sort through the newly discovered messages and draw some investigative conclusion about their merits, he wanted it done.

Technical experts at the FBI's Operational Technology Division created a software program that would allow investigators to upload the new emails to a computer system and compare them with the Clinton emails previously in the FBI's holdings. This "de-duplication" process would rapidly cull the overwhelming majority of emails that had already been investigated.

Over the course of about a week, investigators and analysts reviewed each message by hand and searched for any evidence that Clinton had knowingly broken the law. Once the process had been completed, the team briefed Comey on their findings and their assessment that, despite finding new classified information sent via an unsecured system, nothing they had found in the new batch of emails changed their original recommendation that Clinton not be charged.

Comey immediately advised Congress of this finding. At Trump campaign headquarters, the real estate mogul's acolytes smelled a conspiracy. "IMPOSSIBLE: There R 691,200 seconds in 8 days," Trump adviser and retired lieutenant general Michael Flynn tweeted after word of the new letter to Congress became public. "DIR Comey has thoroughly reviewed 650,000 emails in 8 days? An email / second? IMPOSSIBLE."

Trump parroted this line of attack against the FBI, angrily exclaiming at a rally in Michigan, "You can't review six hundred fifty thousand new emails in eight days!"

But it was two days before the election. Early voting in some states had already begun. For the Clinton campaign, the damage had already been done.

As ROBBY MOOK and I finished our lunch that afternoon in Los Angeles in the summer of 2018, I wasn't about to leave without asking his view on how my former employer may have ultimately played a role in the defeat of his candidate.

I was expecting venom—many people blame Comey to this day—but instead, Mook offered measured analysis.

"It certainly could have decided the election," he said, "but we'll never know for sure. We know rules were broken, and these major events were a breach of protocol. We can debate that endlessly, or we can spend our energy preventing a similar occurrence. We need to reflect on how we make sure something like this doesn't happen again."

However, the FBI's investigation into Hillary Clinton's use of a private email server was only one effort that posed an existential threat to her candidacy. The other was something much more sinister. As the public would eventually learn, while the FBI was toiling away investigating her emails, a hostile foreign government was secretly working feverishly to deny her the presidency.

# CHAPTER 4

# Espionage to Sabotage

A TWENTY-MINUTE DRIVE east along the A12 motorway in the Netherlands will take you from the Binnenhof complex of federal government buildings near The Hague's municipal capital center to the city of Zoetermeer. Rising above one of the city's thoroughfares is a building that looks nothing like the others in its vicinity. Perched across the street from apartments, shops, and corporate offices, it resembles a series of ash-colored battleships lined bow to stern in zigzag formation, each adorned with a myriad of antennas and satellite dishes atop their massive superstructures. The unusual yet conspicuous mixture of heavy wrought-iron fencing, brick facade, and security barricades surrounding the headquarters of the General Intelligence and Security Service (AIVD) leaves no question that there are important secrets inside worth protecting.

AIVD is the vanguard of Dutch national security—an agency of fewer than two thousand people whose mission is to protect its citizens and allies from a range of terrorism, counterintelligence, and cyber threats both at home and abroad. With a classified budget and broad authority to monitor and neutralize malevolent actors, the organization is a major player among Western intelligence agencies. Although difficult to compare to any one US intelligence counterpart, AIVD can be best understood as an outfit that puts together under one roof the domestic intelligence function of the FBI, the international intelligence duties of CIA, and the signals intelligence role of the NSA.

Although AIVD serves the public, it is cumbersome for average citizens to make contact with the agency. Its compound is designated a "prohibited place" under Dutch law, which makes being on its grounds without prior authorization a felony. Citizens cannot email the agency or submit a tip online, but must instead pick up the telephone or physically write to a post office box. Its officers make reaching the agency through digital means nearly impossible, as such communications are vulnerable to covert eavesdropping by adversaries. And if anyone knows about eavesdropping on the enemy, it's the cyber sleuths at AIVD.

During a visit to The Hague in the spring of 2015, I had traveled the four thousand miles from Washington to the Dutch capital to meet with my law enforcement and intelligence counterparts from several Western nations. We were preparing for a joint enforcement action that would collectively disrupt the efforts of cybercriminals who were stealing personal information from unsuspecting victims and wreaking havoc on the global financial system. Recognizing that malicious cyber actors care little about international borders, several allied nations had partnered to shrink the world, share intelligence, and take down websites and communication facilities used by those exploiting the internet. Although our primary goal for this gathering was transparency and coordination, these joint operations were always a bit of a dance: first we had to determine what investigative information we could share with each other without jeopardizing sensitive sources and methods, and then we had to agree to what details we could release to the public without endangering future investigations. It was a dynamic I had often experienced working overseas with international partners—giving and taking without giving too much.

After a long day of exhausting discussions, aggravated by the fact that I'm the world's worst sufferer of jet lag despite years of serious work travel, I packed up my notes and prepared to depart the government office where we were meeting and head back to my hotel for the night. On my way out, an exceedingly affable Dutch law enforcement officer named Willem grabbed me by the arm and asked if he and a colleague could buy me a beer to celebrate a lengthy day of interagency cooperation. "*Natuurlijk!*" I replied, testing the Dutch I had been studying off and on since my first visit to Amsterdam several years prior. "Of course!"

The three of us walked to a pub about five blocks away and slid onto the high stools surrounding a glossy cherry-oak table next to the bar, where draft beer was flowing freely for a packed house. A Green Day song blared from the speakers above, a fact that would have normally been cause enough to make me run for the exits, but I was the guest and did not want to offend. When our frosty amber beverages arrived, we chatted with excitement about the cyber operation being planned—leaving out the sensitive specifics, for fear of being overheard by neighboring patrons—and talked about the individual paths in life that had led us to careers in law enforcement.

After about an hour had passed, Willem recognized a customer walking through the pub's entrance and motioned him over to our table. As the lean man of about forty years of age with spiky blond hair and darting eyes navigated his way through the crowded bar, Willem whispered that he was a friend.

The intelligence officer—whom I'll call Jeroen—grabbed a seat and introduced himself. The three of them exchanged greetings, slipping into Dutch as they described their day. "English, please," I exclaimed with a smile. "Otherwise, I won't know if you three are plotting something." The group erupted in laughter, followed by a flurry of apologies.

We chatted and sipped beer for about another hour, briefing Jeroen on aspects of the multinational cyber enforcement action. He listened intently, nodding regularly while his eyes swept the room like a human radar system.

As the conversation was winding down, Jeroen cleared his throat and said something I would fully appreciate only months later, once it became known that foreign cyber villains were laying the groundwork to upend a US election. "The criminal enterprises are terrible and must be stopped," he said, "but we cannot take our eyes off the nation-states. We are at war. We cannot forget that cybercrime backed by the resources of a hostile government is a thousand times worse than your everyday hacker."

He was right, of course. Nation-state cyber intrusions are far more destructive than anything a lone hacker could ever hope to achieve.

IT WAS THE ultimate "pwn" (pronounced "pone"), cyberspeak for conquering an adversary. From their fortified compound in Zoetermeer, sleuths at AIVD had managed to penetrate the electronic barriers of a group of Russians who were not your run-of-the-mill hackers. These were the ultimate professionals, working at the behest of Kremlin officials hell-bent on interfering in the affairs of governments across the West. Details of the operation were highly protected—kept in a proverbial silo, secret from those without a justifiable need to know—until the operation finally became public in explosive reporting by the Dutch newspaper *de Volkskrant* in January 2018. As the world learned, skilled intelligence operators in the Netherlands had managed to beat the Russians at their own game.

As reported, the operation that would lead intelligence officers in the Netherlands deep into the networks of one of Russia's most dangerous hacking teams began in the summer of 2014. The target was known as APT 29 (Advanced Persistent Threat 29), a group various analysts had nicknamed "the Dukes" and "Cozy Bear." Experts believe that the Dukes have been operating against foreign governments, diplomatic establishments, and corporations since 2010, and that the outfit is run by the SVR, Russia's foreign intelligence agency, which formed from remnants of the old KGB following the collapse of the Soviet Union. Once they had penetrated the Cozy Bear network, Dutch government hackers were able to surveil multiple aspects of the group operating in Moscow, including network traffic and efforts to plot and plan cyberattacks against enemy targets. Remarkably, *de Volkskrant* sources indicated that the Dutch were also able to gain access to security-camera footage from inside the Russian intelligence facility, providing them with live visibility into the inner workings of the operation, and the faces of Russian hackers and visitors alike.

In November 2014, *de Volkskrant* reported, Dutch intelligence officers witnessed something astonishing: the Russians were in the process of launching a cyberattack on the US Department of State, aspects of which the team at Zoetermeer could see in real time as the Russians stole email log-in credentials from unsuspecting State Department employees and maliciously entered the State Department's unclassified computer network. Dutch authorities relayed what they were seeing to officials at the US National Security Agency, who worked alongside the FBI and IT personnel at the State Department to fend off the attack.

As the NSA's then deputy director later told the *Washington Post,* the event "was hand-to-hand combat." Over a twenty-four-hour period, US officials sought to lock down the State Department system and eradicate the intruders. Each time they tried to sever the connection between the infected State Department computers and the Moscow-run command and control systems directing the attack, the Russians would establish a new line into the infected systems. Eventually, US officials decided to pull the plug and bring the entire network down, which caused mass communications disruptions around the world as officials worked to reconstitute the network and mitigate the damage.

Inside the intelligence community, we debated how to respond to the attack. People emailing the State Department, an agency with about seventy thousand employees, started receiving undelivered bounced-back messages; there was simply no way such a major disruption would stay quiet for long. At this time, my role at the FBI was chief spokesperson for cyber matters. Following some dozen coordination meetings with my counterpart, Ned Price, at the National Security Council, we decided that the State Department would take the lead in responding to any initial inquiries about the attack, and the FBI's response would come later. On Sunday, November 16, the department indicated to inquiring reporters that "activity of concern" had been detected on the State Department network and was being mitigated. The following day, I issued a statement from the bureau announcing that we had opened an investigation into the incident.

At the FBI, we thought our public-facing work was done. In cyber investigations, especially those involving national security implications, there is nothing more the bureau was generally comfortable doing other than acknowledging we were investigating a matter and then declining further comment. If the government wanted to call out and "name and shame" a foreign adversary, that decision would come from policy makers at the National Security Council, not the FBI. For instance, in the case of the Sony Pictures cyberattack by North Korea that occurred later that month, we spent weeks working with the victim company to investigate and help reconstitute its systems, but the ultimate decision to announce the perpetrators of the attack came from the White House. In the case of the State Department attack, it was far too early to even consider the implications of pointing a finger at the Kremlin.

Behind the scenes, the intelligence community's work was far from over. Russian hackers were able to capitalize on their breach of the State Department system and gain access to the unclassified network at the White House by sending a simple phishing email to a White House employee, who mistakenly clicked on an embedded link in the message. Unlike our public statements during the State Department hacking, and understanding the sensitivities and myriad ramifications of the Executive Office of the President facing a cyber intrusion, we in the FBI declined to acknowledge our involvement altogether, instead referring all responses to Price at the NSC. At that point, it looked like the damage was limited to the White House's unclassified network.

Thanks to the timely warning from our counterparts in the Netherlands, it appeared that the US government had, in the final analysis, dodged a proverbial bullet. The attacks on the State Department and the White House were costly and disruptive, but the impact was minor compared to the alternative of the Russians having been successful at burrowing into US government networks and remaining in place undetected. Although the Russians had been alerted to the fact that US authorities had discovered their offensive cyber efforts, Dutch visibility into the Cozy Bear operation had not been blown. AIVD continued to monitor the group—watching and cataloguing its every move.

According to *de Volkskrant*, by mid-2015 the Dutch would again find themselves picking up the phone to alert their US counterparts to a new Russian line of attack. This time, the victim would be one of the two major political parties in the United States. It would be the first wave in a brazen effort to disrupt the 2016 presidential election.

WE MAY NEVER know for sure, at least not in its entirety, what specifically prompted an FBI cyber agent, whose name I am choosing not to reveal, to phone the Democratic National Committee in September 2015. His purpose was to warn the DNC that the FBI had evidence of an intrusion into one of its computers, but the source of that intelligence was and remains highly protected to this day. What we do know is that the bureau had become aware that Cozy Bear—the same Russian hackers being monitored by intelligence officials in the Netherlands—had managed to defeat the cybersecurity protocols in place at the DNC and were in one of its systems. According to *de Volkskrant*, the AIVD intelligence service had witnessed the Russians launching a cyberattack against the DNC and then had notified the United States. Although neither US nor Dutch authorities will comment on the information sharing, the timeline for when AIVD reportedly notified the US government and when the FBI subsequently notified the DNC squarely lines up.

In some ways, the call from the FBI reflects the manner in which the US government typically handles notifying potential victims of such crimes. Once malicious activity is detected—either directly by the FBI or by one of its domestic or foreign counterparts—the government has to undergo a cost-benefit analysis in order to assess whether it is best to surveil the criminal actors and determine the full scope of their activity, or to contact the victims of the intrusion and make them aware of danger to their systems. Similar to other national security threats such as terrorism, there is a delicate balance involved: watching and waiting in order to fully illuminate a network of bad actors, or deciding to risk further intelligence collection by going overt in order to prevent imminent damage.

When the FBI notified the DNC that its systems had possibly been compromised, however, it was less the sounding of an alarm and more a whispering into the wind. The special agent phoned the DNC, explained the nature of his call, and was then transferred to the in-house help desk. The

IT contractor he spoke with at first didn't even believe he was really with the FBI. The agent explained that the bureau suspected that a DNC computer had been infected by the Dukes and asked the IT person to check the computer system logs for any indication of the hacking group's presence. The IT specialist was not an expert in cyber intrusions and had to Google "the Dukes" to find out who they were. Still not quite sure whether the call from the agent was a hoax, he then conducted only a cursory search of the DNC's network logs.

What followed was a series of missed opportunities that would have been laughable had the consequences not been so dire. The agent repeatedly placed calls to the IT official, who simply decided not to call him back. As the official indicated in an internal DNC memo viewed by the *New York Times*, "I did not return his calls, as I had nothing to report." By November, the FBI cyber agent was growing increasingly frustrated and called with even worse news: one of the DNC's computers was "calling home," signaling that the malicious code inserted into its network was communicating with the hackers back in Russia. The DNC's tech team again scanned its systems for the indicators provided by the FBI, but came up with no hits. Months would pass will little meaningful progress by either the FBI or the DNC IT staff. All the while, Russian operatives were living on the DNC network, and were about to be joined by a different set of Russian intelligence hackers who would soon turn the Democratic Party's world upside down.

In March 2016, FBI agents arrived in person at the offices of Democratic candidate Hillary Clinton and warned that the campaign had been the target of phishing emails by Russian hackers. However, what neither the Clinton camp nor the FBI knew at the time was the Russians had already scored a major win in a spear-phishing effort aimed at Clinton campaign chair John Podesta's Gmail account. Because Podesta had clicked a malicious link, the Russians now had access to over fifty thousand emails sitting in Podesta's inbox, which would come back to haunt the campaign as the election drew closer. This time, however, it was not the Cozy Bear actors the Dutch had previously been monitoring, but an entirely different set of hackers from the Russian military intelligence agency, known as the GRU. This new threat—dubbed "Fancy Bear" by cybersecurity professionals—was much more aggressive than the intruders that had previously burrowed into the DNC network. When the cybersecurity firm CrowdStrike was eventually brought in by the DNC to mitigate the intrusion, a stunning discovery was made: not only were Cozy Bear and Fancy Bear both inside the DNC network, but neither group of Russian hackers appeared to know of the other's presence.

Over the next several weeks, CrowdStrike worked with a small team at the DNC to assess the damage and rid the intruders from the network. The operation was conducted in secret. If tipped off to the fact that they had been discovered, the Russians might have inflicted serious damage before forensic examiners were able to fully scrub them from the system. If the public became aware, the DNC would find itself in crisis-management mode, fielding calls for information while at the same time trying to win an election.

Late on the afternoon of June 10, approximately one hundred staff members filed into a packed conference room at DNC headquarters in Washington for a mandatory meeting. As described by the Associated Press, Lindsey Reynolds, the DNC's chief operating officer, opened by saying, "What I am about to tell you cannot leave this room." All staff members were required to turn in their laptop computers immediately— no exceptions—and they were warned not to utter a word about it. "Don't even talk to your dog about it," Reynolds said.

What the employees didn't know was that CrowdStrike was preparing for the final step in its remediation efforts to eradicate Russian intelligence operatives from the DNC system. The company would spend the weekend making this final push.

Within a matter of days, the DNC was ready to let the world know that it had been the victim of a massive breach by a foreign nation-state. Although it was ultimately the decision of party officials, the Clinton campaign had been briefed and was on board with the plan. "We were okay with it going to the press," Robby Mook told me. "By that point, we were concerned that the Russians were going to start pushing out information they had stolen. We were leery of their close association with Trump."

As part of their media strategy, the DNC opted to brief one journalist who could lay out the story in a thoughtful way and provide a thorough overview of the cyberattack. For this, they turned to veteran *Washington Post* reporter Ellen Nakashima—someone who was extremely familiar with the intricacies of state-sponsored cyber intrusions. Nakashima is widely known in media circles as one of the best in the business. When I worked in public affairs at the FBI, I would periodically receive calls from her on a number of cyber-related issues, and each time I felt a bit of hesitation before answering the phone, because I knew that she was extremely well sourced and that whatever she was seeking comment on had already been vetted a hundred ways from Sunday.

Nakashima's piece, titled "Russian Government Hackers Penetrated DNC, Stole Opposition Research on Trump," ran in the *Post* on Tuesday, June 14, 2016. It laid out the operation in detail, and noted that "the depth of the penetration reflects the skill and determination of the United States' top cyber-adversary as Russia goes after strategic targets, from the White House and State Department to political campaign organizations." The story also included an all-too-familiar full-throated denial from a Kremlin spokesperson, who completely ruled out any Russian involvement.

Although the initial story rocked official Washington and cybersecurity circles, it was partially eclipsed by a national tragedy that had struck two days earlier. In Orlando, Florida, an ISIS sympathizer had opened fire at Pulse, a gay nightclub, killing forty-nine innocent people and wounding over fifty others. The attack consumed the news cycle as investigators and reporters worked to unearth details of the shooter's past and determine the motivation behind the mass murder. At the time, it was the deadliest shooting by a single perpetrator in US history.

In the aftermath of this horror, FBI director James Comey had let me know that he intended to travel to Orlando and meet with the investigators who were still working to process the heartbreaking crime scene, and to thank the dozens of first responders who had tried to help save lives. With little advance notice of Comey's trip, I'd decided to travel ahead of him in order to iron out the logistics of his visit and help scout a location where he could meet privately with over one hundred law enforcement officers involved with the incident. At the time, my mind was focused on the tragedy that had befallen the LGBTQ community and the FBI's investigation into the terrorist who had wreaked so much havoc on innocent civilians.

I'd had little time to check the headlines, but as I sat waiting to log in to a computer terminal inside the FBI's satellite office in Orlando, I overheard a group of agents in the squad bay next to me discussing the DNC hack. "This is really bad," I heard an agent say to one of her colleagues.

Wrongly assuming they were still talking about the *Washington Post* story, I peered over the cubicle and asked if there were any new developments.

"Oh yeah," she replied. "The dam is about to break."

THE DEMOCRATIC DAM did indeed start to rupture on June 15. An anonymous person using the online persona "Guccifer 2.0" published a WordPress blog post titled, in part, "DNC's Servers Hacked by a Lone Hacker." The post dripped with sarcasm and snark, refuting the claim by CrowdStrike that sophisticated Russian hackers had been behind the attack and claiming that it was Guccifer 2.0 who had done it. The post included what Guccifer 2.0 called "a few docs" from the DNC network, along with an ominous warning: Guccifer 2.0 had given stolen material to WikiLeaks, the organization created by Julian Assange that had become famous for publishing sensitive government and private information.

Although not known at the time, the FBI was later able to tie Guccifer 2.0 to the GRU hacker group, based on technical and link analysis. For cybersecurity experts, any lingering doubt about whether Russia was indeed behind the DNC hack was put to rest when Guccifer 2.0 started publishing the stolen documents. One former intelligence officer I spoke with summarized the thinking at the time among national security professionals. "When individuals engage in hacking, the goal is often to steal information they can then profit from," he explained. "Publicizing the information they have stolen makes no sense. Similarly, governments who steal information for intelligence purposes almost universally use that information to inform their own worldview." The exception to this rule occurs, he told me, when a foreign government seeks to use stolen information for the purpose of launching an influence operation—to manipulate and shape the public opinion of another country. "When the DNC information was released in mass quantities, I immediately saw the hallmark of a Russian influence operation," he said. "This had now moved from traditional espionage to sabotage."

Among the first batch of stolen material released was a DNC opposition research file on candidate Donald Trump. More than two hundred pages long, it laid out a scathing assessment of Trump's past business dealings and personal failings. Trump was described as an unscrupulous businessman and a misogynist.

At first, the release of the information seemed to run counter to the prevailing view that the Russians were seeking to help Trump and hurt Clinton, whom the Kremlin had loathed ever since her time as the United States' chief diplomat under President Obama. But those of us who worked national security investigations saw the release as a wise move by Russian intelligence. Dropping the document in full would help cloud their own role while also inoculating Trump from all of the damning revelations the DNC had been compiling. Publicizing all of the opposition research at once in June—five months before the election—would be much better for Trump than had the DNC been able to time the release for right before voters went to the polls.

On July 22, just days before the start of the Democratic National Convention in Philadelphia, WikiLeaks announced its new "Hillary Leaks series," unloading a trove of stolen emails, including hacked communications from seven key DNC figures. The documents were damning for the party, as they contained private exchanges that appeared to be evidence that the DNC was working to undermine Clinton's main Democratic challenger, Bernie Sanders, including one exchange where an official thought questioning the candidate's religious faith might be good strategy. In one leaked message, then DNC chair Debbie Wasserman Schultz referred to

Sanders's campaign manager as a "damn liar" and "particularly scummy." In another, she indicated that Sanders "isn't going to be president." The negative fallout from the revelations forced Wasserman Schultz to resign her post just before the start of the convention.

The Democrats were haunted by these hacks all the way up to Election Day. In early October, WikiLeaks began releasing the stolen emails the Russians had taken from the account of DNC chair John Podesta. It was the ultimate slow bleed, with new tranches of communications trickling out on a daily basis. The messages contained information about the campaign's strategy and embarrassing remarks Podesta had made in describing Clinton's terrible instincts. The messages also contained information about large sums of money Clinton and her husband, former president Bill Clinton, had made on the speaker circuit.

Meanwhile, as David Corn and Michael Isikoff describe in their best-selling book, *Russian Roulette*, Trump was stirring the pot and piling on to the criticism of Clinton. He was reveling in the chaos, all too happy to use the stolen information as a wedge to separate Democratic Party leadership from its base. Speaking to reporters in Florida, Trump famously suggested that the Russians should up their game and engage in more hacking. "Russia, if you're listening, I hope you're able to find the thirty thousand emails that are missing," Trump said, referring to the messages from Clinton's private server that her team had deleted. "I think you will probably be rewarded mightily by our press."

As Clinton policy adviser Jake Sullivan remarked at the time, "This has to be the first time that a major presidential candidate has actively encouraged a foreign power to conduct espionage against his political opponent. . . . This has gone from being a matter of curiosity, and a matter of politics, to being a national security issue."

INSIDE THE INTELLIGENCE community, we were grappling with the brazen attack on the US electoral process by the Russians, but we were also shocked by Trump's cavalier approach to national security and the way one of the leading candidates for president continued to downplay the significance of the attack. During a debate with Clinton, Trump uttered a line that would effectively sum up his approach to Russian election interference. "I mean, it could be Russia, but it could also be China," he said. "It could also be lots of other people. It also could be somebody sitting on their bed that weighs four hundred pounds, okay? You don't know who broke in to DNC."

With the benefit of hindsight, many critical questions remain. What if the DNC IT personnel who were initially warned by the FBI in 2015 had taken the issue more seriously? What if the FBI had escalated its warning to party leadership, rather than relying on a low-level staffer in tech support? Anyone looking at the issue honestly would conclude there were missed opportunities all around.

While important, these questions pale in comparison to a much larger issue that still evokes bitterness from Democrats who fell victim to the unprecedented efforts of a hostile foreign government. Their candidate, who had been publicly investigated by the FBI, had lost possibly in part because of the bureau's actions close to Election Day, yet, behind the scenes, the FBI was also secretly investigating the Trump campaign itself and its alleged ties to the Kremlin. The public would know nothing of the Trump investigation until well after Trump was sworn into office. Why, many still furiously wonder, was this bombshell kept hidden from the public?

# CHAPTER 5

# Crossfire

IT WAS NOT the first time the former spy had been contacted by a total stranger and asked to do something illegal. People would occasionally reach out electronically and solicit his deep expertise for help with the commission of a crime. Perhaps it was hacking into the email account of a significant other. Maybe they sought to tap the cell phone of a boss or a colleague. Sometimes, they just didn't like someone and wanted to cause mischief by breaking into a Twitter or Facebook account. Regardless of their motivation, his answer each time was the same: absolutely not.

"Lots of people have these incredibly stupid ideas and think you will help them," Matt Tait, a former analyst with the United Kingdom's signals intelligence service, exclaimed in melodic British-accented English as we sat near Washington's Dupont Circle over a couple of beers.

But the mysterious caller who reached him in London that September afternoon in 2016 had a request that seemed not only incredibly stupid, but possibly treasonous: Would Tait be willing to help sift through copies of the missing thirty-three thousand emails deleted by Hillary Clinton's lawyers and assess their authenticity? Tait could hardly believe what he was hearing. At first, he didn't even quite understand it. The caller told Tait that he had obtained the batch of messages from hackers operating on the dark web, who claimed they'd successfully hacked into Clinton's private email server and exfiltrated the data, but he needed a cyber expert to review the messages and determine if they were real or fake.

The caller was Peter W. Smith, a well-connected Republican operative who bragged about his association to retired lieutenant general Michael

Flynn. By this point in the campaign, Flynn was a senior adviser to candidate Trump on national security issues. Earlier in the year, it was reported that he had even been vetted as a potential running mate for Trump. With his sights now set on a different senior posting—possibly the job of national security adviser in a future Trump administration—Flynn was all in on the campaign, stumping for Trump and helping craft the candidate's policy positions.

Believing Hillary Clinton had deleted many of her messages in order to cover up instances of wrongdoing and to prevent embarrassment, Smith assembled a team to hunt for the missing emails and release them to the public. Perhaps someone had successfully broken into her unsecure server. Perhaps they would offer them to the highest bidder. Smith had to find out. As he would later admit to the *Wall Street Journal*, Smith's team found five groups of hackers who might have had the emails, including two groups of Russians.

Although the US intelligence community had not yet publicly acknowledged that Kremlin intelligence officers had burrowed deep into computer systems at the Democratic National Committee and the Democratic Congressional Campaign Committee, the Democratic Party had vocally announced that it was the victim of Russian hackers. Anyone reading the news that year would have known about the serious allegations of Russian interference. But this didn't appear to faze Smith. He didn't care about the nationality of the hackers. He simply wanted the emails.

As Matt Tait listened, Peter Smith explained that material from one of the hacker groups in particular seemed especially promising. "We're pretty confident these are legitimate emails," Smith said, "but we need to be sure before we publish them. We need to publish them before the election."

Several thoughts raced through Tait's mind. Most interesting was the fact that Smith was not seeking his help to go find the emails, but was instead asking him to read through material already in his possession. "Based on strange requests I've received in the past, I could understand some idiot coming to me asking for help finding them on the dark web," Tait told me. "In that case, I would have told him this is not a productive conversation. Goodbye. But here he was saying he already had them."

Tait also wondered why Smith had contacted him specifically, particularly with the large number of cybersecurity professionals available for such an endeavor. It occurred to the former spy that he was not being enlisted for help because of his national security expertise—he had previously spent several years at the United Kingdom's Government Communications Headquarters (GCHQ) alongside plenty of other young whip-smart analysts conducting operations against hostile adversaries—but, rather, because of his accumulated knowledge and insight into the mind of Hillary Clinton. Although he was now a tech security consultant by day, by night he was engaged in another line of work, geared toward educating the public about the inner workings of government. One of his favorite pastimes involved poring over documents released by US government agencies under the Freedom of Information Act and then analyzing and synthesizing them for the public. Topics had included CIA's enhanced interrogation program, the Benghazi attack investigation, and Hillary Clinton's email server, to name a few. Using the Twitter account @pwnallthethings, Tait would post screenshots of interesting revelations, sometimes buried within hundreds of pages of government data, and then explain to the public what it all meant.

"So you're basically a journalist," I said, envisioning his efforts as similar to those of a beat reporter scanning government records for newsy items.

"Much different," he responded with a smile. Reporters on deadline don't have the same luxury of time, he explained. "What I would do is simply start from the beginning and work my way through the entire document," he said. "Rather than looking at the sections I was interested in, I would just read the whole thing, because it forces you to see everything. It doesn't force you to comment on everything, but it forces you to see everything."

Asked what motivates him to spend hours conducting his analysis, Tait said he believes that it is important for citizens to understand what is happening in government, but also that reading the email conversations between government agency employees truly gives one insight into the character and psyche of those doing the governing.

Tait's analysis and commentary had always skewed neutral on the political spectrum. He would resist editorializing, and simply describe what the information meant. In the case of the Hillary Clinton emails, which he read and analyzed beginning in 2014, when they first started being publicly released by the State Department pursuant to Freedom of Information Act requests from the media, his blunt explanations sometimes irked those in progressive circles.

"The Hillary Clinton emails were fascinating because you were offered a window into her life that nobody else would have good insight into," Tait said. "You can tell she has these people who are really close to her. You have these other people who are just massive sycophants. Or you have others who are just lying to her face. You can tell the difference between how she replies to the people she likes versus how she replies to the people that she doesn't. That was the whole reason why I was going through the Hillary Clinton stuff. This is someone who was likely to be the next president."

It was this unique knowledge into the inner thoughts of Clinton that would make Tait so attractive to Smith. Tait knew Clinton's writing style, her syntax, and her vocabulary. He would surely be in a position to analyze the batch of communications Smith had and determine whether they were truly Clinton's or forgeries.

Rather than help a political campaign of either party gather and amplify dirt about an opponent—Tait was not even a US citizen and therefore unable to vote in the presidential election—he thought it instead important to warn Smith that he was playing with fire. "You need to be aware that this is probably Russian intelligence," Tait cautioned. He explained that the circumstances Smith had outlined, about how he had received the emails belonging to Clinton, had all the hallmarks of a Kremlin operation. Tait had spent much of his intelligence career targeting Russian operatives and knew the characteristics of their offensive operations. Weaponizing stolen information for sinister purposes was their modus operandi.

But how could the Kremlin specifically benefit from enlisting someone in Trumpworld to harm Clinton? Tait described his thinking for me by outlining a series of hypotheticals. Assuming for a moment that the emails were real and Russian operatives had somehow managed to hack the Clinton server, right before the election would be the time to release any potentially damaging information. Doing so might hurt Clinton's chances of winning, or at the very least sow chaos and discord among the electorate. "Of course, you wouldn't want to publish everything," Tait said, "because if you're the Russians, you would still want to hang on to a few items that may help you blackmail Clinton once she got elected." But apart from keeping in reserve a few extra arrows in your quiver, this would be the time to unload and start dumping all of the Clinton material.

What concerned Tait most of all was the apparent shortsightedness of Smith and his associates, who failed to see what seemed so glaringly obvious: If the Russians really wanted to leak stolen Clinton emails, they had multiple outlets to do so. Why would they go to the Trump campaign and use it as a platform for dissemination? To compromise the Trump campaign, of course.

With opposition research a natural part of any campaign, the Russians would clearly understand the appetite on the part of Clinton's opponent to gather and distribute damning information. If Russian intelligence officers could convince the Trump campaign to play ball in a blatantly illegal operation involving the exfiltration and distribution of stolen private personal conversations, they would assume leverage that might become beneficial in myriad ways. If Trump actually won, the Russians would stand to benefit from the ability to blackmail the president, who might fear the consequences of the public disclosure of his campaign's collusion with a foreign government. If Trump lost, the Kremlin would still benefit by having leverage over associates who would no doubt continue to operate in Republican circles, and the ability to shape the narrative and agenda on the new conservative television news network many people assumed Trump would establish if he lost.

If the above circumstances were true, the information the hackers were claiming to have did not actually need to be genuine. Even if they had not actually exfiltrated emails from the Clinton server, the Russians' ability to conscript the Trump campaign in a collusive conspiracy to take the White House would be all the leverage they would need. Tait warned Smith that this was a dangerous road to travel.

"What did he say?" I asked, staring at Tait in amazement.

"Smith said he didn't care," he replied. Smith and his team were going to move forward no matter what.

"You need to be aware that these guys don't f*ck around," Tait asserted, hands waving dramatically as he talked about the Russian hackers. "People who get in their way end up dead on the curb. Be aware of who you're playing with."

Tait's admonishment had no effect on Smith. Once it became clear that the former British spy wouldn't go along with his request, Smith emailed Tait a nondisclosure agreement, asking him to sign and return it. Tait saw the ploy for what it was—an effort to silence him, to keep him from ever revealing their discussions. He refused to sign.

Tait never heard from Smith again—until Smith made a mistake a few weeks later. For reasons unknown, Tait accidentally received an email containing a document titled "A Demonstrative Pedagogical Summary to Be Developed and Released Prior to November 8, 2016," which detailed the formation of a limited liability corporation named KLS Research. The document described the Delaware-based LLC as a vehicle with the purpose "to avoid campaign reporting," and contained a list of four groups of people who were somehow involved in the operation. One group was labeled "Trump Campaign" and contained the names of several senior Trump associates, such as Steve Bannon, Sam Clovis, Kellyanne Conway, Michael Flynn, and Lisa Nelson. Another group, labeled "independent groups / organizations / individuals / resources to be deployed," included Tait as a member. As he read the document, Tait quickly concluded that KLS Research was a company established for the purpose of helping the Trump campaign obtain opposition research on Clinton, but one that would operate at arm's length from the campaign in order to skirt any federal elections laws requiring the documentation of campaign expenditures.

ON MAY 14, 2017, just over a week after speaking with the *Wall Street Journal* about the Clinton email operation, and more than a month before the story would finally publish, Peter Smith, who was eighty-one, killed himself at the Aspen Suites hotel in Rochester, Minnesota. According to the *Chicago Tribune*, Smith left behind a suicide note that read, in part: "NO FOUL PLAY WHATSOEVER—ALL SELF INFLICTED. NO PARTY

ASSISTED OR HAD KNOWLEDGE AS AN ACCOMPLICE BEFORE THE FACT." His death would leave many unanswered questions about the effort to obtain stolen Clinton emails, specifically regarding the scope of the operation and who else may have been involved.

Although it remains unclear to this day whether Michael Flynn was actively involved in the operation, Smith certainly portrayed himself as someone familiar with intimate details of Trump campaign operations that only Flynn would know. For example, in his conversation with Matt Tait, Smith claimed to have insight into discussions Flynn was having with the campaign about possibly seeking the role of CIA director. Smith laced his storytelling with color commentary of Flynn's internal decision-making processes, his disdain for other government officials, and even his personal views on Trump. Smith also described to Tait specific details about Flynn's operational security habits—for example, how he required everyone on his team to use the encrypted email service ProtonMail. As far as Tait was concerned, Smith was either a close associate of Flynn or a proficient liar.

Although Tait's specific connection to the KLS Research operation was fleeting, his involvement in the affair was far from over. At the time of the 2016 election, Tait could not have predicted that one day he would find himself sitting across from federal prosecutors and recounting his Smith connection. The former British intelligence analyst would become a key witness in a special counsel probe working to unearth malicious activity by the Kremlin, and the clandestine KLS Research effort would become the focus of investigative reporters trying to unravel the mystery by following the money.

Smith's dirt-gathering actions appeared to represent an effort by someone connected to the Trump campaign to willingly sidle up to Moscow for the purposes of winning the election. For the FBI, all signs pointed to a gathering storm as each new day seemed to bring some new revelation about a Trump-Russia connection. Indeed, by the time of the Smith revelations in June 2017, a full-fledged investigation had already been underway inside the bureau for almost a year, homing in on several Trump associates. Rather than simply circling one counterintelligence target—the typical way espionage investigations are conducted—the FBI was looking at a possible conspiracy: Was Trump himself involved in an effort to collude with the Russian government in order to win the presidency? In mid-July 2016, the answer to that question was unknown, but it was something the bureau had to find out. And when FBI director Comey finally publicly confirmed the investigation eight months later, Trump would erupt.

Like the Russian DNC hacking operation brought to the attention of US officials by the Netherlands' AIVD, it would be yet another foreign intelligence service that would prove instrumental in tipping off the US intelligence community to the possibility that something sinister was afoot inside the Trump campaign.

AT THE WEST end of London's Hyde Park sits Kensington Palace, a seventeenth-century mansion that has long served as a home to the British royal family (Prince William and Kate Middleton and their brood are among its current occupants). A walk of less than a mile, toward Notting Hill Gate, around a series of homes and shops, will take you to the Kensington Wine Rooms, a ritzy bar tucked away at the intersection of two busy streets with narrowing sidewalks. Inside, historical elegance meets modernity, and patrons atop tall barstools or in overstuffed leather chairs can choose from an array of reds and whites flowing from new age electronic dispensers.

In May 2016, Alexander Downer, the Australian high commissioner to the United Kingdom, stepped from the bustling street corner into the swanky establishment to grab a drink with a visiting official serving as one of candidate Donald Trump's foreign-policy advisers. George Papadopoulos was at the time a brash twenty-eight-year-old former energy consultant who served a stint on Ben Carson's 2016 presidential campaign and then went to work for Trump after Carson dropped out of the race.

The actual purpose of the meeting remains a bit of a mystery. Downer says he was interested in meeting with someone from the Trump foreign-policy team because the Aussies were curious about what Trump's approach to Asia would be. Unlike former secretary of state Hillary Clinton, who had served as the torchbearer for the Obama administration's policy decision to focus more on the area, Trump was largely unknown to officials in Canberra, beyond his hit reality-TV show and beauty pageants. For his part, Papadopoulos suggests a sinister motive behind Downer's invitation to have a drink. The former campaign aide says he was targeted by Western intelligence services as part of a campaign to stop Donald Trump, although he has provided little by way of corroborating information.

Whatever the genesis of the meeting, an evening of diplomatic chitchat over gin and tonics (with weak pours, Downer notes) would be the beginning of the road to convicted felonhood for George Papadopoulos. As the *New York Times* outlined in a major report on the origins of the FBI's Trump-Russia investigation, at one point during the discussion Papadopoulos told Downer that the Kremlin had dirt on candidate Clinton. In diplomacy, as in spying, one often gleans tidbits of interesting information during the course of a conversation, and one must decide what follow-up questions to ask and which threads to pull without tipping off the other party that something they just uttered might be explosive. Downer filed the Clinton tidbit away, perhaps at the time unsure of what to make of it, much less its utility.

According to court records, Papadopoulos learned of the information that the Russians reportedly had on Clinton at a meeting the month before with Joseph Mifsud, a mysterious Maltese professor with ties to the Russian government. The two had originally met in Italy and eventually realized their shared interests. Upon assuming his role with the Trump campaign, Papadopoulos had been told that one of Trump's key foreign-policy positions would be improving ties with Russia. Perhaps he thought that Mifsud's apparent connections to the Kremlin might prove beneficial to Trump, whereas Papadopoulos's connection to one of the key presidential candidates in the United States could have its own benefits.

Although much about Mifsud is shrouded in secrecy, at one point he told Papadopoulos that the Russians possessed dirt on Clinton in the form of thousands of emails. This meeting came just prior to the night of drinks with the Australian high commissioner in London, making it almost certain that the information Mifsud told Papadopoulos was the same information the young campaign aide was boasting about to the Aussie official.

For his part, Downer did what any good diplomat would do after meeting with an aide to someone who might become the next president of the United States: he wrote up a cable documenting his discussions and fired it off to his bosses. It was not until Guccifer 2.0 and WikiLeaks began pushing out stolen DNC emails that the Australian government put two and two together and thought it possible that the offhand remark by the Trump aide that May night at the Kensington Wine Rooms might have been referring to the stolen Democratic communications now consuming international headlines. The Australians decided it was time to notify their US counterparts of the comments made by Papadopoulos.

This decision underscores the special relationship between the United States and Australia. The two nations are part of the so-called Five Eyes arrangement—a consortium of nations that also includes the United Kingdom, Canada, and New Zealand. These five allies routinely share highly classified information.

In addition to being great partners, the Australians are simply damn good intelligence officers. Their operators and analysts are among the best in the business, bringing to each task a sense of rigor one doesn't find everywhere in the world. When I worked investigations, I served on a team responsible for liaising with Australian law enforcement, intelligence, and military personnel, and found them to be experts at their trade. When I learned it was an Aussie tip that helped launch the FBI's Trump-Russia investigation, I wasn't the least bit surprised at Australia's willingness to come forward and share critical information about a potential threat to US national security.

BACK AT FBI headquarters in July 2016, FBI counterintelligence agents and analysts were staring at disparate pieces of raw intelligence and trying to determine whether all of the dots connected. The bureau was well aware of the Russian cyberattacks against the DNC and was now witnessing along with the rest of the world the mass release of stolen messages in an effort to influence a US election. With the new information from the Australian diplomat, stating that Papadopoulos claimed to know about dirt the Russians had on Clinton, was it possible that the Trump campaign knew in advance that the Russians had sought to undermine Clinton and throw the election in Trump's favor? Was Team Trump somehow involved? It would have been dereliction on the part of the FBI to ignore the potential connection. And so Crossfire Hurricane was born.

Crossfire Hurricane would soon come to focus on four individuals in Trump's orbit: Michael Flynn, campaign manager Paul Manafort, George Papadopoulos, and another foreign-policy adviser for the Trump campaign named Carter Page. "You have to remember that it was early in the investigation and we weren't entirely sure what to make of these four," said a former official. "They all seemed to have *some* connection to Russia, but it was unclear if they were conduits for Russian intelligence. It was also unclear whether they were all working together on an effort involving the Russians, or if they just coincidentally had historical ties to Moscow." Either way, the FBI had to find out.

Investigators were initially unsure what to make of Carter Page. Prior to joining the Trump campaign, he had been closely linked to Russian interests, including the Russian state oil company Gazprom. As the *New York Times* reported, he was a Trump foreign-policy adviser with a history of travel to Russia and had previously been targeted by the Russian intelligence services. In a 2013 visit to Moscow, Page met with one of three people the FBI would later charge with being Kremlin intelligence officers. In court filings, investigators described the transcript of a secret recording they made of the Russian spies, in which they referred to Page as a useful "idiot." Page was later interviewed by the FBI about his dealings with the Russians but denied any wrongdoing.

In July 2016, he again caught the attention of the FBI after traveling to Russia to give a pro-Kremlin speech at a Moscow institute. "Washington and other Western capitals have impeded potential progress through their often-hypocritical focus on ideas such as democratization, inequality, corruption and regime change," Page said in his remarks. Media reports indicated that during his visit Page also met with two top allies of the president of Russia, Vladimir Putin.

"Deciphering Page's involvement was something we were all interested in," the former official told me, "but at the beginning of the investigation, nothing was crystal clear. He was sort of a screwed-up dude who lived with his mother, and the Federal Bureau of Investigation had already previously looked at him, but here he was traveling to Moscow while working for Trump, so of course it was a possible red flag."

Paul Manafort was the most experienced political operative of the four subjects rolled into the Crossfire Hurricane case. With a law degree from Georgetown, he had spent a career in Republican political circles, with roles in the presidential campaigns of Gerald Ford, Ronald Reagan, George H. W. Bush, and Bob Dole. He had also been a lobbyist, with a résumé that reads like a who's who of consulting for governments widely deemed repressive and corrupt, working for firms linked to the Saudi royal family, the klepto-cratic presidency of the Philippines' Ferdinand Marcos, and, most recently, the campaign of Russian-backed Viktor Yanukovych in Ukraine. Known as a hard-nosed take-no-prisoners negotiator, Manafort had been brought on board the Trump campaign in March 2016 and then assumed the role of campaign manager in June.

According to media reports, Manafort had been the subject of FBI investigation and surveillance as far back as 2014, based on his work with Yanukovych, with new Foreign Intelligence Surveillance Act (FISA) wiretap-ping authorities covering 2017 and parts of 2016. After reports surfaced in August 2016 that Manafort had received millions of dollars in undisclosed cash from officials in Ukraine, he stepped down from the campaign.

The Crossfire Hurricane gang of four was rounded out by Michael Flynn. Pushed out of his role as director of the Defense Intelligence Agency in 2014, reportedly for his constant clashing with the Obama team, he started the Flynn Intel Group, a consulting firm with clients in Russia as well as clients linked to the governments of Recep Tayyip Erdogan in Turkey.

Flynn had caused jaws to drop in December 2015 when he traveled to Moscow to attend a gala honoring the Kremlin-backed television network RT, where he was seated next to Russian president Vladimir Putin. It would later be learned that Flynn was paid an estimated $45,000 to take this trip, and in 2017 he would find himself under investigation by the Department of Defense for allegedly failing to report the income when renewing his US government security clearance. But for now he was caught up in the bureau's quiet effort to determine whether Team Trump was colluding with officials in Moscow to sabotage Clinton's election chances.

By AUGUST 2016, more and more about the FBI's investigation into the Russians had been seeping out into the public domain, but the bureau was not confirming anything; the investigation was still very much in its infancy. On August 27, Senate Democratic leader Harry Reid wrote a letter to James Comey, in which he pleaded with the FBI to be more forthcoming about what the FBI knew about any potential ties involving Trump. "The prospect of a hostile government actively seeking to undermine our free and fair elections represents one of the gravest threats to our democracy since the Cold War and it is critical for the Federal Bureau of Investigation to use every resource available to investigate this matter thoroughly and in a timely fashion," the letter read in part. "The American people deserve to have a full understanding of the facts from a completed investigation before they vote this November." He specifically mentioned concerns about Carter Page and longtime Trump buddy Roger Stone, who had recently boasted about being directly in contact with WikiLeaks founder Julian Assange.

The day we received the Reid letter, Comey was scheduled to spend time at Quantico with a large gathering of FBI leaders from field offices around the country. Addressing the group on various aspects of leadership, he returned to a topic he had spoken about to audiences earlier in the year during the Clinton investigation. "Look," he said, Senator Reid's frustration clearly top of mind, "when doing your work, you are constantly going to have critics pushing you to work harder and work faster. You have to constantly remind your teams that when faced with the choice between doing something fast and doing it well, always choose well."

After Comey's October 28 letter to Congress announcing the reopening of the Clinton email investigation, Reid erupted. He was apoplectic, firing off an angry letter to Comey blasting him for the perceived double standard in how the FBI was treating Clinton and Trump, and accusing Comey of breaking the law.

"In my communications with you and other top officials in the national security community," Reid wrote, "it has become clear that you possess explosive information about close ties and coordination between Donald Trump, his top advisors, and the Russian government."

As journalists David Corn and Michael Isikoff describe in their 2018 book *Russian Roulette*, the Reid letter caused them to wonder more about this "explosive information" that Reid was citing—which he presumably would have obtained as a member of the Senate Select Committee on Intelligence. Corn reached out to Glenn Simpson of Fusion GPS, a consulting firm that Corn knew was collecting opposition research on Trump for the Democrats, including any about potential ties to Russia. Corn asked Simpson if there was anything he should be working to investigate.

Over lunch, Simpson described astonishing information he had obtained from retired MI6 spy Christopher Steele. As part of his contract with the Democratic National Committee to gather opposition research on Trump, Simpson had enlisted the help of Steele, who had set about tasking a network of Kremlin sources and subsources. Simpson showed Corn a series of reports from Steele, which included allegations that the Russian government had compromising material on Trump related to his finances and sexual proclivities.

Corn then spoke with Steele, who confirmed that he had provided this same information to the FBI. Unsatisfied with any noticeable progress in the bureau's investigation into the Republican presidential nominee, and believing that US citizens had a right to know this information before Election Day, Steele provided the basis for the October 31 *Mother Jones* article written by Corn, headlined "A Veteran Spy Has Given the FBI Information Alleging a Russian Operation to Cultivate Donald Trump." Although Corn did not report on the unverified salacious details involving Trump's sexual activities in Moscow, his story was the first to detail information in the now infamous Steele dossier.

As Corn and Isikoff recount in their book, this potential blockbuster was overshadowed by an article in the *New York Times* that dropped the same day, titled "Investigating Donald Trump, F.B.I. Sees No Clear Link to Russia."

Eight days later, the Clinton campaign limped to the finish line in what would be for many an unexpected defeat.

ONE LINGERING QUESTION that still infuriates Democrats to this day is: Why the apparent double standard in how the bureau treated Clinton and how it dealt with Trump? How could the FBI so publicly reopen the investigation into Clinton's handling of classified information while seemingly shielding the fact that it also had *four* Trump campaign aides under investigation?

One former FBI special agent involved in both investigations explained it to me like this: "To maintain success in a counterintelligence investigation, we require it to remain hidden and covert, so the potential bad actors continue to conduct activity that will further help us understand the extent of the threat and identify others higher up who may be involved." He went on to describe the critical aspect of fairness central to our legal system. "FBI counterintelligence investigations are opened based on a very low predicate of information. It would be completely inappropriate for every time we open up an investigation for us to announce that. That would defeat the whole innocent until proven guilty thing, right?"

The Clinton case, he pointed out, was potentially a criminal one; the Trump case was a counterintelligence investigation. "That's a nuance that is glossed over in the public all the time. It leads to, 'How could you treat the two things differently?' They were treated differently because they were different. One was an apple; one was an orange."

In an interview with James Comey for this book at his home on the outskirts of Washington, DC, he, too, cited these differences in the two investigations, as well as what he calls hindsight bias. "With the Trump campaign investigation," he said, "we had just started. We didn't yet know what we had."

I pressed him on why he didn't offer even *minimal* notice to the American people that Trump may have ties to Russia. In a spirited back-and-forth reminiscent of my time on his staff, Comey challenged the premise. "What would I have said, exactly?" he inquired. "Should I have said: 'We've just opened a case on these people, we don't know if there's anything to it, none of them is the candidate, they might end up being cleared, and, oh, by the way, it's classified, and that is all you're going to get from us'?"

While these explanations make sense to anyone who has ever conducted an investigation—one of the most frustrating things for any FBI agent is when someone tries to compare your case to something unrelated—I'm confident even these sober assessments will likely not satisfy those who still feel the sting of defeat. Many regular Americans will forever blame Comey and the FBI for Clinton's loss. I can only offer this inside insight into the bureau's calculus and let readers draw their own conclusions.

ALTHOUGH TRUMP HAD just been elected president, the FBI's work was far from over. While the Crossfire Hurricane team continued sifting through intelligence collected on Papadopoulos, Manafort, and Page, it was retired lieutenant general Michael Flynn who posed the most acute challenge. Here was someone poised to become the next national security adviser to the president of the United States—someone who would have access to the most closely guarded secrets in government. If there was a nefarious connection between Flynn and the Kremlin, the bureau had to identify it and act quickly. The FBI owed that to the American people. Indeed, bureau leadership believed we owed it to the new president.

# CHAPTER 6

# Collusion

THE WHITE HOUSE was desperately trying to make sense of something that had not happened. Certain it was about to ignite a major diplomatic row with the Russian Federation, it was caught by surprise when President Vladimir Putin—a ruthlessly calculating former spy who frequently lashed out at even the hint of provocation—instead acted in a manner opposite to what many experts inside government had predicted. As one former Obama official told me, "Any time you impose costs on an adversary, you take into account how you expect them to respond." But the response that came surprised almost everyone.

On December 29, 2016, less than one month before Donald Trump would be sworn in as the forty-fifth president of the United States, Barack Obama took action against Russia in retaliation for Moscow's attack on the 2016 election. Describing the Kremlin's efforts to subvert US democracy as a "national emergency," Obama signed an executive order imposing economic sanctions on the Russian intelligence services responsible for hacking the DNC. He also expelled almost three dozen suspected Russian intelligence operatives from US soil and shuttered facilities suspected of being used for spying efforts. The president said that his actions did not constitute the full US response, but merely represented the first wave of a larger series of actions that would unfold at the time and place of the United States' choosing. The effort was the culmination of months of planning and debate inside the US national security apparatus about what costs should be imposed on the Kremlin for its brazen belligerence in cyberspace. It would be described as one of the most serious diplomatic confrontations between the superpowers since the end of the Cold War.

The Obama team readied itself for the proportional tit for tat that typically follows such actions. In conducting foreign policy, especially the employment of punitive measures aimed at holding a regime accountable for violating international norms, the notion that a sanctioned government will respond in kind is typically baked into the planning process. "You eject our spies, we eject your spies," another former administration official told me. "You sanction us, we sanction you."

After the sanctions were announced, a Kremlin spokesperson presaged the retaliation that would follow, saying that there would be "official statements, countermeasures, and much more." A Putin associate described the approaching storm in equally dire terms, noting that "the principle of reciprocity applies here absolutely, without alternative."

But the retaliation never came. Instead, Putin publicly indicated that he would work to restore relations between his country and the new Trump administration and ignore the actions of the Obama team. "While we reserve the right to take reciprocal measures," Putin said, "we're not going to downgrade ourselves to the level of irresponsible 'kitchen' diplomacy."

Inside the US government, officials were keen to learn exactly what was going on. Why were the Russians ignoring US sanctions and the humiliation of the suspected intelligence officers the White House had sent packing? It was no secret that Trump had historically been friendly toward Russia, but was there more to the story? What followed next represents the classic work our intelligence professionals perform each and every day to connect dots and fill gaps in order to guard against national security threats.

A request from the director of national intelligence went out to the intelligence community for information the agencies might have that could help explain Russia's lack of retaliation. FBI analysts pulsed our systems and found their answer. A piece of collected intelligence stored in a bureau computer database shed light on the entire affair. It also became the smoking gun that would lead to the demise of Trump's national security adviser.

ON THE DAY Obama signed the sanction orders, Sergey Kislyak, Russia's ambassador to the US, picked up the phone to call Michael Flynn, who was then assisting with transition efforts as he waited to assume the role of Trump's new national security adviser. Kislyak was presumably concerned about the government's approach to his country and likely sought input from Flynn on how the new Trump administration would act. The call between Flynn and Kislyak was intercepted, providing US government officials with a transcript of communications between a foreign official and a then private citizen.

The same day, Flynn called a senior member of the Trump transition team at the president-elect's Mar-a-Lago resort in Palm Beach, Florida. What, if anything, Flynn wondered, should he tell the Russian ambassador? Flynn and the other senior official discussed Obama's sanctions, and the fact that the transition team did not want Russia to do anything that might escalate the situation.

Immediately following his call to Mar-a-Lago, Flynn called Kislyak back and relayed the team's hope that Russia would not go overboard in its response, but would only respond reciprocally. After the call, Flynn again telephoned the transition team to provide a readout of his communications with the Russian ambassador.

Once Putin publicly released his statement on the matter, Kislyak again called Flynn to report that the Russian government would not be retaliating. Flynn closed the loop with senior members of the transition team, relaying the information Kislyak had provided. The public would first learn about these intercepted communications in a column by David Ignatius in the *Washington Post* on January 12, 2017. Legal experts debated whether Flynn's actions in lobbying a foreign government as a private citizen constituted a felony.

Flynn's calls with Kislyak about US sanctions were not the only instances in which he had reportedly lobbied foreign governments on US foreign-policy issues while still a private citizen. On December 22, 2016, a senior Trump transition official (later identified as Trump's son-in-law, Jared Kushner) directed Flynn to contact various foreign governments and work to influence their vote on a pending United Nations resolution regarding Israeli settlements. As part of this effort, Flynn called Kislyak to convey the Trump team's disapproval of the resolution and requested that the Russians either vote against it or delay their vote until Trump assumed office.

Although details of the Flynn affair would eventually make it into the public domain via court filings, at the time, people inside the intelligence community were enraged at how this information had made its way into a US newspaper. One former official captured the mood among those dealing with the fallout. "We protect our intelligence sources and methods like nothing else," he told me. "At the same time we were trying to determine the extent of the Trump-Russia connection, critical details were being made public. It was a pure disaster."

Worries about the disclosure would soon take a back seat to an even more startling turn of events. While the FBI and the Justice Department were working to piece together Flynn's relationship with Russia, Vice President Elect Mike Pence joined CBS's *Face the Nation* on January 15, 2017, to address the Flynn-Kislyak connection and the larger Russia issue. Pence got warmed up by critiquing people in government and the press who he claimed were trying to undermine the legitimacy of Trump's election. When asked by host John Dickerson if there were any contacts between the Trump campaign and Russians trying to interfere in the election, Pence responded categorically, "Of course not. And I think to suggest that is to give credence to some of these bizarre rumors that have swirled around the candidacy." He went on to suggest that the narrative was largely being pushed because of media bias. Dickerson then asked Pence directly about Flynn and whether the incoming national security adviser's communications with the Russians had an impact on Putin's decision not to retaliate against Obama's sanctions. "I talked to General Flynn about that conversation," Pence said. "They did not discuss anything having to with the United States' decision to expel diplomats or impose sanctions." When pressed for clarification, Pence stated clearly that the conversations "had nothing whatsoever to do with sanctions."

Pence's comments raised eyebrows at both FBI headquarters and across the street at Main Justice. As one former Justice Department official told me, "We were like, wait a minute. What the hell?" Our investigators knew the vice president elect's comments were inconsistent with evidence in their possession. So did Flynn lie to Pence when directly questioned about the media reports? Or was Pence lying to the American people? There was no question in the mind of the intelligence community that the Flynn-Kislyak conversations had taken place, but why would Flynn or Pence lie about them if the discussions were indeed sanctioned by the Trump transition team?

JANUARY 19—ONE DAY before Trump would be formally sworn in—was one of the busiest days for the FBI director during my time on his staff. It began with an early morning helicopter flight out to Quantico to swear in a new class of freshly minted special agents, who had just completed their training. James Comey shook hands and took pictures with the hundreds of family members and friends in attendance while I kept a sharp eye on the clock, aware that the airspace in and around DC was gradually being shut down as security preparations for the inauguration intensified. After the graduation, we were quickly back in the FBI helicopter and skids-up en route back to Washington, where Comey would soon receive a briefing from dozens of operators from the FBI's elite Hostage Rescue Team, who had strategically positioned themselves in a warehouse in DC's outskirts, ready to respond to any attempted terrorist attack on the inauguration.

As our helicopter approached the Wilson Bridge, an air traffic controller squawked a terse warning to our pilots, indicating that the airspace was currently restricted, and requested further identification. Satisfied with the information provided, he gave us clearance to land. As we neared the helipad and passed a barrage of surface-to-air missile platforms below us on the banks of the Potomac River, I marveled at the staggering amount of preparation that goes into ensuring the protection of our nation's chief executive. And as we hovered near the Lincoln Memorial, waiting for an approaching US Park Police helicopter to pass, I could not help but think of the dozens of new special agents who had just taken an oath to support and defend everything the monuments below us stood for. I also recall having a difficult time processing two competing realizations: on the one hand, the government was expending untold amounts of time and money to guard against external threats to our nation's changing of the guard, while on the other hand, it was working to determine whether the incoming president's team had colluded with a foreign adversary to obtain the keys to the kingdom. This contradiction haunts me to this day.

"SO, WHAT EXACTLY is the Logan Act?" I asked my boss, flipping through a folder of briefing papers as we departed the meeting at the warehouse with Hostage Rescue Team operators and headed for our final event of the day at the command center of the FBI's Washington Field Office. During my FBI career, I had investigated numerous violations of federal law at home and abroad, but Flynn's particular predicament was blurry to me.

Comey took me through the technicalities surrounding Flynn's alleged actions with the Russians. The revelation of the Flynn-Kislyak intercepts presented US authorities with a unique situation, he explained. Although it was common for incoming administration transition teams to speak with foreign governments in order to make introductions and discuss policy priorities, Flynn's request that the Russians limit their response to official US sanctions had technically risked placing him in legal jeopardy. The Logan Act—an obscure federal law enacted in 1799—prohibits private citizens from certain acts involving foreign governments. The law states that anyone acting without the authority of the US government, who communicates with foreign officials "with intent to influence the measures or conduct of any foreign government . . . in relation to any disputes or controversies with the United States, or to defeat the measures of the United States," has committed a crime, punishable by up to three years in prison.

Despite a few hairy situations involving protesters—including one setting a limousine on fire near the White House, which caused thick black smoke to billow into the air, making witnesses wonder if the executive mansion had been targeted—Inauguration Day went smoothly. For the FBI and the rest of the country's national security apparatus, it was all hands on deck. Agents, analysts, and professional staff manned the command centers at FBI headquarters and the Washington Field Office while investigative teams roved through the city. My office at the FBI was on the corner of Pennsylvania Avenue and Ninth Street Northwest, providing a sweeping view of many of the festivities.

Once the oath was taken, I walked the few blocks to my apartment and joined my dad, who was visiting from Texas. Up on the roof of the building, we watched as now former president Barack Obama and his wife, Michelle, lifted off from the Capitol grounds in a dark-green Marine Sikorsky helicopter and made a pass over our heads en route to Joint Base Andrews.

"God bless America," my dad whispered as we both considered the peaceful transfer of power that sets the United States apart from so many other nations.

Lighting a Paul Garmirian Soiree cigar and waving the match to extinguish the flame, I replied with one of the most hopeful, yet naive, predictions of my professional life: "I hope Trump is good for the FBI."

ON THE SUNDAY following the inauguration, Comey had been invited to attend a White House function being held to thank the law enforcement agencies that had assisted in planning and executing the event. The director appreciated the sentiment but was initially hesitant. He felt that socializing with the new president might not be good for the FBI's reputation of independence. Many in the country believed (and still believe to this day) that Comey was responsible for Trump's election, and pictures and video of the two together would likely only further this narrative. However, after consulting with his senior leadership team, Comey decided he had to go. Declining the invitation might risk insulting both the president and the other law enforcement chiefs who would be in attendance.

About thirty officials gathered in the Blue Room of the White House, shaking hands and catching up. Trump entered and began heaping praise on the attendees as cameras rolled and photographs were taken. Comey spent most of the time trying to avoid the new president, relegating himself to the far end of the room. For a while at least, Trump avoided calling out Comey, which the director later learned was likely because he was wearing a blue suit and standing in front of a curtain of the same shade, but the president eventually noticed the director, welcoming him over with a dramatic extension of his arms.

"Jim!" the president exclaimed. "He's become more famous than me," Trump said to widespread laughter.

As Comey later described, he approached the president with an outstretched hand and held firm, trying to preempt a presidential hug. "I'm really looking forward to working with you," Trump told him.

The president's comments to Comey in the Blue Room—however brief and insincere—are important for a couple of reasons. First, during both the presidential transition and his first months in office, Trump had made a practice of saying positive things about Comey and insisting that the director stay on and continue to lead the organization. Second, by telling Comey that he wanted him to continue in the role, Trump was signaling that he had no understanding of or appreciation for the time-honored independence the White House typically affords federal law enforcement.

The FBI director's statutorily mandated ten-year term is meant to ensure that a new president won't simply clean house upon arrival and install a crony in the position. Custom held that a director could be fired for specific reasons—such as in the case of Director William Sessions, who was fired by President Bill Clinton in 1993 after various ethical violations came to light—so it was a generally accepted norm that a director would be removed only for cause. By telegraphing to Comey that Trump himself would be making the decision on whether Comey would remain in the job, he was chipping away at an important institutional norm, which he would altogether obliterate in four months' time.

Contrary to the narrative since promoted by Trump, the FBI did not set out to bring down the incoming national security adviser. Quite the opposite. In fact, one former official described Flynn as the Crossfire Hurricane investigation subject the FBI actually felt the most comfortable about. Prior to the discovery of his calls with the Russian ambassador, it appeared as though Flynn had exercised puzzling behavior vis-à-vis the Kremlin, but the FBI had yet to discover anything that would warrant prosecution. Nevertheless, with knowledge that Flynn had potentially run afoul of the Logan Act and with the strange *Face the Nation* development suggesting that Flynn had lied to the incoming vice president (or worse), the FBI had to do what it does best: go have a conversation and gather facts.

The question of how to proceed with interviewing Flynn was the subject of intense discussion inside the director's suite. Comey and his counter-intelligence team thought it was imperative to get Flynn's side of the story, but there were two issues that first had to be resolved.

The first was what notice, if any, the FBI should give to Flynn and the White House before conducting an interview of the president's chief national security aide. A key aspect of determining someone's truthfulness is maintaining an element of surprise in order for agents to assess for them-selves whether the subject of an interview is attempting to hide something. For many FBI agents—myself included—the real-time analysis of words and physical reaction to an agent's line of questioning is one of the most fascinating and enlightening parts of the job. An entire block of instruction at the FBI Academy centers not only on asking good questions, but also on studying a subject's reaction to a particular topic. In the case of Flynn, if he got wind of the bureau's specific purpose in speaking with him, he might have time to concoct and rehearse a fictitious narrative explaining his actions.

Another issue: one does not just walk up to the front gates of 1600 Pennsylvania Avenue and ask for entry into the West Wing—even if you're an FBI agent. Concentric rings of security ensure that anyone actually mak-ing their way into the White House compound has an authorized purpose that has been vetted well in advance. One thing the FBI had going for it was the fact that White House staff were still settling into their new roles, and the place was abuzz with personnel eager to get started on a host of initia-tives and a press corps cataloguing the frenetic pace.

"With all the chaos," Comey told me, "we thought we might actually get away with sending agents over to the White House to sit down with Flynn."

Typical protocol would involve sending over a request to the White House counsel's office, explaining the nature of the inquiry, and then waiting by the phone for clearance. After much discussion, Comey gave the green light to his deputy, Andrew McCabe, to call Flynn and tell him the FBI was sending over two agents to speak with him about something important. "We just decided, you know, screw it," Comey said. Flynn would not be in custody— any interview would be voluntary—so there would be no requirement to tell him that he had a right to remain silent and the right to counsel. If Flynn refused to talk, so be it.

Comey's next decision was equally gutsy and would land him in the familiar position of ruffling feathers over at the Justice Department. Comey always studied each high-profile move by the FBI—studying each issue through the lens of how it might be perceived by differing factions—and then sought to land on decisions that would ensure public confidence in the FBI as an apolitical and independent institution. Comey told me that his decision in the Flynn episode centered on his concern that taking overt investigative steps against the new national security adviser might be perceived as a last-ditch effort by holdover Obama administration officials at the Justice Department to target Team Trump. One of those officials was Sally Yates, Obama's deputy attorney general, who had been elevated to the position of acting attorney general after the inauguration while the White House found a replacement for Loretta Lynch. Yates is an accomplished government lawyer who rose through the ranks of the Justice Department in a career that spanned nearly thirty years. She would soon become a household name after standing up to the Trump administration over the "Muslim ban"—ultimately leading to her firing—but at the time she was merely known in DOJ and FBI circles as a respected apolitical career public servant.

Despite the confidence in Yates inside the FBI, Comey worried that bringing her into the decision-making process on the Flynn matter might risk the perception of an Obama appointee leading the charge against Flynn. He also thought that not telling Yates would offer her deniability, ensuring that Comey would take whatever heat came from the administration if the

Flynn affair turned into something major. So he decided not to tell her—at least not yet. Despite his good intentions, being kept out of the loop would anger her.

ON ANY GIVEN day, the White House national security adviser spends hours on end gathering information necessary for the nation's chief executive to respond to global conflict and manage crises large and small. On this particular day, however, Flynn was facing a crisis of his own making as he sat in a West Wing office across from two stoic federal agents who had come to ask about allegations of impropriety.

Surprisingly, it did not appear as though Flynn had told anyone else—including the White House counsel's office—that FBI agents were coming to see him. By this point, Flynn would have been well aware of the firestorm surrounding the original *Washington Post* column claiming that he had spoken with Kislyak during the transition, as well as subsequent reporting claiming that the US intelligence community had actual transcripts of the call. As the former director of the powerful Defense Intelligence Agency, Flynn certainly would have known the capabilities of the US government when it comes to spying on the conversations of diplomats from hostile countries. Furthermore, with questions swirling around whether Flynn had violated the Logan Act by attempting to influence a foreign government while still a private citizen, one would think he would have at least ensured that a lawyer was present when he talked with the FBI. But Flynn seemed unconcerned, possibly thinking he could outsmart the agents before him and just make the whole thing go away. He could not have been more wrong.

According to a person familiar with the interview, the goal of the FBI in speaking with Flynn was not to trap him in a lie but to find out whether there was criminal intent in his conduct with the Russian ambassador and to shed light on his thought processes. No one seriously thought Flynn would be charged under the Logan Act—only two people have ever been prosecuted in the law's history, the last in 1852—but it was necessary to hear directly from him.

During the interview, the national security adviser committed a serious crime when talking to the FBI agents seated before him, one of whom
was Peter Strzok (more on him later). Flynn stated that he had not asked
the Russian ambassador to refrain from escalating tensions between the
two governments after Obama had imposed sanctions. He also said that
he could not recall the follow-up call during which Kislyak indicated that
Russia would moderate its response to the sanctions based on Flynn's original request. These were flat-out lies.

Incredibly, a person familiar with the interview later told me that the
agents had telegraphed to Flynn that they knew the contents of his communications with the Russian diplomat, based on the series of questions they
had posed. In one instance, the agents had tried to jog Flynn's memory by
asking specifically about his call with Kislyak regarding the Israeli settle-
ment playing out at the United Nations. "Yes, good reminder," Flynn had
said. Despite this signaling, he opted to lie, claiming he had indeed discussed Israel but did not ask the Russians to vote a certain way.

Another interesting part of the exchange, which has since been spun
by partisans attempting to paint Flynn as the victim of FBI entrapment,
pertains to his demeanor during the interview. The agents asking the questions noted that Flynn did not appear to be exhibiting any indicators of
deception, meaning there was no outward manifestation of sweating, stam-
mering, or the like. But this did not mean Flynn was telling the truth. The
US government had the telephone call transcripts. They knew he was not
telling them the truth. If anything, Flynn's calm and composed demeanor
suggested that he was actually really good at telling lies. But it didn't mean
he was innocent.

Comey told me that while the interview was still underway, he phoned
Yates across the street at Main Justice and told her that agents had been
dispatched to the White House and were currently with Flynn. The acting attorney general was furious. "How could you possibly do this without
consulting me?" she asked Comey. It was too late to recall the agents from
the West Wing, but Yates ordered that she be briefed the moment they
returned.

When the interview was over, Strzok and his colleague raced back to FBI headquarters and briefed the leadership team. Flynn was now in serious legal jeopardy. Armed with the evidence, the bureau was now staring at violations of 18 US Code, section 1001, which makes lying to an FBI agent about a material fact in an investigation a crime punishable by up to five years in prison. One member of the leadership team told me they actually wondered if Flynn was suffering from dementia, or whether he had been intoxicated when he spoke with Kislyak. What else would explain such a blatant misrepresentation of the facts that had already been publicly reported? After kicking around various possibilities and motivations, the investigative team packed up its notes and headed across the street to meet with Yates.

One interesting aside is how much more serious Sally Yates thought Michael Flynn's lies to Mike Pence were than did James Comey. In their discussions about Flynn, Comey couldn't fully wrap his mind around the FBI's role in internal White House deception. "I kept saying, 'Why do I care if Flynn lies to the vice president or if the vice president lies to the American people?'" Comey told me. "I mean, I care as a citizen," he added, "but the FBI's job is not to police the statements an administration makes to the American people." Yates, on the other hand, was adamant that the lies were extremely serious, not only because letting Pence know he was repeating lies would be the right thing to do, but also because Flynn was increasingly placing himself in a compromising position in relation to the Russians.

# CHAPTER 7

# Collision

LESS THAN ONE week into the Trump presidency, Acting Attorney General Sally Yates telephoned White House counsel Don McGahn and indicated that she had a sensitive matter she needed to brief him on. Despite the availability of encrypted telephone and video systems that permit government agencies to communicate with each other about highly classified topics, Yates explained that the matter at hand was not something she wanted to discuss by phone.

That afternoon, Yates and a member of her national security team traveled the short distance to the White House, where they met McGahn. His office was deemed a Sensitive Compartmented Information Facility, or SCIF—government lingo for the type of room certified for the discussion of classified information. These special rooms provide officials with a secure place to discuss classified matters without fear of eavesdropping by foreign intelligence services. (Fans of the FX hit series *The Americans* will recall FBI special agent Stan Beeman routinely meeting with his colleagues in "the vault.")

Yates said she began the conversation by explaining that the government was in possession of material that suggested that the statements being made by Vice President Pence about Michael Flynn and the Russians were untrue. She said she explained the nature of the sensitive information the government had and how it had been acquired. Yates said she also told McGahn that Flynn had been interviewed by the FBI about the matter at hand, that McGahn had asked how the interview had gone, and that she had declined to answer. She said she made clear that she did not believe

Pence was deliberately lying (a view shared by other insiders) but she felt he was entitled to know that whatever he had been told by Flynn was a lie, and that she was troubled by the fact that the American people were being lied to as well. Lastly, she expressed concern that Flynn might be in a potentially compromising situation that might make him prone to blackmail by the Russians, because they would also have known Flynn was lying to the vice president.

Yates said McGahn took all this in, then asked whether she thought Flynn should be fired, and she responded that it was not her decision to make—it would be up to the White House—but she felt compelled to make sure the White House was aware of the troubling information now in the DOJ's holdings.

The next morning, she said, McGahn phoned her and asked if she would come back to his office to go back over the information she had presented. Yates said she again ticked through her concerns, noting that each time Flynn's lies had been repeated, they made the possibility of compromise even stronger. She said McGahn expressed his concern that taking a personnel action against Flynn—such as firing him—might negatively impact the FBI's investigation into the matter, and she assured him that was not a concern to DOJ because Flynn had already been interviewed. In the mind of investigators, if the White House decided to send Flynn packing, it would not hinder their case. Yates said McGahn asked if it would be possible to review the underlying material that indicated Flynn was being untruthful, and she said she would make logistical arrangements for him to come see the information for himself.

She would ultimately be unable to oversee the process of sharing the underlying intelligence, however, as her tenure as acting attorney general was about to come to an abrupt end.

THE SAME DAY as Yates's second White House meeting, back at FBI headquarters, James Comey received an odd request. Just after lunchtime, I walked over to the director's suite to chitchat with Althea James, Comey's executive assistant. Althea is exactly the type of assistant that government executives and Fortune 500 CEOs would kill to have on their staff. She has the superhuman ability to exhibit kindness and focused attention while also juggling forty different things in her mind at the same time. Having spent time working overseas in austere environments, she also has a certain professional rigidity—a defined limit to her patience when she senses she is dealing with a bully or someone trying to game the system.

As I approached Althea's desk, her head was slightly tilted and an eyebrow was raised. "What is it?" I asked, wondering what had managed to leave this unflappable woman speechless. "The director is going to the White House for dinner," she replied, eyes widening, followed by a smile. A short time earlier, Althea had patched through a call from President Trump, who asked Comey whether he wanted to come over for a meal.

I walked into Comey's office and plopped onto one of the chairs facing his desk. "I don't think we spend enough time together," I said, as he gave me a puzzled stare. "Want to grab dinner?"

We both laughed, and he lamented that he'd had to cancel a dinner date with his wife, Patrice, after the call from Trump.

"Good luck," I said with a salute as I hit the door. "See you next week."

Comey told me he thought Trump's call was odd—presidents don't usually socialize with FBI directors—but he hoped to just get through the evening by letting the other dinner guests do all the talking. Little did he know, Trump had arranged dinner for two.

THE NEXT WEEK, Comey boarded the FBI's executive jet bound for Scottsdale, Arizona, where he was to address a large group of state judges who had traveled in from around the country. I had flown home to Los Angeles that weekend, so I hadn't yet had time to get a full readout of his dinner with the president. I anxiously awaited an update. I caught a commercial flight to Phoenix and linked up with the security advance team that was making final preparations for Comey's arrival. The team typically consists of agents and communications specialists dispatched from Washington, but also members of the local field office. The primary job of these agents and analysts is to work investigations and arrest criminals, but they also volunteer to help with security and logistics whenever the director happens to be visiting their territory. Traveling outside the bubble of the director's office was always a welcome experience for me, because it allowed me to connect with colleagues in the field who do the important work. I had been assigned to work as Comey's special assistant for eighteen months; then I would go back to the field to join these men and women.

After Comey's room had been swept for any possible security threats, the large crew of local and DC-based staff joined me on my balcony, where we all unwound with a bottle of cabernet from my minifridge (not paid for by the taxpayers, I'll add) and Jimmy Buffett playing on someone's iPhone. We ticked through the schedule for the coming day, and then agreed to dispense with the shoptalk and just enjoy each other's company and the cold Scottsdale night.

Our efforts to refrain from talking about work didn't last long. We soon received word that our ultimate boss—Sally Yates, the acting US attorney general—had been fired by Trump that same evening after her refusal to defend a presidential executive order banning certain immigrants and refugees from primarily Muslim-majority countries. Although many of us had assumed the Obama holdover would eventually be replaced by someone loyal to Trump, her time in office had now come to an abrupt end. It was another signal that anyone not in step with the administration's party line would soon be shown the door, regardless of the experience and expertise they brought to the table.

Comey landed the next day, along with Eric Smith—the senior-most agent in the director's office, who managed the staff responsible for coordinating Comey's every movement. Although this former Green Beret was now a high-ranking member of the FBI's Senior Executive Service, he was a field agent at heart and, like me, enjoyed joining Comey outside the DC bubble. Although I wanted to hear everything about the director's dinner with Trump the Friday before, I didn't want to distract Comey before his speech, so I contained my curiosity.

After he spoke, we mingled for a while with the attendees, listening to the various law enforcement challenges facing the judges' respective states.

After taking pictures and saying goodbyes, we rolled back to our bank of hotel rooms, where Comey wanted to unwind for a bit and do some work. *Darn*, I thought. *I'm never going to hear about this Trump dinner.*

A mere twenty minutes after settling into my hotel room, I looked down at my phone and saw an incoming call from the boss. "Let's go for a hike," he said, explaining that he needed some fresh air.

I phoned Eric and the security detail and told them we should suit up, as the director wanted to go climb Mummy Mountain, a rugged hill with trails starting at the base of our hotel. I'd been on many walks with Comey—walking is one of his favorite ways of clearing his head and test-driving new thoughts and ideas—but this one would become the most memorable for me.

The security detail fanned out in front of and behind us, providing a wide berth for private conversation while also ensuring they were at the ready in the event that a potential threat presented itself. One of the agents jokingly insisted that I walk just in front of Comey in order to detect any loose rocks, and to serve as a human shield against snakes.

As we wound our way up the mountain, stopping regularly to look out onto the sprawling Phoenix cityscape below, Comey finally got me up to speed on dinner with Trump. As was later revealed, this was the scene of Trump's now-infamous request for a "loyalty pledge." Comey told me he was immediately uneasy after realizing upon his arrival that he and Trump would be dining alone. The meal was awkward from the beginning, he said, with Trump asking him before the main course had even arrived, "So what do you want to do?" The president was referring to Comey's job and his future as director of the FBI. The president said he knew he could "make a change at FBI" if he so desired, but he was interested in Comey's thoughts. To Comey, the entire dinner was a setup—Trump was lording his power over him and wanted something in return.

Trump monopolized the conversation, Comey told me, moving from topic to topic, sometimes without any logical segue: At one point, he brought up the Steele dossier that Comey had originally briefed him on at Trump Tower; he was fixated on the unconfirmed report that he had been with prostitutes in Moscow, calling the story "fake news." At another point, he said something that made Comey's blood boil. "I need loyalty," Trump said. "I expect loyalty." (The president, who has reportedly surpassed more than ten thousand false or misleading statements since taking office, disputes this claim.) Despite the fact that the FBI was investigating members of his own Trump campaign, the president had no qualms about sitting across from the director of the agency and demanding personal loyalty in a manner that Comey later described in his book, *A Higher Loyalty*, as reminiscent of Mafia tactics.

Comey was not about to submit. His refusal meant the clock on his tenure as director was now rapidly ticking toward his professional demise. As I walked next to him on Mummy Mountain, listening to him recount this story, I was at first confused. *Was the president that obtuse?* I thought. *Who told him it would be a good idea to treat his FBI director this way?* I could feel the blood starting to rush to my face in anger.

Comey appeared equally perplexed and disgusted as he described an event that at that time remained a closely guarded secret among a few trusted advisers. While we hiked the steep trail, he would regularly stop in midsentence and regard the view as he tried to process his thoughts.

And when we returned to the hotel, it was clear he was not ready to call an end to this therapeutic stroll outside the political muck and mire of the DC beltway. "Let's do another lap," he said.

IT WAS FEBRUARY 13—just eighteen days since Sally Yates first put the White House on notice about the intelligence surrounding Michael Flynn's calls with the Russians—and Flynn was on the phone with reporters from a conservative website, boasting about the continued confidence Trump had in him. The twenty-fifth US national security adviser had no intention of going anywhere. Rather than trying to get out in front of the fact that he had lied to both the vice president and the FBI (the former, not particularly career-enhancing; the latter, a crime), Flynn was railing against "criminal" media leaks involving his past conversations with the Russian ambassador.

Trump's confidence in Flynn would take an abrupt nosedive later that day after the *Washington Post* contacted the White House requesting comment for a story it was preparing, which would report that Yates had warned the administration about Flynn's lies and his potential to be blackmailed, yet somehow Flynn had remained on the job. By the end of the day, Flynn had turned in a resignation letter, acknowledging that he had "inadvertently briefed the Vice President Elect and others with incomplete information regarding [his] phone calls with the Russian Ambassador." The letter made no mention of the fact that Flynn had also lied to the FBI.

Inside the bureau, officials privately wondered how the Flynn departure would affect the FBI's relationship with the new administration. Trump had clearly cast himself as a fair-weather friend of law enforcement—criticizing the handling of the Hillary Clinton investigation when he believed that certain decisions impacted him negatively, and boasting about the agency when an action appeared to him as politically advantageous—but now the FBI was in part responsible for bringing down Trump's trusted national security adviser less than a month into the administration. "Brace for impact," one of my colleagues, an accomplished investigator who had served under several administrations, noted sourly. Many of us felt similarly uneasy. Trump was someone who mostly saw the world through the lens of favors. Would he let the bureau do its job, or would he find a way to put his finger on the scales of justice? We would soon find out.

The day after Flynn was fired, Comey was at the White House for a previously scheduled briefing on counterterrorism threats. As the meeting with Trump and other senior officials was drawing to a close, the president indicated that he wanted to meet privately with the FBI director. "I just want to talk to Jim," he said. Both the new attorney general, Jeff Sessions, and Trump's son-in-law, Jared Kushner, attempted to stay behind, but Trump waved them off.

Once the door had closed, Trump brought up the issue of Flynn. He said that Flynn had done nothing wrong in speaking with the Russian ambassador but he'd nevertheless had to be let go because he had misled Pence. Trump insisted that Flynn was "a good guy" but then followed his praise of Flynn with what many experts—myself included—considered to be a clear attempt to interfere with an ongoing FBI investigation and shut down the Justice Department's efforts to hold Flynn accountable for his actions. "I hope you can see your way clear to letting this go, to letting Flynn go," Trump said.

The shocking, inappropriate nature of this request cannot be overstated. The president of the United States—Comey's boss—was asking the FBI to end a criminal investigation into a confidant, despite the fact that Flynn had violated federal law. Trump was threatening the independence of federal law enforcement, which for decades had helped distinguish the United States from banana republics around the world. And this would not be the last time the White House would try to use the FBI in an inappropriate way.

THE NEXT DAY, Comey and I were in the air on the way to a meeting in Seattle with the National Organization of Black Law Enforcement Executives. He had been on his Samsung Galaxy smartphone nonstop since takeoff, going back and forth with our team in Washington about a *New York Times* article that had dropped the day before indicating that members of Trump's campaign were in contact with Russian intelligence officials prior to the election. The FBI's deputy director, Andrew McCabe, had been at the White House after the article came out and spoke with Chief of Staff Reince Priebus about it. McCabe indicated that the *Times* had overstated the FBI's knowledge of contacts between Trump campaign members and the Russians, and Priebus wondered if the FBI could put out a statement refuting the claims.

Reaching for the in-flight Airfone next to his seat in front of me on the FBI's executive jet, Comey called McCabe to discuss the matter. As the conversation went on, Comey became increasingly agitated, and his voice began to rise. "This is not what we do," Comey barked, making it clear that the FBI would not be used as a pawn to knock down news stories critical of the White House. Comey was not about to drag the FBI into the mix while the sensitive Crossfire Hurricane investigation was still underway. "I'll talk to Reince," Comey finally said, shoving the phone back into its cradle.

A few minutes later, we heard the piercing sound of an incoming call, and Comey snatched the phone from the wall. He and Priebus talked about the issue, and Comey held firm. If the administration wanted to tell reporters that the intelligence community was casting doubt on certain details in the article, he said, that was fine, but the FBI would not be issuing any statements. Doing so ran counter to his view that the FBI remain independent of politics. In fact, the White House communicating directly with the FBI itself, rather than going through the attorney general, violated long-held custom.

Following the conversation, Comey hung up the phone, head shaking, as I received a readout of the call. "They just don't get it," he said with a sigh, as I moved forward and settled into the seat next to him. He muttered again about the importance of independence. "Look, some people might think I'm crazy," he continued, "but the FBI as an institution cannot be viewed as a political tentacle of the White House. We are *in* the executive branch, but we are not *of* the executive branch."

Up to this point, I had seen Comey visibly upset on only one other occasion. In that other instance, he was running through an important speech with the staff and clearly was off his game, stumbling over words, getting the cadence wrong. Afterward, he polled the team for thoughts on how he was doing. "Outstanding," one person gushed. "I know that's not true," Comey replied in an uncharacteristically raised voice. "I need feedback. I expect brutally honest feedback."

Back on the airplane, seeming to realize that his tone could suggest that he was allowing the White House to get the best of him, he quickly turned positive. "They'll learn the appropriate way to deal with us," he told me. "We'll train 'em."

"HAVE YOU SEEN the tweets?" Michael Kulstad, senior adviser in our Office of Public Affairs, texted me early on the morning of March 4. Mike was a Comey confidant who had first worked with him when Comey was US attorney in Manhattan, and had been brought to the FBI to lend his media and communications expertise to our press operation. "The tweets" to which Mike was referring could mean only one thing: the president of the

United States was up early speaking to the world on his favorite communication platform. I quickly opened Twitter and braced for what I would find.

"Terrible!" Trump had tweeted. "Just found out that Obama had my 'wires tapped' in Trump Tower just before the victory. Nothing found. This is McCarthyism!" The tweetstorm continued. "How low has President Obama gone to tapp [*sic*] my phones during the very sacred election process," Trump wrote. "This is Nixon/Watergate. Bad (or sick) guy!"

"What in the world is he talking about?" I tapped out in reply to Mike. If the president had just been briefed on electronic surveillance conducted against him at Trump Tower, presumably such a briefing would have come from the Justice Department or someone else in the know. This made no sense. I scanned the major headlines from the past week, wondering if I had somehow missed a report claiming that Trump had been the subject of illegal wiretapping. Nothing.

"Don't know," Mike replied, "but I let the boss know." Kulstad often served as an early-warning system for Comey, devouring large quantities of news and then flagging items that might eventually become of interest to him. These tweets were a flashing red light. Court-ordered surveillance in the United States is conducted at the federal level by the FBI, so if Trump was claiming he had been illegally spied on, the train was now coming down the tracks and headed straight for the bureau.

As CNN's Brian Stelter outlined in a piece dissecting the origins of the Trump Tower wiretap claims, the entire issue got its start based on unsubstantiated allegations set forth by right-wing media circles. What started as nonsense spewed by a far-right talk radio host quickly snowballed as more mainstream conservative outlets seized on the issue and turned a spark into a raging wildfire. As Stelter noted, the original peddler of the claim "cherry-picked news stories that supported his thesis and omitted information that cut against it." Despite the fact that most serious media outlets were unable to verify the reports, Trump took them at face value. Although he could have picked up the phone and demanded a briefing from the attorney general or the director of national intelligence, he instead chose to spread rumor and innuendo on Twitter.

Trump's outlandish claims ignited a firestorm inside the US intelligence community. I spoke that weekend with several colleagues at the FBI, CIA, and the NSA, all of whom were completely dumbfounded by what the president was saying. More than that, we were furious. The president of the United States was in effect claiming that the intelligence community violated its oath and engaged in criminal activity by illegally spying on him at the behest of President Obama.

Part of me thought, at the time, that Trump might actually believe what he was hearing because he probably wished he had the power to order the FBI and other agencies to do whatever he willed. He had by now learned that the FBI was not going to be his lapdog; maybe he had convinced himself that the FBI had pledged loyalty to Obama but was now refusing to pledge loyalty to him.

It is true that there were associates of Trump under FBI counterintelligence investigation, which included a variety of sensitive techniques since declassified, but nothing was unlawful. Indeed, techniques used in the Crossfire Hurricane investigation would have had to have been signed off on either at the highest levels of the Justice Department or by independent federal judges, depending on the level of intrusiveness.

Comey was furious, too, but he held his fire.

Things would soon change, thanks to an unexpected intervention by Senator Chuck Grassley. The senior senator from Iowa, who then chaired the powerful Senate Judiciary Committee, was becoming increasingly frustrated at reading headlines about suspected Trump-Russia connections but not getting any substantive information from the bureau. He finally signaled that he would hold up the confirmation of incoming Deputy Attorney General Rod Rosenstein until Congress received answers from the FBI. The Justice Department then gave Comey the green light to go public; he would make an announcement at an upcoming congressional hearing on worldwide threats.

On Saturday, March 18, I worked from home, reviewing Comey's draft opening statement. After making some edits, we exchanged notes, and then he spent the next day preparing for his testimony. On Monday, he took his seat at the witness table before the House Intelligence Committee.

When appearing before Congress, Comey rarely, if ever, read from prepared notes. He was typically comfortable enough in his understanding of the subject matter at hand to field an array of questions and either answer assertively or make a note to get back to the questioner with a more detailed answer at a later date. On this day, however, he hewed closely to the written script before him, mindful that he was discussing a sensitive investigation that had not yet been completed. The room fell silent as he keyed his microphone and dropped a bombshell.

"I have been authorized by the Department of Justice to confirm that the FBI, as part of our counterintelligence mission, is investigating the Russian government's efforts to interfere in the 2016 presidential election," Comey said, "and that includes investigating the nature of any links between individuals associated with the Trump campaign and the Russian government, and whether there was any coordination between the campaign and Russia's efforts."

Due to the classified nature of the investigation, he would not say anything more of substance on the topic, except to indicate that the investigation had begun the previous July. He did, however, use the occasion to dismiss Trump's ridiculous claim that he had been the subject of illegal wiretapping.

Back at FBI headquarters, Comey sank onto the faux leather couch in my office, exhausted from having testified for so long before Congress while having to sidestep specific questions about the investigation that he could not answer in an open hearing. We watched some of the coverage on television, flipping between CNN, MSNBC, and Fox News, taking in the historic implications of an FBI director publicly confirming that the campaign of a sitting president was under investigation. After all the leaks and all the spin, here was the FBI placing down a marker, confirming that its counterintelligence professionals were hard at work trying to safeguard the nation from external threats.

If confirming the investigation was akin to turning a pressure-release valve inside the Justice Department, at the White House it was the start of a five-alarm fire. The administration was now in damage-control mode.

Press Secretary Sean Spicer—whose reservoir of credibility had been running increasingly low ever since his first day on the job, when he'd battled the press over the size of the crowd at Trump's inauguration—sought to downplay Comey's announcement. The White House claimed there was no coordination with the Russians and then immediately pivoted to the leaks, suggesting that public knowledge of the matter was due to malicious actions by former Obama officials.

Ten days after the hearing, Trump phoned the FBI director. He wanted to know why Comey had testified about the case before Congress, and Comey responded that congressional leaders had been demanding answers. The director also advised the president that he had privately informed congressional leaders that Trump himself was not currently the subject of the investigation. Trump said that he wanted to get that fact out publicly, and Comey demurred, thinking this would be a difficult course of action to take because he might then be faced with a duty to correct the record down the road if Trump at some point became caught up in the case.

As Comey later described in his book, Trump then brought up a topic that had been the subject of several of his past interactions with Comey: FBI deputy director Andrew McCabe. Although McCabe was a registered Republican, his wife had run for public office in Virginia and had received a substantial amount of money from a political organization controlled by then governor Terry McAuliffe, who was closely tied to the Clintons. Trump was obsessed with McCabe, repeatedly musing that McCabe was out to get Trump because his wife had run for office as a Democrat. If it sounds ludicrous, it's because it is.

Inside the FBI, some of us seethed at Trump's failure to see this powerful, accomplished woman as separate from her husband. Jill McCabe was a physician who had been recruited to run for office because of her skill and abilities. Trump, however, believed there had to be something sinister behind Jill McCabe's husband now serving in such a powerful position at the FBI. Trump seemed to think Andy McCabe had gone easy on Clinton during the email investigation to help his wife, or was simply out to get Trump, or perhaps both. There was no rational way to explain his obsession with Andy. Trump acted like a man seeing enemies everywhere, even where they did not exist.

On April 11, in what would be the last time Comey ever spoke with the president, Trump called in an irritated mood. Although Comey had sensitized both him and Chief of Staff Reince Priebus to the reality that directly phoning the FBI director was not customary—and that the White House should instead work through Justice Department leadership in its dealings with the FBI—the president ignored these suggestions and made the call. Unlike previous instances, in which Trump had started the conversation heaping faint praise on Comey, this time he got straight to the point. Why, Trump wondered, was the bureau not publicly confirming that Trump was not a subject of the Russia investigation, lamenting at how "the cloud" surrounding the investigation was inhibiting his ability to do his job. Comey said he had presented the president's original request to DOJ and was not sure where it stood. The president pondered whether the White House should go directly to DOJ officials, and Comey suggested that was the best course of action. The investigation was clearly weighing on the president, but it remained unclear whether it was merely an annoyance to him or something that genuinely frightened him because of where it could lead.

That same day, the *Washington Post* ran a story announcing that Trump campaign adviser Carter Page had been the subject of surveillance under FISA. Unlike typical search warrants in criminal investigations, FISA orders are instead handled by a secret court in Washington, DC, established to handle sensitive national security investigations. In my FBI career, I handled numerous FISA orders and investigations, and to say that they are onerous is putting it lightly. The process of getting a FISA warrant is a labor-intensive one, which involves crafting an application often several inches thick, fact-checking every single word and declaration made in the application, and then getting the request through a series of FBI and DOJ lawyers whose jobs are to scrutinize each request for accuracy and efficacy.

The Page news, therefore, was especially damning for a White House already under fire following Comey's public confirmation of the Russia investigation. Trump had tried to distance himself from Page, with Spicer claiming that the president didn't even know him, but the idea that Trump campaign officials might have colluded with Russia to throw an election was now the subject of nonstop media coverage.

And for good reason. There were now many questions about Trump's ties with Moscow: Did the Russians have dirt—sexual and/or financial—on Trump? Why did Trump seem so unconcerned by Russia's brazen efforts to interfere in the presidential election? Did the fact that Trump wouldn't release his tax returns—despite previously vowing to do so—have anything to do with the Kremlin?

TRUMP WOULD LATER interact suspiciously with Russian president Vladimir Putin in a way that would cause many former spies to question whether Trump was compromised, but by May 2017 the White House was merely faced with lingering doubts and a brutal news cycle. For a president who was frequently glued to the headlines and constantly gauging how he was being portrayed in the press, the churn of Russia stories must have made him feel as if the walls were closing in.

In his final call with the FBI director, Trump returned to the familiar language of loyalty. "I have been very loyal to you, very loyal," he told Comey. "We had that thing, you know," he said, conjuring up some mutual pledge of loyalty that Comey had not actually accepted.

For a person motivated by the pursuit of power above everything else, if you're not a friend, you're a foe. Trump must have begun to realize that there would be no public statement from the FBI announcing his innocence, at least not while the investigation was still underway. The president would have to do something else to relieve this great pressure.

# CHAPTER 8

# "You're Fired"

INFURIATED BY A Russia investigation that was not going away, Donald Trump took to Twitter on May 2, 2017, to vent his frustration. It would be the first time the president lambasted James Comey on social media since taking office, signaling to many inside the FBI that the president was getting ready to blow. "FBI Director Comey was the best thing that ever happened to Hillary Clinton in that he gave her a free pass for many bad deeds! The phony . . . ," he wrote. ". . . Trump/Russia story," he continued in a second tweet, "was an excuse used by the Democrats as justification for losing the election. Perhaps Trump just ran a great campaign?"

Inside the FBI, people were furious. All at once, the president was landing two blows against an agency that prided itself on fairness and independence. In the span of two tweets, he had managed to accuse the FBI of helping cover up criminal activity vis-à-vis Clinton and then claim that the FBI was somehow involved in a partisan ploy to manufacture a counterintelligence investigation into his campaign's ties to Russia. "This guy just isn't well," a colleague of mine remarked as we sat at dinner scrolling through our Twitter feeds. "I'm as Republican as they come, but this guy has simply lost it."

An uneasiness was building about the president and his increasingly heated rhetoric toward the bureau and our investigation. But, we thought, what exactly could he do about it? It would be political suicide—and possibly obstruction of justice—for the commander in chief to order the Justice Department to shut down an investigation into his campaign. We knew Trump was unpredictable, but that seemed a bridge too far.

The next day, Comey was back on Capitol Hill, testifying before the Senate Judiciary Committee. I watched the hearing from the "war room" back at FBI headquarters—essentially, a conference room where members of the team gather around a giant TV eating unhealthy snacks and taking notes. People came and went throughout the hearing, catching snippets of Comey's testimony and stepping out to juggle their other daily tasks. The goal for the director's staff was to watch the testimony in real time, take note of any follow-up requests for information Comey received from the senators, and then start tasking those requests out to the appropriate FBI operational division. It was rare for Comey to misspeak or say something that needed clarification, but when it did happen, a member of the staff in the war room would fire off a text message to someone seated behind Comey, who would in turn jot down a note and set it on the table in front of the director.

As was usually the case, Comey was staffed at this particular hearing by Greg Brower, the FBI's head of congressional affairs. Brower is a former state senator and US attorney in Nevada who, thanks to his stellar legal acumen, was recruited for the position of deputy general counsel at the FBI in 2016. He would be tapped the next year to lead the division responsible for working with Congress on a multitude of criminal, national security, and intelligence issues. A former naval officer, Brower is a quiet yet confident professional who was known on the seventh floor of FBI headquarters for his unflappable demeanor, even in chaotic situations. These personality traits were well suited for the person charged with dealing with an increasingly irate Congress and the seemingly endless requests for details of FBI operations from both sides of the political aisle.

By that point, Comey had already briefed the so-called Gang of Eight— the House speaker and minority leader, the Senate majority and minority leaders, and the chairs and ranking members of the House and Senate Intelligence Committees—on the details of the investigation, so he felt he was keeping congressional leadership adequately informed. The goal in briefing congressional leadership is to permit them the ability to execute their important oversight functions without broadcasting sensitive operational details to all 535 members of Congress. I can say, having been aware of a number of issues briefed to the group, that the information provided to the Gang of Eight rarely, if ever, leaks. This is quite a compliment for a branch of government known for leaking like a sieve.

Shortly after Brower took the FBI congressional affairs post, Comey said he wanted to brief the Gang of Eight on the Russia investigation, and Brower found himself accompanying the director to Capitol Hill. As Comey laid out the FBI's Russia investigation, Brower told me, the Gang of Eight was riveted. "He had an incredible ability to confidently brief without using notes," Brower said.

Although there was much Comey could *not* say about a classified investigation while in the open Senate Judiciary Committee hearing on May 3, the public heard from him on a wide range of topics, including the Trump-Russia case, Attorney General Jeff Sessions's recusal from the investigation due to his campaign ties, the FISA warrant authorizing surveillance of Trump adviser Carter Page, the Steele dossier, and why some members believed the Trump case was being treated differently than that of Hillary Clinton's email server. Comey was asked several times about Trump's direct involvement with Russia and declined to provide specifics. Asked about Trump's comments that the hacking of the DNC could have been done by China or a lot of other groups, Comey responded, "The intelligence community with high confidence concluded it was Russia." He was then asked about and went on to explain his rationale for why Putin favored Trump over Clinton. Finally, Comey was asked whether he stood by his original claim refuting Trump's accusation that the intelligence community had illegally wiretapped Trump Tower. "Correct," Comey responded tersely.

THE COMEY HEARING was not the only event on Capitol Hill that would reflect negatively upon the president. The following Monday—May 8—fired acting attorney general Sally Yates and former director of national intelligence James Clapper appeared before a Senate Judiciary subcommittee to answer questions about Russia's role in the 2016 election. Likely worried about what the former Justice Department and intelligence professionals might say, Trump tried to get out ahead of the spectacle by shifting the narrative away from possible collusion with Russia and instead focusing on media leaks. "Ask Sally Yates, under oath, if she knows how classified information got into the newspapers soon after she explained it to W.H. Council [*sic*]," Trump vented on Twitter, before deleting the tweet and replacing it later with one with his chief lawyer's title spelled correctly.

Speaking calmly but forcefully, Yates walked the senators through the timeline of her interactions with the White House in the run-up to Michael Flynn's firing, describing her efforts to sound the alarm that Flynn might have placed himself in a compromising situation by lying to the vice president. Her testimony appeared at odds with the description of her interactions provided by White House Press Secretary Sean Spicer and Chief of Staff Reince Priebus, who had described her notifications about Flynn's troubling behavior as merely "a heads-up."

Regardless of the spin, the truth of the matter was that the highest ranking official in the US Department of Justice had warned the White House that the president's most senior adviser on national security matters was potentially in a situation where he could be blackmailed by a foreign adversary. I can recall in my time with the FBI many moments in which I called my counterparts at the National Security Council to give them a heads-up on something, but advising them that someone close to the president with access to highly classified information was prone to blackmail wouldn't fit the benign description of merely flagging something for their general awareness. The White House had waited eighteen days from the time the acting attorney general first notified them of the Flynn lies before showing him the door, and it did so only after a newspaper indicated that it was about to run a story on the original warning. If people in the Trump administration had chosen to ignore Yates's warning, that was their decision, but to characterize her good-faith effort to sound the alarm on a major national security vulnerability as only a heads-up was disingenuous to the core.

For his part, President Trump was clearly rattled by the public testimony coming from Yates. Again taking to Twitter, he downplayed the hearing and sought to discredit both her and the media. "Sally Yates made the fake media extremely unhappy today—she said nothing but old news!" he railed. But he wasn't finished: He then again brought up the claim that he had been illegally spied on by the national security community. "Biggest story today between Clapper & Yates is on surveillance," Trump tweeted. "Why doesn't the media report on this? #FakeNews!"

By this point, people inside the intelligence community had lost all patience with Trump's bluster. I was on several group chats with friends in the FBI and at other intelligence agencies; these were fast becoming the digital equivalent of evening therapy sessions for government employees perplexed by the president's erratic behavior. In one exchange the night after the Yates hearing, an intelligence analyst buddy of mine rhetorically asked, "When will he stop calling us criminals?" Despite Trump's repeated claims that there's a mythical deep state inside government that is actively working against him, that was not what was going on here. Rather, our chats were simply the real-time reflections of public servants concerned with the chief executive's rhetoric, which was growing more and more dangerous and unhinged by the day. If a CEO at any company in the world spent his or her day publicly bashing employees and calling them corrupt, you can bet those very same employees would be talking about it at the proverbial water cooler.

JAMES COMEY'S FINAL day as director of the Federal Bureau of Investigation began just like any other in his nearly four-year post as the agency's head. It was Tuesday, May 9, 2017, and he had an early morning flight to Florida for a meeting with law enforcement executives, with plans to continue west to California for a special-agent diversity recruiting event being hosted by the FBI's Los Angeles field office.

While official Washington was still asleep, I met Damien Walke, the chief of Comey's protective detail, and Eric Smith, Comey's senior special assistant, at FBI headquarters to prepare for the trip. While Damien and Eric filled a bureau SUV with long guns, ballistic vests, and a medical kit, I ran upstairs to grab the electronic tablet containing the President's Daily Brief—the top-secret threat briefing compiled each night for the president and a select group of senior national security officials—which had just been dropped off for Comey by a CIA analyst. This highly sensitive document used to arrive in a hard-copy binder, but now state-of-the-art digital technology from the wizards at Langley allowed those authorized to read the PDB to do so in an electronic format, complete with rich graphics and organizational charts. Although the electronic tablet it was on was password-protected, ensuring its physical security was one of the most stressful parts of my job. Losing it would be a cardinal sin. On one very memorable occasion, I yelled to one of our drivers to bring our motorcade to a halt on the freeway because I couldn't find it in my bag. Thankfully, I had merely placed it in the wrong pocket, and disaster was averted. There was no greater feeling of relief than after Comey had finished reading it for the day and I was able to hand it off to our traveling communications specialist for safekeeping.

While the "pickup team" fetched Comey from his house, Damien and I made the short drive across the Potomac to a private terminal at Reagan National Airport. As I passed through the electronic sliding-glass doors from the terminal out onto the tarmac, I was at first confused by the unusual aircraft occupying our regular spot, which was obscuring the FBI's Gulfstream executive jet parked behind it. Rather than seeing the bureau airplane, I was instead greeted by a blue-and-white four-engine Lockheed WP-3D Orion belonging to the National Oceanic and Atmospheric Administration. This was one of the famous "hurricane hunters"—the aircraft flown into gathering storms to survey wind conditions and other data important to forecasters.

"Are we expecting a bumpy ride?" I wondered aloud as Damien and I walked past the majestic aircraft.

Comey arrived a short time later, and as I peered out a window on the Gulfstream's starboard side, I could see him dragging his luggage and steadying a cup of coffee while he stared at the hurricane hunters' black space-shuttle-like nose cone.

"What is that thing?" he asked as he climbed aboard, tossing me his bag.

"That's one of those special weather airplanes," I replied with unscientific precision. "There's no telling how many times that thing has been tossed and battered by violent storms."

"I know the feeling," he responded wryly.

As he removed his jacket and settled into his seat, he reached into his Tumi laptop bag and grabbed a bottle of red wine, which he proudly held up before returning it to the bag. Somewhere along the way during our travels, I had remarked that he should consider bringing his own wine on these government trips. It wasn't for reasons of security, but for frugality. No matter where we traveled, Comey was the kind of person who would almost always eschew going out at night, seeing the sights, and grabbing a nice meal. He knew that just going out to dinner in any given city would mean taking along bodyguards, drivers, and possibly local police officers. Rather than burden the security detail—who themselves also needed to eat and maybe wanted some downtime in an exciting new city—he would opt to stay at the hotel, order room service, and let the team go out and enjoy the evening. His doing so was admirable, but it was also expensive. I finally pointed out to him that one glass of wine purchased from hotel room service was probably the same price as an entire bottle he could bring along from home. On this particular trip, he had finally decided to pack a bottle of red.

It was rush hour at the airport, and as we taxied out toward the runway, we took our place in line behind a dozen jets waiting for takeoff. A running joke of ours had been how undignified it was that the FBI director had to wait in line behind commercial jets. Poking fun at other senior government officials, whose egos could often fill an entire airplane hangar, we would often talk about the theoretical cabinet official asking his or her pilot to cut the line and bypass the commoners.

"I can call the control tower," I said, as we inched forward during what seemed like an interminable wait.

"I bet that hurricane airplane doesn't have to wait in line," Comey joked.

"It's okay," I said, reaching for my headphones and sliding back into my seat. "At least we're not heading into a storm."

AFTER OUR BRIEF stop in Jacksonville, we headed to Los Angeles International Airport and taxied to a secluded section of the airfield, where we were met by Deirdre Fike, the assistant director in charge of the local field office, a group of FBI SWAT agents, and officers from the California Highway Patrol, who would be flanking the motorcade with marked police cruisers.

The first stop would be the field office headquarters, near UCLA in Westwood, where Comey would have the chance to meet with employees and learn about some of the investigative operations currently underway in the region. The diversity recruitment event was scheduled for later that evening in West Hollywood, which meant Comey would have a couple of hours beforehand to walk the floors of the building and talk with the troops. We took the elevator up to the eleventh floor for our first stop, a conference room, where Comey met with a group of senior leaders who managed personnel and operations in the seven-county Los Angeles area.

These were my friends and mentors—people I had worked for and with during my earliest years in the field, when I had been stationed there. Ever the raucous bunch, as they went around the table introducing themselves, many could not help but poke fun at how Comey's hiring standards for his staff seemed to have plummeted with my arrival on his team. After the meeting, Deirdre walked Comey around the rest of building, where he stopped at the desks of employees to introduce himself, check in on what they were working on that day, and take pictures. (Many already had pictures with the boss from previous visits hanging in their cubicles.)

As WE HUMMED along, working our way from floor to floor, Comey stopped in at the fourteenth-floor operations center, where a large group of employees had gathered. He had been speaking for only a short time when he abruptly stopped. After working closely with him for over a year, I had perfected the art of listening to him speak while multitasking on my FBI phone. His silence snapped me out of my focus on the document I was browsing, and I looked up to see him staring at me, nodding in the direction of one of the large television screens on the wall at the back of the room.

COMEY RESIGNS, the Fox News Channel banner read. For a brief second, Comey told me later, he thought it was a joke, perhaps the work of some mischievous LA FBI tech agent trying to pull a fast one on the director. Then a second television, programmed to CNN, broadcast the breaking news that Comey had been fired. Senior Washington correspondent Jeff Zeleny explained what was currently known of developments on the ground in DC: that President Trump had fired the FBI director.

There were gasps heard throughout the operations center as employees tried to process the news.

While Comey continued addressing the group—he didn't want to rush off the stage, understanding the terrible message that would send to a room full of employees who had technically just lost their leader—I stepped into a quiet corner and phoned Chief of Staff Jim Rybicki back in Washington. Rybicki was perhaps Comey's closest confidant in the FBI, someone who had been with him off and on for over a decade at Main Justice and the bureau. When I reached him, he was on his way home for the evening and had not yet heard the news, but he quickly turned around and raced back to the Hoover Building.

I knew I didn't want to leave Comey out in a large group while he was still trying to make sense of what was going on, so I asked Deirdre if we could take over one of the supervisors' offices adjacent to the operations center so we could make calls and find out what was happening. Comey, Eric Smith, and I gathered in the office, closed the door, and just sat for a moment looking at each other.

"I hope this isn't true," Comey said, in a tone that conveyed both annoyance and sadness.

I told him we were still trying to gather the details but would report back just as soon as we heard something official. I handed him his iPhone, and he dialed his wife, Patrice. When he connected, Eric and I stepped outside and shut the door, leaving him to speak with her in private.

I grabbed Damien from the security team and we went over our options. The original plan was for us to travel about ten miles to the diversity recruitment event, and then to Marina del Rey, where we'd planned to overnight before flying the next morning to Monterey. Understanding the anguish Comey must have been experiencing that moment—hell, we were all crushed—I proposed that we scrap the plan and focus on getting Comey home. Damien started working on logistics.

Eric and I went back inside the office and sat with Comey for a while. He connected with the staff back in DC and learned officially that he had indeed been relieved of his duties. Rather than summoning Comey back to the White House and firing the director himself, Trump had ordered one of his longtime bodyguards to drop off a letter at the FBI visitors' center informing Comey of the president's decision. I later learned from my CNN colleagues that a member of the reporting team had just happened to be walking by the Hoover Building at the time, saw a dark-colored sedan illegally parked in front of FBI headquarters with its police lights flashing, and recognized the bodyguard from the president's team. By his presence, the reporter knew something important was happening.

"There was so much left to be done," Comey said as he sat shaking his head. His lips were pursed, signaling to me the combination of both pain and disgust that he was experiencing. I told him we were going to move to Deirdre's office, which was much larger than the small space we were presently jammed into, and then offered a suggestion.

"Sir, I don't know where your mind is right now," I said. "I can't even imagine. But you have only seen about a third of the employees in this building, who no doubt wanted to see their director today. If you're okay with it, may I suggest to Deirdre that any employees who want to see you before we depart come down here to the operations center?"

"Absolutely," he said. "I would love that. But make it clear this is optional. Don't ask her to summon everyone down here."

I stepped out and found Deirdre, who was upset like the rest of us, and furious at not only what had happened, but also at the humiliating manner in which it had transpired. I conveyed my idea, and Deirdre said to give her ten minutes.

I went back into the office and found Comey staring out the window toward the Hollywood Hills. We just sat there in silence, periodically catching each other's gaze and then shaking our heads. There was nothing to say. I had asked the team back in Washington to scan and email over the letter from the president, but it had not yet arrived. After a couple of minutes, I asked Comey if he was ready to go. He stood, put his coat back on, and nodded.

Upon opening the door, I expected to see several people—Comey was highly regarded in the field—but the large operations center was packed wall to wall with dozens of employees. As Comey stepped out, the room erupted into applause, which lingered while some employees shifted from clapping to brushing away tears to clapping again.

"Look, I don't know what is going on in Washington," Comey said as the room fell silent. "But just remember this: your mission of protecting the American people and upholding the Constitution of the United States continues. May you do it forever, as long as you can. Serving as your director has been the most rewarding experience of my professional life."

There was more applause, and Comey shook hands and returned hugs. Before exiting, he abruptly stopped and poked his head into an adjacent room where a handful of employees were busy working. These were the operations staff who were servicing the needs of the agents currently in the field, working surveillance, locating wanted criminals, and interviewing witnesses. Understanding that they had been unable to drop what they were doing to come hear his final message, he repeated what he had told the larger group about the importance of the bureau's mission.

"Please keep doing the mission," he said, embracing one sobbing employee on his way out the door. With that, we headed downstairs to quickly regroup in Deirdre's office before departing for Washington.

"WE HAVE A problem," Damien said, as we stood outside Deirdre's office, where Comey was seated talking on the phone. Since the FBI pilots had been flying all day long—first to Florida and then to California—they were now on the verge of pushing the maximum number of hours permitted in one day. Damien was working to scramble another crew or see if the FAA would grant a waiver for the flight back home.

"Whatever it takes, let's get him home," I said, and he nodded in agreement. "If any of us had been fired, we would want to be home, not sitting in some Marriott in Marina del Rey, far away from our families."

Damien said he was on it and would circle back once he had learned more.

I went in and explained to Comey the conundrum we were now facing and how it was possible we might be stuck in Los Angeles for the night. As we sat talking, our phones buzzed with an incoming email from the DC team containing an attachment with the letter from the president.

"It is essential that we find new leadership for the FBI that restores public trust and confidence in its vital law enforcement mission," the president wrote. But the file contained much more than just a letter from Trump. Also included was a memorandum from Attorney General Jeff Sessions and a lengthy treatise from Deputy Attorney General Rod Rosenstein outlining why he was recommending that Comey be relieved of his job. Rosenstein's rationale? In his view, Comey had mishandled the Hillary Clinton email investigation and had to go in order to restore trust and confidence in the FBI.

We were irate. Actually, there is a stronger description of just how angry we were, but it would not fit the general decorum of this book. The Clinton case! An investigation that had been closed some six months earlier. The sham could not have been more obvious to us.

That Trump had managed to enlist the assistance of Rosenstein in the charade was striking. Not too long before the firing, I had joined Comey in Maryland after Rosenstein had invited the director to come speak to a group of lawyers on the topic of effective leadership. Now, Rosenstein was saying Comey was a terrible leader who was no longer effective. The deputy attorney general was widely known inside the FBI as a smart lawyer and a political animal, and it was that latter trait that likely had him placating a president who was looking for any excuse to send Comey packing.

We would later learn an astonishing detail: the president had met with Rosenstein before the firing and wanted the deputy attorney general to reference the Russia investigation in his letter recommending the firing, but Rosenstein had reportedly said that detail was not necessary. This suggests that Rosenstein *knew* the Russia investigation was on Trump's mind when making the decision to fire Comey, but decided instead to focus on Clinton rather than admit that the president was possibly obstructing justice by firing the person investigating his campaign.

Rosenstein would not be the only one in Trump's orbit believed to have sacrificed personal principles. As Comey was reading over Rosenstein's memo a second time, I received a call from one of the team members in Washington, who indicated that then secretary of homeland security John Kelly wanted to talk to Comey. Kelly was a retired Marine Corps general who had once served as a Pentagon combatant commander before joining the Trump administration as head of the Department of Homeland Security. He would also later do a five-month stint as Trump's chief of staff after the departure of Reince Priebus. At this time, however, he was a colleague of Comey's, leading a department that the FBI worked with very closely on any given day. I gave Comey a phone number for Kelly and sat next to him as he spoke with the DHS secretary.

It was clear from the end of the conversation I could hear that Kelly had called to express his regrets that Comey had been fired and was questioning whether he himself should remain in office. Comey urged him not to leave, saying that the country needed good people of principle surrounding Trump. The call ended with Comey reassuring Kelly that all would be well, rather than the other way around.

This issue is important because once details of the phone call came to light after the release of Comey's book, the White House disputed the claim that Kelly had called the president dishonorable and talked of leaving, instead claiming the call between the two officials was perfunctory in nature and merely meant to wish Comey good luck. I knew that this was false.

After the Kelly call, Comey told me he wanted to draft a final all-employee farewell message to the FBI family and asked me to notify headquarters to be ready to send out an email that evening, just as soon as he had written it.

Comey's internal emails to the entire FBI were a mainstay in the organization. He always wrote them himself and considered them one of the ways he could stay connected to the employees serving around the world. Personnel would often reply to him directly, and he welcomed the back-and-forth. He lived in constant fear of being trapped inside a bubble and looked to these exchanges as an opportunity to obtain ground truth.

I tapped out a note to the public affairs internal-communications team and copied a couple of the senior officials on the executive corridor, advising them that a draft note would soon be forthcoming. A reply soon came back: request denied.

Jeff Sessions had decided that there would be no further communications from Comey to the FBI; instead, he himself would send out an email to the bureau formally advising us of the president's decision. I told Comey of the AG's decision and that he would be unable to communicate a final time with the troops. He was crushed.

Damien and I did another quick aside, and he advised that it looked like we would be able to fly back to DC that night after all, but with a brief stop in Colorado. He had identified another set of FBI pilots in Denver rated for the Gulfstream, so it was just a matter of using the current crew for the first leg and the Denver crew for the second. The initial crew would technically be a bit over their maximum hours that day, so as I understood it we were still waiting on a waiver from the FAA.

I relayed this news to Comey and then stepped out to take one of the more ridiculous phone calls of my life. One of the FBI lawyers in DC had called to tell me that there was apparently an issue brewing over at Main Justice regarding whether Comey would actually be allowed to fly back home on an FBI aircraft. Since he was technically no longer employed by the government, there were some officials over there suggesting that he should instead fly back commercially.

"Are you freaking kidding me?" I said. I walked him through how incredibly asinine and juvenile the argument was, and how it smacked of last-ditch retribution. I explained that flying Comey home was not only the ethical thing to do, but that we also had eight other FBI employees now stuck in Los Angeles—Eric Smith, the air crew, security agents, and me— and we were going to board that airplane and fly home. What difference did it make if we added one more person—who just so happened to be the former leader of the organization?

The lawyer assured me that he was merely the messenger and he would get back in touch with further guidance. I had now had enough. Things were moving from unprofessional to just plain cruel. I turned off my phone and threw it in my bag (probably a little harder than I should have), the better to ignore any follow-up call with official orders to abort the flight.

Before we packed up, I had a realization that seemed trivial at the time, but it was important nonetheless. We had no food. We had flown all day and were now preparing to make another six-hour flight across the country, but we had nothing to eat for the ride home. Unlike some corporate jets that come with flight attendants and fine dining, the FBI jet had none of that. If we were lucky, there might be a few bottles of water and granola bars stashed somewhere in the cabinets, but I wasn't betting on it. I called one of the LA SWAT agents, whom I had known since my early days in the office, and told him I had the most menial request and felt bad even asking. Would he be able to grab Comey a sandwich?

"A sandwich?" he replied incredulously. "After what he's been through, we're going to get him a steak, and shrimp, and—"

"Great sentiment," I said. "And I know he appreciates it, but you have to beat our motorcade to the airport, so any plain old turkey sandwich will do."

"Okay, what does he want on it?" he asked.

"Nothing," I replied. "He's the most boring eater there is. Just a regular turkey sandwich will do."

It was time to go, and I gave Comey the thumbs-up. By this time, Deirdre, the head of the field office, had already departed for the originally scheduled diversity recruiting event, where she had the unenviable task of being the first FBI official to publicly address an event being covered by the national press since word of Comey's firing had been made public. As we walked to the door of her office to head to the elevators, Comey stopped, and walked over to her desk. He sat down, grabbed a slip of personalized stationery from her shelf, and penned a farewell note thanking her for everything. With that, he stood, and we left.

I would soon learn from my headquarters colleagues that President

Trump had barred Comey from ever again entering FBI space, making this moment his last inside the bureau.

As LOS ANGELES rush-hour traffic was just getting underway, our motorcade rumbled out of the federal building's loading dock and looped onto the freeway for the drive back to the airport. I opened a news app on my personal iPhone, and we watched in real time the live helicopter coverage of our procession of two black Suburbans and two highway patrol cruisers slowly inching down the 405 freeway.

When we arrived at the airfield, we snaked through a series of news trucks and photographers staking out the entrance. A security agent told Comey we were going to pull directly up to the steps of the plane so he could rush on board.

This bothered me for a couple of reasons. I didn't like the optics. *Why should he run?* I thought. *He hasn't done anything wrong.* And on countless trips to dozens of cities and towns across the US, Comey had always asked me to ensure that there was time left over in the schedule so he could personally thank the local police officers who had helped protect him on a given trip. It was nonnegotiable. Rushing onto the plane now would deprive him of that great joy, probably for the last time.

As we neared the airplane, I didn't want to offend my good buddy on the security detail who had instructed us to head directly to the plane, so I quickly scratched out a note and handed it to Comey: "You've never ignored the cops." He gave it a read, and slowly nodded.

Those watching the aerial news footage of our arrival that day may have noticed a brief awkward moment when Comey stepped out of the SUV. While the security agents moved toward the airplane, Comey took a different path, veering around the nose of the vehicle and over to the California Highway Patrol officers standing by. He shook hands and thanked them for their service.

I was later told that this very moment infuriated President Trump, who was watching the live coverage back in Washington. I guess he'd expected Comey to shrink away.

As the stairs of the Gulfstream were raised and the door closed, we made a hard turn and headed to the end of the runway. A pilot up front flipped a switch and the onboard TV screen flickered from an in-flight route map to CNN, where Anderson Cooper was anchoring coverage on half the screen, with a live video feed of our airplane on the other. I looked out the window and could see the television news helicopters stacked on the outskirts of the LAX airspace. To describe the experience as surreal would not do it justice.

It wasn't until the airplane had banked across the skies above Los Angeles and leveled off that the gravity of the entire situation really hit me. The president of the United States had taken the FBI out at the knees, removing someone who had refused to pledge loyalty and publicly announce the president was not under investigation. I was obviously sad for Comey and thought his departure a great loss on a number of fronts, but I feared for the future of the organization. *What will Trump do next?* I thought.

None of us spoke until about an hour into the flight. I moved to a seat across from Comey and recounted the past year, and we talked about all the important work still left to be done. I then got up and traded places with Damien, whose work was just beginning. He explained that the FAA had given clearance to our pilots to continue all the way to Washington, so a stopover in Denver would not be needed. A former Green Beret, Damien is used to being in fast-moving and unpredictable situations, and he handled the Comey firing like a consummate professional. He was now faced with the realization that he was immediately responsible for ensuring the protection of two high-profile people—Comey, who would continue receiving security for the time being, and Andrew McCabe, the bureau's deputy director, who had now been elevated to the position of acting director.

After Damien and Comey had finished talking through security issues, Damien returned to his seat. Noticing that everyone was now either napping or on the verge of it, I pressed the button on the master control panel, plunging the cabin into darkness. Comey switched on an overhead reading lamp, and I returned to the seat across from him.

"What are you going to do now?" I asked.

"I have no clue," he said. "Maybe teach."

He then reached into his bag and was reminded of the bottle of wine he had brought along. "Do we have any cups?" he asked.

I walked to the back of the plane and searched through the cabinets in the galley. Nothing. In one drawer I found a bag of disposable coffee cups, which by their coloring looked like they had been in there since the age of the Wright brothers. I also noticed ten foot-long Subway sandwiches that the SWAT team had managed to buy and bring to the airplane before our departure. *I love those guys*, I thought, reflecting on the spirit of camaraderie that makes employment at the FBI so special. I walked back to Comey and handed him a sandwich, and one of the sketchy coffee cups.

"What the hell is this?" he joked.

"FBI Airline's finest," I replied.

"You know what?" he said. "After today, this is perfect."

He opened the bottle and poured himself a glassful—well, a Styrofoam cupful—and sipped it as we continued to commiserate about all that had transpired.

After a while, I returned to my seat and turned on my phone. Once I connected to the Wi-Fi, a flood of emails poured into my inbox like a tidal wave. *No way*, I thought, turning the phone back off. I reclined the seat and just sat there in silence. I was now technically Andy McCabe's de facto special assistant, although I didn't really know him. He was a friendly and witty man, and we had chatted here and there on the margin of meetings as he came and went into Comey's office, but I had probably spoken with him for even a total of twenty minutes during my entire time on the director's staff. I wondered what he was thinking as this new role was suddenly thrust upon him.

I looked around and noticed that Comey was the only other person still awake, just staring out the window in the glow of his reading lamp. I fetched myself one of the dilapidated coffee cups and returned to the seat across from him, firmly setting the cup down in front of him.

"I thought you'd never ask," he said with a smile, reopening the wine bottle and offering a generous pour.

"It just dawned on me that I no longer work for you," I replied, "so you can't punish me for drinking on duty."

We offered each other a cheers and continued conversing over refills. After the conversation had faded, he broke the silence by offering me his hand, which I shook.

"I just want to say thank you," he said. "For everything."

I replied that working for him had been a great honor, adding how unusual it was that he had surrounded himself with people who were not afraid to challenge or correct him. I later learned that was one of the key reasons he had hired me on his staff: because I had once had a chance encounter with him when he asked my opinion of something and I gave him blunt critical feedback.

I regaled him with a story from my first day on the job as his special assistant, when I'd walked into my new office, which I was to share with Tommy Mayes, another supervisory special agent who was in charge of operations for the director's office. As I carried in a box and set it on my new desk, Tommy, a no-nonsense former cop from Tennessee who had also served as a SWAT team leader in the FBI, was on the phone arguing with someone.

"Yeah, we're not going to be able to do that," Tommy barked as I eavesdropped on his conversation. Whoever he was speaking with was definitely getting Tommy's unvarnished opinion on the travel arrangements for an upcoming Comey trip.

"My job is to plan all this stuff and make sure it's done well. And things work a lot easier when I'm allowed to just do my job," he said, becoming more agitated as the conversation continued.

When he finally hung up, I asked him who he had been arguing with.

"The director," he said, eyes returning to the computer screen as he tapped on his keyboard.

Upon hearing the story, Comey let out a hearty laugh.

Well past midnight of the longest day ever, on our approach to DC, Comey walked to the front of the plane. He chatted with the pilots and the communications specialist who had staffed him on every out-of-town trip.

For years, the pilots had been offering to let him ride in the cockpit on the way into Washington, describing it as one of the most incredible sights one could witness. Realizing that this would be his last trip, Comey now asked if he could take them up on the offer. They threw a lever and pulled out the sliding jump seat for him.

As we banked around the nation's capital on final approach, I looked out on the still city and focused in on the Washington Monument, which I used as a reference point to then move my gaze slightly northward to the White House. The executive mansion sat in near darkness for the night. I wondered if Trump was sleeping soundly now that he had fired the man leading the investigation into his campaign's suspected ties to a foreign adversary. I wondered if he was ready for the political upheaval he had set in motion.

The wheels of the Gulfstream slammed down hard on the runway, and the pilots reversed the engines. As we turned to taxi toward a side entrance of the airport, unsure of whether reporters would be staked out waiting to catch a glimpse of the fired FBI chief, Damien pressed a switch on the master control panel behind his seat, which instantly lowered all of the airplane's window shades to the closed position. Although Comey was no longer director, his safety and privacy were still the security detail's responsibility.

We were unable to peer out to see where we were, so the transit across the airfield felt like an eternity. I stood to put on my jacket and to gather the classified briefing books we had brought along during the trip. Next to me, Ryan McDonald, one of the security agents, was busy moving several high-powered rifles toward the front of the airplane. Unlike most trips, where we would chat as we went about our business, no one said a word. Awkwardness hung in the air.

True to form, Comey decided to put everyone at ease. "Gentlemen, we are still on an active taxiway," Comey loudly announced. "I am going to have to ask you to please return to your seats, as your safety is our primary concern."

The tension we were all feeling was cut in an instant as the cabin filled with laughter. But although we had made it back safely, the tumultuous weeks and months ahead would prove that we were on far from solid ground.

# CHAPTER 9

# Mueller Time

THE DARK BMW carrying the special guest rounded the corner of the FBI headquarters' subterranean parking structure, its tires emitting an earsplitting, echoing screech as they attempted to gain traction on the slick polished pavement. The vehicle slowed as it passed the fleet of armored SUVs that had served as protective battlewagons for the BMW's occupant in days gone by, and came to a halt near an elevator reserved for VIPs. The door swung open, and out stepped Robert Mueller.

To the relief of many of us rank-and-file bureau employees, after it became known that the president had tried to obstruct the Flynn investigation, the former director of the FBI was appointed by the Justice Department as special counsel overseeing the Russia investigation. Crossfire Hurricane would now belong to Mueller. His written mandate would be to determine whether members of the Trump campaign had colluded with the Kremlin. Unwritten, but equally important, was his role in protecting the investigation from outside political interference by either DOJ leadership or the president's inner circle.

By the time Mueller came on the scene, however, the investigation of the Trump campaign was only one aspect of the increasingly complex case. Leadership inside the FBI was so alarmed by Donald Trump's removal of James Comey they thought it possible that the actions of the president might constitute a threat to US national security. Among their questions: Was he wittingly or unwittingly doing the bidding of Vladimir Putin by terminating the person leading the Russia investigation? In an unprecedented move, the bureau reportedly opened an investigation aimed at determining whether

Trump was a counterintelligence threat. Many FBI critics have called this alleged action an emotional response to Comey's removal. However, those who truly know the FBI understand that the agency would have been derelict in its duties if it had failed to investigate this glaring issue.

Everything about Mueller's arrival that day at FBI headquarters was chilling. For one thing, these were familiar surroundings for the man who had first taken the reins of the organization one week before the September 11 terrorist attacks, appointed by President George W. Bush, and it was he who had worked to lead the most resource-intensive investigation in bureau history while at the same time shaping the organization into an agile force that could identify and neutralize potential attacks before they occurred. His battle rhythm his entire time as director involved shifting his attention from one threat to the next, managing investigations into known bad actors while simultaneously trying to deal with new ones as they cropped up.

One day in August 2006 that I remember vividly (I was then a junior staffer in his public affairs office), Mueller had started his morning by reading through the US government's "threat matrix"—the daily compendium of all major national security threats known to US intelligence agencies—followed by a case briefing on a particular target of interest, and then we raced up Connecticut Avenue to DHS headquarters, where Mueller, then homeland security chief Michael Chertoff, and then attorney general Alberto Gonzales briefed the press on a major plot, which had been uncovered by British authorities, to bomb several commercial airliners bound for the United States.

This was a typical day: Mueller's entire twelve-year tenure as FBI director—he had served the statutory ten-year term before being extended another two years—was marked by unprecedented external threats like these.

Now, in May 2017, he had returned to the FBI once again to investigate a possible national security threat. Only this time, the threat came from within.

As Mueller exited the car, I stood next to a six foot three former Navy diver who had served on the FBI director's protective detail under both Mueller and Comey.

"Can you believe this?" he asked.

Mueller approached us with his famous ramrod-straight Marine Corps posture and cadence, and a rare smile crossed his face as he recognized us. After a few years of relatively peaceful existence in his quiet private-sector post-FBI life, the new special counsel in charge of the investigation into the Trump campaign's possible collusion with the Russian government was now being thrown back into the Washington political muck, which had only gotten more toxic since he had last been in government. To say that his role came packed with a set of built-in enemies would be an understatement.

"Finally, some friendly faces," he joked as he extended his hand, and we escorted him upstairs.

THIS WAS NOT the first time Mueller had returned to the building since leaving office, but it was certainly the most dramatic. About a year earlier, he had come to receive a briefing on cyber threats in the wake of intrusions into companies like Sony Pictures, JPMorgan Chase, and Anthem Blue Cross. His private-sector work had included speaking on the topic of cyber-security and sensitizing corporations to the need to call in law enforcement quickly to mitigate intrusions once they've been detected. Wanting to ensure that he was equipped with the latest publicly available information, he asked for, and received, a briefing on current threats from the chief and deputy chief of the FBI's Cyber Division.

I was the bureau's chief national press spokesperson for cyber issues— the person responsible for crafting communication strategies to explain to the world how the FBI was combatting cyber threats from hackers and hostile foreign intelligence services. Having an amplifying voice like Mueller making sure clients in corporate America recognized the importance of engaging with the FBI should they become victims of cybercrime was a huge force multiplier.

Mueller and I sat in a secure room, listening intently to a prepared briefing from two of the bureau's top cyber experts. Then, in true Bob Mueller fashion, he began his famous rapid-fire direct questioning while taking copious notes.

After the briefing, I walked him out through the courtyard and to the street. The courtyard was undergoing massive construction, so we had to navigate a maze of chain-link fencing and makeshift barricades.

"What's going on here?" he inquired.

"A renovation project," I said. "The new version is going to be much better than ever before."

Unimpressed, he continued his interrogation. "What was wrong with the way it was before I left?" he asked.

Sensing that he was beginning to take it personally, and thinking it a battle not worth fighting, I opted for levity. "The place is crumbling," I said. "It has been battered by the elements for forty years. I assure you no one here thinks it a reflection upon your leadership."

He erupted in laughter, perhaps realizing the ridiculousness of his inquisition. He said his goodbyes and stepped out to Tenth Street to hail a taxi. Little did we know, he'd be back in approximately one year's time to help revive the organization's crumbling reputation, which was now being battered by political winds.

UP ON THE seventh floor, Mueller stepped out of the director's elevator. He didn't need to be told where to go; he had walked these hallways thousands of times before. Typically, guests of the director don't actually make it the entire way to the director's private office without stopping to look at the pictures adorning the walls. The corridor is full of images of the FBI in action—tactical operators rappelling from helicopters, bomb technicians disposing of incendiary devices, FBI agents in the field arresting dangerous fugitives, and victim specialists caring for those impacted by crime. Mueller walked briskly past.

We wound through a series of hallways and into the main reception room, where Mueller was met by acting director Andy McCabe and the bureau's head of counterintelligence. They exchanged greetings, and Mueller commented on being back in the building.

"The place hasn't changed a bit," he said.

"Maybe not physically," McCabe replied, highlighting the discomfort most of us felt after Comey's firing, the public revelation of the attempts by Trump to inappropriately influence the Flynn and Russia investigations, and now the appointment of a special counsel.

McCabe invited Mueller into his conference room, where a team had assembled to begin briefing him on the current status of Crossfire Hurricane. Mueller headed toward the door but then stopped next to a television that was tuned to a news program carrying a live feed of a speech by Trump. Mueller watched it for a moment. Trump was offering his standard one-liners, much to the enjoyment of the rowdy, cheering crowd. Mueller turned and shot me a long, steady look. In its seriousness and silence, the look spoke volumes to me. The former director is a very impatient man, and he almost certainly knew he would soon find himself on the receiving end of invective spewed by the president of the United States. His new position would turn him into Trump's primary target.

Everyone in the FBI knew that you didn't sit down to brief Mueller unless you were fully prepared. If you were going to encroach on his time by suggesting that a particular topic was important, you had better have done your homework and be fully prepared to answer any questions he might ask.

I found this out in a (now) amusing way when I was fresh out of college and early in my FBI career. I was required to compile open-source news about FBI operations from across the globe, creating a product that would accompany Mueller's daily threat briefing. At 6:30 a.m. one day in 2005, my lack of preparation and Mueller's grouchiness came together in one of those teachable moments I will never forget. I walked into Mueller's office as he sat before a large pile of wiretap authorizations and handed him the daily news briefing.

"Just tell me what's in it," he said, tossing the papers on his desk and pointing to the mountain of other briefing notes before him.

"News," I said, in a way that must have unintentionally sounded like a wiseass response. The truth was I had been running late that day and hadn't fully digested everything in the briefing, and I was certainly not prepared to verbally give him the highlights in a concise manner.

Upon hearing my response, Mueller's eyebrows lurched skyward in a not-so-subtle way.

"Not helpful," he said, as he snatched up the news briefing and began flipping through it himself—a move that told me it was time to exit.

The next morning, he gave me a mulligan. "Let's try this again," he said with a half smile as we repeated the exercise, this time with a different result.

I never made that kind of mistake again. To this day, when I think about giving even the most menial task anything other than my very best, I can still envision Mueller's forehead folding up in disappointment.

Although Mueller could run roughshod over people as he worked at breakneck speed, there were limits to how far he could go. As he later recounted to a group of senior staff (which quickly made its way around FBI headquarters, as most good gossip did), he had once made the mistake of accidently slipping into his work demeanor after arriving home one evening while catching up on the day's events with his saintly wife, Ann. She was explaining something that perturbed her and was going into great detail. After listening to her story for several minutes and unsure of where it was headed, his impatient FBI director instinct kicked in.

"What's the issue?" he snapped, deploying the phrase he had used countless times at the office when signaling to someone briefing him that they had finally exhausted his patience. As the story goes, Ann's response made it clear to Mueller that their home was not FBI headquarters.

While Mueller's edges were anything but smooth, deep down one could tell that he was a genuinely decent man. My position as a junior staffer in the director's office during Mueller's tenure gave me a vantage point others more senior in the chain of command did not enjoy. Many simply lived in fear of disappointing the man, whereas I was new enough not to be afraid to make mistakes or ask seemingly amateur questions. I'd also had the occasion to travel with Mueller outside the DC beltway bubble and see him interact with the rank-and-file agents and analysts during field office visits. There were none of the tyrannical features on display during these exchanges. That's not to say he was touchy-feely—far from it—but it was clear he had a good heart and appreciated those who were doing dangerous work to protect the nation.

In one poignant moment I'll never forget, late one night in June 2006 I was sitting in a makeshift command center across the hall from Mueller's hotel room in San Diego, chatting with three agents from the local SWAT team and watching the news on TV. We were talking about Mueller and how stressful the job of FBI director must be, when suddenly his hotel room door sprang open and he darted our way carrying several bottles of alcohol. It seemed he had swiped all the adult beverages from his mini-bar and brought them over to the command center.

"I figured you guys might like these," he said, as he set the bottles down on the counter.

"You came to have a drink with us?" I asked incredulously.

"Not *with*," he said, making it clear he did not intend to stick around and shoot the breeze.

And with that, he turned and went back to his room without saying another word.

ONCE SEATED AROUND the same mahogany conference table Mueller had used every morning back when he was director, the Crossfire Hurricane team ticked through where things stood on the Russia probe. According to someone present, Mueller and his longtime aide—former FBI special agent Aaron Zebley—took notes as they listened to the presentation of facts, evidence, and investigative theories. Some members of the team would be detailed to Mueller's newly formed special counsel group, so it was unnecessary for Mueller to write down every single fact discussed, but it was clear that he wanted to know anything significant. Again, he launched right into intense questioning.

It was only after nearly two hours that Mueller was satisfied for the time being with his knowledge of the case, logistics for his new operation, and the amount of staffing support he would be receiving from the bureau. One member of the Crossfire Hurricane team summed up Mueller's performance in the following way: "It was almost like he was still the director, quizzing members of the team and then firing off follow-ups in rapid succession."

On the way out, Mueller and Zebley were presented with a set of forms formally reinstating their access to FBI files. When Mueller had finished signing his documents, he joined me and Zebley in the hall. It was hard to fathom the responsibility that had now been placed on this man. I had seen him several times at meetings and events since he'd left office, and one thing people had always commented on was how much better he looked after no longer having to bear the stress that came with the role of protecting the nation. That weight had now returned in an instant, but he looked steeled by the counterintelligence briefing he had just received. He was back in the familiar role of protector.

Damien and I walked him to the elevator for the ride back to the basement garage. As we descended into the bowels of the building, Damien and I flanking him, Mueller dramatically looked to his left and then to his right, gazing at our shirts. We both knew what was coming. During Mueller's tenure as director, he had worn a solid-white oxford dress shirt every single day, and the unofficial rule was that senior executives would follow suit. When he came across someone with even the hint of a patterned shirt or a color other than white, he would enjoy pointing out their departure from his strict standards. As he now surveyed Damien and me, standing next to him in nearly matching purple patterned dress shirts, he couldn't resist.

"What the hell happened to this place?" he said, before bursting into a loud belly laugh.

THE EIGHT DAYS between James Comey's firing and Mueller's appointment as special counsel now seem like a blur. However, at the time, living each day in full in the aftermath of the removal of the FBI director was an extremely difficult period for the organization. Our leader was gone. For over three years, Comey had worked to drive into the soul of the organization a renewed commitment to improving its leadership development, operational agility, and technological innovation. He communicated his vision regularly via in-person visits and messages he sent organization-wide. For far too long, the bureau's culture had allowed insecure bullies with giant egos to work their way up the ladder. Not under his watch. Although his new approach of finding and promoting leaders who were both kind and tough would occasionally draw fire from some of the old guard—including some retired agents who continue to represent the tiny cottage industry of Comey haters trying to remain relevant on the media circuit—many others embraced his "servant leadership" principles.

"Kindness is not a weakness," Comey once told me as we sat in his office talking. To him, there was an important distinction. "I am a very kind person," he said, "but I am not a weak person. There are some people out there who will confuse kindness for weakness in order to take advantage of you. Those are the people you need to crush. But, in the main, treat everyone you meet with kindness."

One incident that vividly illustrates Comey's style occurred during a 2016 field office visit, when he was meeting with several federal, state, and local partners operating in the area. I could tell that one official in particular was really starting to grate on Comey as he ran roughshod over everyone else in attendance, interrupting to talk about himself at every turn. He was a bully straight from central casting. Each time the bombastic offender opened his mouth, Comey would shoot me a disdainful look.

Incredibly, as we all stood to leave the meeting, the official turned to Comey and said, "Director, I understand you're flying back to Washington now. I'm also headed to Washington, so I'll just ride with you."

I tried to suppress a laugh, knowing full well there was no way this guy would be traveling back with us. "I'm sorry, sir," I interjected, and explained all the policies and procedural hurdles that would unfortunately prevent him from flying on our jet with such short notice.

As we boarded our plane, Comey turned to me and said, "Can you believe that guy? Where does that kind of ego even come from?" We removed our winter outerwear and threw our jackets onto one of the half dozen empty seats in the plane's cabin. "Besides, if that guy was here, where would we put our coats?" he quipped.

With Comey's firing, his view of ethical leadership and his priorities for the organization were suddenly placed in jeopardy. Would they continue under his future successor? No one knew.

"He took Comey from us," a former colleague of mine said of the president shortly after the firing. "Donald Trump has likely never spent a minute of his life thinking about effective leadership principles and the building and caring for teams. But, just like that, he robbed the FBI of someone who thought about little else."

Interestingly, even FBI employees who didn't know Comey personally, or who vehemently disagreed with decisions he'd made during the 2016 election season, were aghast—at both the manner in which his firing had taken place and also the underlying reason for his removal. Of the many people I spoke with at the FBI and the Justice Department, not one bought into the notion that Trump had fired Comey over the Hillary Clinton investigation. It simply wasn't believable. At this point, only a small circle was aware of Trump's previous efforts to shut down the Flynn investigation and influence the Russia probe, but even many of those not aware suspected that the president was in effect attempting to get rid of the person taking a close look at his campaign.

The question that remained on everyone's mind was how the White House had persuaded DOJ leadership to go along with the president's plan.

On March 2, 2017, a day after the *Washington Post* reported on two contacts between Attorney General Jeff Sessions and the Russian ambassador to the United States during the 2016 campaign, Sessions had publicly announced that he would recuse himself from any investigations involving Russia and the Trump campaign.

Sessions faced intense criticism, because the reports on previous contact with the Russians stood in stark contrast with comments he had made under oath before Congress, during his confirmation hearing, indicating that he had *not* had contacts with the Kremlin during the election. With the revelation of the Sessions-Kislyak meetings, the attorney general's candor was now being called into question.

It would later be learned that even though Sessions had insisted he had not spoken with the Russian about campaign issues, Kislyak saw it differently. Intercepts by the US intelligence community, documenting conversations between the ambassador and his superiors in Moscow, indicated that the two men had in fact talked about campaign matters. Even though Sessions had recused himself from anything pertaining to Russia, he had been actively involved in efforts to remove James Comey—the person leading the investigation into ties between Russia and the Trump team.

Rod Rosenstein was another puzzle. As mentioned in chapter 8, he set forth the rationale, in a memo accompanying Trump's letter firing Comey, that the director was being removed because of the Clinton investigation, but Rosenstein *knew* the Russia investigation was on Trump's mind when deciding to eliminate Comey, because the president himself had asked Rosenstein to include a passage declaring Trump's innocence in the case. Knowing that his boss—the attorney general—was recused from all matters relating to the Kremlin and knowing that the Russia case was part of Trump's calculus, how could Rosenstein possibly go along with what seemed like such a blatant attempt to subvert justice? The deputy attorney general was widely known as "the survivor" inside the FBI—someone who had managed to dodge sticky situations and ingratiate himself with members of both political parties—so was it possible he was living up to this nickname? We may never know for sure what ultimately motivated Rosenstein's decision-making, but there is a large enough body of evidence available to justify skepticism.

I had my own experience with the deputy attorney general that left me feeling both sad and repulsed. On February 3, 2018, the day after I resigned and went to work for CNN, I received a phone call from a number I didn't recognize. The caller left a voice message. It was Rosenstein. Though he technically reported to Attorney General Jeff Sessions, Rosenstein was by far the most powerful man in the entire department. By then, Sessions had recused himself from anything related to the 2016 campaign, and so it was Rosenstein that Robert Mueller reported to. He was also in the middle of a firestorm of his own, under attack by the president at the time for launching, and then failing to shut down, the special counsel probe.

That Rosenstein was calling a field supervisor like me was odd. That he'd somehow obtained my personal cell phone number bordered on inappropriate. The FBI works through protocol; the appropriate thing for a person in Rosenstein's position to do if he wished to call me would be to go through the director of the FBI, the deputy director, or the head of the field office in which I last served, then on down the line. I didn't know precisely what Rosenstein's motives were in calling me that day—there's no way to get in his head—but as someone who is suspicious of unsolicited flattery in general, especially accolades from political appointees I don't even know, I found this phone call bizarre. I debated whether I should call Rosenstein back, but I finally did.

"Josh," he said, "I heard you were resigning, and I want you to reconsider." He went on to say I was a "fantastic" special agent. "We cannot lose you," he said.

I immediately sensed an insincere pitch. I was a complete stranger to Rosenstein. He had no idea what kind of agent I was. But, upon leaving the FBI, I had written a fairly scathing article in the *New York Times* pointing out the danger of the president's continued attacks on law enforcement. That article, coupled with my new position working for a major news outlet, probably concerned Rosenstein, who (rightly) assumed I would be critical of him, too. In my mind, the purpose of his strange phone call was not to dissuade a "fantastic" special agent from leaving; it was all about preserving his reputation.

I told Rosenstein I greatly appreciated his kind words but that I wasn't going to change my mind. Then, because I had nothing to lose, I added, "I completely disagree with the way you and other Justice Department leaders have handled attacks on the bureau. It's crickets over there. At a time when the FBI is facing unprecedented political attacks by politicians in survival mode, our DOJ leaders have remained silent. That's why I'm resigning. To do what *you* should be doing."

I then mentioned a memo by Representative Devin Nunes, which had been made public the day before. "Here we have a totally biased, one-sided memo in the press that essentially accuses the FBI of criminal activity, and we've heard nothing from you at all."

Rosenstein tried to deflect—insisting that the Republican attacks on the

FBI were "old news" since Nunes was now moving on to vilify the so-called deep state inside the State Department. I told him I didn't see the attacks on DOJ abating anytime soon. He quickly got off the phone.

This was the leadership of the US Department of Justice. Image-conscious, timid, and contributing by its silence to the attacks on the nation's, indeed the world's, premier law enforcement organization. I have since come to somewhat appreciate the courage Rosenstein later displayed in his many clashes with the White House, but at the time he was still the political appointee whose motivations seemed untrustworthy.

ONE OF THE most significant aspects of the Comey firing was just how badly the White House had misjudged Democrats and public opinion. It was reported by the *Wall Street Journal* that Jared Kushner was privately pushing for Trump to can Comey, apparently believing that Democrats would celebrate the dismissal based on their view of Comey as someone who had been unfair to Hillary Clinton, but the move backfired, highlighting Kushner's ineptitude and political naivete.

One other character in the saga whose credibility quickly hit rock bottom within the FBI was White House Deputy Press Secretary Sarah Sanders, who took to the podium after the firing and claimed that the rank and file inside the bureau had lost faith in Comey and that she had heard from "countless members of the FBI" who were grateful for Trump's decision to fire Comey.

"What a load of bullsh*t," a senior agent bellowed as several of us sat around a television watching reports of Sanders's comments. "To think people inside the FBI are picking up the phone to call Sarah Huckabee Sanders and tell her 'thank you' is complete garbage."

I realize that I was close to Comey and other senior FBI leaders, and that it's possible that my personal biases might be at work here, even as I try hard to arrest them. So let me share some hard data. Each year, bureau employees submit anonymous reports containing their personal views on the quality of FBI leadership and their overall satisfaction with the agency. These "climate surveys," as they are called, allow employees to rate the abilities of their bosses and provide feedback on what is needed to make the place better, without fear of retribution. The *New York Times* obtained three years of these surveys under a Freedom of Information Act request, which showed that agents and analysts around the country gave Comey high marks "as both an inspiring leader and someone more interested in leading than being liked." The lies told about the views of FBI employees were just that—lies, crafted to manipulate public opinion.

After Comey's firing, we received word from the White House that President Trump wanted to address employees at FBI headquarters. Maybe Trump believed in his own sales skills and the ability to persuade a suspicious audience that he knew more about Comey than they did, or perhaps it was just based on ignorance about how we actually felt, but the request created a lot of chatter around the building. Many of us privately wondered if such a visit was a good idea, because (a) we could not be sure that employees would even want to come hear from Trump, and (b) we worried that they would vocalize their displeasure at how Comey's firing had been handled. We had absolutely no concern that employees would be disrespectful—the bureau is an organization built on strict adherence to respect for the chain of command—but asking people whose careers are dedicated to finding the truth to come to an auditorium and hear from someone who had been peddling lies was a recipe for an uncomfortable encounter. Bureau leadership diplomatically warned the White House about the widespread anger within the agency, and the idea was quickly tabled.

ALTHOUGH SOME OF the events I am recounting may now be familiar to readers, it is worth remembering that at the time of Comey's firing, the public did not yet know about his memos—his notes that recount how the president had demanded loyalty, interfered in the Flynn investigation, and was growing increasingly angry at Comey for not publicly announcing that Trump himself was not under investigation. The Trump administration had attempted to manipulate the public into believing Comey had been removed because he had been *too hard* on Hillary Clinton. That was the company line, until it wasn't.

By Thursday, May 11, the wheels came off the wagon for the White House. Just forty-eight hours after telling the American people that Comey was terminated because of the email server case, Trump sat down with NBC's Lester Holt and claimed that not only had he decided to fire Comey before receiving the recommendation letters from Sessions and Rosenstein, but that it was because of the Russia investigation. "When I decided to just do it," Trump explained to Holt, "I said to myself, I said, 'You know, this Russia thing, with Trump and Russia, is a made-up story.'"

There it was. In all the cases I had worked, never had someone related to an investigation go on national television and admit that what was stated two days earlier wasn't the truth. I can only imagine the angst felt at the White House and down the street in the offices of Sessions and Rosenstein after the president sat before a reporter and laid the whole thing bare. It would later be reported by the *New York Times* that Trump had actually met in the Oval Office with Russian Ambassador Sergey Kislyak and Foreign Minister Sergey Lavrov the day after Comey was fired and told them that getting rid of the FBI director had relieved the "great pressure" the Russian investigation had been causing Trump.

The same day as the NBC interview, Americans learned for the first time that Trump had dined with Comey after the inauguration and had asked him for a pledge of loyalty. I was relieved that the entire reason behind the firing was finally coming into full view. I had been privy to Comey's startling version of his interactions with the president, and I was one of only a handful of agents who knew he had documented these exchanges in writing. Until this information became public, I felt like I was keeping a deep secret from those I cared about most. I had met with and consoled many FBI employees the day after Comey's firing, but I hadn't felt comfortable disclosing that there was likely something more sinister behind the move—that after demurring and refusing to pledge his loyalty to Trump, and after publicly testifying that Trump's campaign was under FBI investigation, Comey had been terminated. I was glad that I could at last talk with my shell-shocked colleagues. And I was glad the American people could begin to learn the truth.

After news of the Trump-Comey loyalty dinner made its way to the press, Trump became irate, tweeting, "James Comey better hope that there are no 'tapes' of our conversations before he starts leaking to the press!"

The message the president was sending was loud and clear. He was suggesting that the White House might have actually recorded conversations of the president and others inside the executive mansion.

"This is Nixon all over again," one FBI official recalled thinking.

James Comey had the same thought: Was it possible there actually were tapes? Even before his firing, the leadership team had wondered what to do with Comey's memos about his meetings with the president. They clearly revealed possible obstruction by the president of the United States. And although Trump could dispute their accuracy, the fact that they were written contemporaneously after speaking with the president added to their credibility. Investigative notes written by FBI agents are testimonial in nature and are usually given great credence in the minds of judges and juries.

But was there a need to publicize them during the Crossfire Hurricane investigation? Comey had decided to file them away and wait to see if Trump would continue to exert inappropriate pressure. He'd refrained from even letting the midlevel investigators and analysts working the case know that the nation's chief executive had sought to influence it. He did not want that fact to skew the work of the team.

Now, the former director wondered if the public had a right to know that he had his own evidence that Trump had attempted to obstruct justice. And if there *were* tapes, he wondered how the Justice Department could get its hands on them and how he could ensure from the outside that the investigation would be done without even further influence from the White House. His view was that a special counsel, independent of Trump, Sessions, and Rosenstein, would be the only vehicle to guarantee a fair and transparent process for achieving justice.

Although Comey's ultimate goal was transparency, he himself did not behave in an entirely transparent manner. Rather than calling the media directly or holding a press conference, he sought a cutout who could feed his memos to a reporter. He read the contents of one of his unclassified memos (others would subsequently be declassified and released) to a long-time friend, who, in turn, went to the *New York Times*. As Comey would later explain, he didn't want to go to the media himself because at this time a large group of journalists had been camped out at the end of his driveway, documenting his every move and attempting to glean comment from Comey and his family on his firing. He feared that directly addressing reporters would only cause an even greater feeding frenzy.

In my view, Comey's decision to share this information with a news-paper was an avoidable mistake that probably cost him more than he expected. Our investigation was proceeding, and so far, Rosenstein, at that point the de facto head of the investigation, had not attempted to meddle in it; if he had, that would have taken us to DEFCON 1. And even then, I believe Comey should have gone to Congress or the courts first.

My opinion was not universally shared by my colleagues. Many were relieved that Trump had finally been exposed as working to obstruct jus-tice, and did not mind the media involvement. As one senior FBI official said to me at the time: "What were [Comey's] options? He could have gone to Congress, but the Judiciary and Intelligence Committees were led by Trump acolytes." And, the official continued, since he'd been fired, "Comey was a private citizen who was telling the public about his conversations with someone who happened to be the president. He didn't discuss any-thing classified. He simply let the American people know their president had potentially committed a crime."

Whatever the motivation behind his method of disclosure, the gambit worked. On May 16—one week to the day since he had been fired—the *Times* broke the story on the Comey memo documenting Trump's efforts to shut down the Flynn probe. Whether Rosenstein felt boxed in, or whether he recognized that the public was in an uproar at a firing he had person-ally had a hand in orchestrating, he acted quickly, the next day appointing a special counsel to assume primacy over the Russia investigation. Robert Mueller was a logical choice.

The former FBI director was someone whose reputation in and outside of Washington was unparalleled. He had been appointed by a Republican president and then asked by a Democratic president to stay on the job once Mueller's term had expired, in order to provide continuity for the national security community in the high-threat period that was 2011. He had served in high positions in both DOJ and the FBI, and knew how to manage complex multifaceted investigations.

"Rod [Rosenstein] is rightly lauded for picking Mueller," one former senior DOJ official told me. "But we should remember that the only thing one could do was appoint a special counsel. Second of all, clearly the only person in America who could do that job was Mueller. Thirdly, it was the only thing that Rod could do with a prayer of somehow, if not restoring his reputation, at least bringing it back up to some level of equilibrium."

Rosenstein's decision to appoint a special counsel would put him squarely at odds with an increasingly agitated president. According to the Justice Department, after being told of Mueller's appointment, Trump told his attorney general, "Oh my God. This is terrible. This is the end of my presidency. I'm f*cked."

# CHAPTER 10

# Witch Hunt

THE MUELLER INVESTIGATION posed an existential threat to the White House the moment it began. It marked a turning point in the presidency of Donald Trump. For the first time in the history of the country, the US Department of Justice had established a special team to independently investigate whether people associated with a sitting commander in chief had colluded with a hostile foreign government to win an election. Robert Mueller had not only inherited the FBI's legacy Trump campaign investigation, but also the part that dealt with whether Trump himself posed a national security threat. Mueller may now be a household name, but it is important to remember just how unprecedented it was at the time to have government investigators assigned to determine whether a president and his associates had conspired with a foreign adversary.

From the very beginning, Trump made no secret of his disdain for the Mueller team. Where more strategically adept politicians might have seen it as advantageous to insist publicly that a thorough investigation would ultimately prove their innocence, Trump took a different approach. He kicked his campaign of attack against the FBI and the intelligence community into high gear. "This is the single greatest witch hunt of a politician in American history!" Trump tweeted the day after Mueller was appointed, bulldozing any quiet confidence the White House might have wanted to project. The gloves were off.

The phrase "witch hunt" was one the president would promote early and often. As someone more comfortable on offense rather than defense, he had apparently made the calculation that declaring victimhood and trashing the Justice Department would be personally and politically helpful, even if it meant the wholesale destruction of the reputations of thousands of public servants who had dedicated their careers to finding the truth. All he had to do was convince a large enough segment of the population that he was being targeted by corrupt and out-of-control law enforcement officers. In doing so, he may have figured, he might also convince them that whatever Mueller's investigators unearthed was also manufactured by people out to get him.

From our vantage point inside DOJ and the FBI, Trump's motives were transparent. Anyone who has worked a criminal investigation knows that guilty defendants often attack the government when their chips are down. The problem here was that Trump was not just any ordinary potential defendant. He was the most powerful person in the world, whose every utterance was amplified many times over. I had countless conversations with senior FBI leaders and buddies in the field, who all expressed grave concerns at what Trump's relentless campaign of attack might do to the agency's ability to secure public trust in other investigations. With each new attack, even many of the most stridently conservative FBI agents I knew began shifting from a place of frustration to one of building anger.

Despite the president's bluster, however, Mueller had begun to quietly assemble an armada of experts with a diverse array of investigative specialties. He needed prosecutors, special agents, intelligence analysts, and forensic accountants to work the case, not to mention a host of security and IT specialists to get the operation up and running. Apart from the members of the team who had helped with the original Crossfire Hurricane case, Mueller would essentially be building a new operation from the ground up. Inside the FBI, it felt as though we were living an episode of *Lost*— friends and colleagues would be at work one day and then disappear on assignment to the Mueller team the next. As people went over, they would then recommend others they knew to come join them. With FBI personnel being pulled so quickly from all over, it was difficult at first for the director's office to keep tabs on which agents and analysts were on detail to the special counsel.

"How many people do we have assigned to the Mueller investigation?" I recall asking my new boss, acting FBI director Andrew McCabe, not long after the special counsel had been established.

"That is a fantastic question!" McCabe thundered. "I'm running this place and I have no idea how many of my own people are being pulled onto his team."

Mueller's team had a wide-reaching mandate that consisted of two key prongs. The first involved sussing out any links and coordination between the Trump campaign and the Russian government. And because federal law enforcement officers can't simply turn a blind eye if they come across criminal activity unrelated to their original case, the second allowed Mueller to pursue any other potential violations of federal law he might unearth while investigating the Russia connections. It was this second element of Mueller's authority that would prove instrumental in helping uncover a veritable den of thieves operating in the president's orbit. It would also be the catalyst for serious heartburn for Trump and his White House as Mueller continued to rack up indictments against key allies.

For the president's part, he soon had greater things to worry about than the secret activities of the Mueller team. Firing James Comey now meant the former director was unencumbered. Trump, Kushner, and whoever else was behind the harebrained idea to get rid of him failed to appreciate that terminating him would permit him the freedom to speak out about any wrongdoing he had witnessed. He wasn't going away. Quite the contrary. Elected leaders on Capitol Hill and members of the public were now clamoring to hear directly from him about the reports that Trump had sought to improperly influence the FBI's work. The American people would soon get that opportunity in a blockbuster Senate hearing.

On June 8, 2017, I did something that I had rarely had the chance to do during my whirlwind-paced assignment as Comey's special assistant: I put in a leave slip and took the day off. It would be anything but a relaxing vacation day, but it was very important that I made sure I was not working on the taxpayer's dime that morning, because the person I would spend my day supporting was no longer a government employee. Comey was set to break his silence, testify before Congress, and finally tell his version of the insane events that had transpired over the past several months.

"I'm taking the day off," I wrote in a note to one of my colleagues so they would know where I was. "Gonna do my civic duty and go watch a hearing up on the Hill."

I had been in touch with Comey since his firing—partly because I kept getting inundated by FBI employees from across the world wondering how they could send him cards and letters of support. This endeavor alone had proven to be a herculean undertaking. I was uncomfortable handing out his home address, so at first I would tell employees to send me their notes and I would ensure that they got to him. What a mistake. I received boxloads of envelopes, challenge coins (for the uninitiated, these are mementos bearing the insignias of law enforcement and military units that are often bestowed upon others as souvenirs), hats, and other sentimental material from employees who were so moved by his leadership they wanted to thank him for his service in their own way. This was unsustainable, so Althea James, the director's executive assistant, and I set up a system where everything could be collected in one place and then one of the security agents still protecting Comey would make a run out to his house to make a delivery about once a week. With these well-wishing employees in mind, and knowing that Comey had been barred from sending a final all-employee message after his termination, I sent him a note the night before the Senate hearing suggesting that he use this megaplatform to address members of the FBI family.

"You read my mind," he replied. "I look forward to doing just that."

On the morning of the hearing, I awoke early and threw on my workout gear. I had taken up marathon running a few years before, using the hours of training to relieve stress and also to multitask, by listening to my ever-growing list of audiobooks and podcasts. As I ran toward the majestic compound that houses the legislative branch of government, I could see a flurry of activity starting to build. It was only seven, but members of the public were already lining up outside, each hoping for the opportunity to witness history firsthand. Television vans were starting to arrive on the

Senate side of the building, and a noticeable number of white US Capitol Police cruisers were beginning to stage on Constitution Avenue.

Slowing my pace, I stared up at the *Statue of Freedom* perched atop the great dome of the Capitol—her head protected by a military-style helmet, and her sheathed sword at the ready. It was incredible to see the full dome unobstructed, because for the better part of two years it had been shrouded in scaffolding as workers repaired some thirteen hundred cracks in the facade. The renovations had been completed in late 2016, but this was the first time I was seeing the finished product up close. I was reminded of one of my favorite lines from Ernest Hemingway: "The world breaks everyone and afterward many are strong at the broken places." Over two hundred years since its completion, the building was not only still standing, but had been reinforced, making it even stronger than before.

Returning to the office, I quickly showered and changed into one of the suits hanging in my locker in the FBI's basement gym. A couple of friends who had just finished shooting hoops wanted to talk shop about what to expect from the hearing, but I apologized and told them I was running late and had to jet.

"You watching the hearing at your desk?" my buddy Mike asked.

"I'm off today," I said with a wink.

"GOOD MORNING. FBI," said the lead advance security agent, flashing his credentials as we rolled past one of the Capitol Police checkpoints and parked next to the Hart Senate Office Building. Named for the late Senator Philip Hart (D-MI), known in his time as "the conscience of the Senate," the structure is one of the office buildings flanking the north end of the Capitol compound. Above one of its entrances, a tribute to the building's namesake is inscribed, recalling him as "a man of incorruptible integrity and personal courage." When we walked inside, the three security agents I was with made their way around the building's security booth and showed their badges. Rather than follow suit, I turned and headed to one of the magnetometers where visitors are screened.

"Where are you going?" asked one of the agents. "This way."

"Nah, I'm not here in an official capacity," I replied.

I was nearly always armed with my Glock 22 service weapon—except perhaps when running or going to the beach—but I had kept it locked up at home that day, knowing my eventual destination would be the Capitol. Although FBI agents have wide latitude in where they carry firearms throughout the country, the seat of the legislative branch is one of the rare places where an agent can't just walk in while carrying and flash a badge. Although the Capitol has its own police force to protect its 535 VIPs, congressional security officers keep sharp tabs on who in their midst is armed. Since I wasn't a member of the FBI's protective detail, I didn't have a building hard pass that allowed me to come and go. I knew that showing up armed would require a separate meeting with the police and a request that they permit me to enter with my weapon. I didn't want any special treatment, as I was merely there to show Comey some moral support. I also knew I would be surrounded by at least fifteen people with guns.

We entered the hearing room of the Senate Intelligence Committee. The place was jam-packed. This was going to be quite a show. I said hello to the committee's head of security, who had been the key point of contact for our agents in many past hearings. One of his colleagues escorted me to the holding room behind the dais, where they would bring Comey to relax before the hearing began.

Sitting alone, I looked around at the wood-paneled room with a lone conference table and several old wooden chairs spread about. Various trinkets and pictures adorned the walls. Although I felt as if I were sitting in a musty old antique store, I couldn't help but take in the gravity of the moment. The fired FBI director was about to tell the world about his private conversations with an out-of-control president. The hearing would be watched (and his every word picked apart) by millions. Many people in Washington had actually taken off work to head to bars and restaurants in order to watch the entire hearing live. The whole thing just seemed surreal.

A knock at the door shook me from my daydreaming, and a Capitol Police officer poked his head inside. I looked up, and he sheepishly asked if he could hit the restroom in the holding room before Comey arrived.

"Have at it," I said. "It's going to be a long hearing."

He laughed and walked past me. A couple of minutes later, the main door to the room opened without warning, and in stepped Comey. With an outstretched hand and double-clasped handshake (at six foot eight, he's not a hugger), he smiled and said, "Oh, good, I was hoping I wouldn't be stuck in here alone."

He took off his jacket and plopped onto one of the creaky chairs against the wall. Suddenly, the sound of running water and paper towels being pulled from a dispenser reminded me of the officer who had not yet left.

"Who's that?" Comey asked.

Before I could answer, the officer exited the bathroom, apologizing for any disturbance.

Comey chuckled while standing up to introduce himself. The police officer gave his name, followed by "US Capitol Police, sir."

"I'm Jim Comey, unemployed," he said, and we all erupted in laughter, the former director preempting the awkwardness.

As we sat chatting, our conversation was interrupted by another knock at the door, and in stepped Senate Intelligence Committee Chair Richard Burr and Vice Chair Mark Warner (D-VA). They had come to walk Comey through logistics, and to socialize with him before the big show. The Senate has long been known for its collegiality, but it is worth noting—especially in hindsight after witnessing the embarrassing and destructive actions of the House Intelligence Committee that would soon come—that these two gentlemen were exhibiting the type of bipartisanship normally expected of those overseeing the intelligence community. They had come together, unified in their desire to get to the truth and provide answers to the American people, and were going to do all they could to keep partisan politics out of it. Upon their arrival, we stood, and Comey introduced me to both of them. We all sat down and Burr got down to business.

"Our goal here today is to gather the facts," he said, Warner nodding in agreement. "We don't want a circus. We just want to fulfill our important oversight role."

ONCE INSIDE THE hearing room, I took a seat in the row reserved for guests of the witness. A Senate security officer signaled to everyone in the room that the hearing would soon begin. It was game time. As camera shutters clicked and the sound of reporters' keyboards clacked away behind me, Comey entered the room and took his seat. After not-so-brief opening remarks by Senate leadership, and after Comey was placed under oath, the former FBI director began his introduction.

Donald Trump must have hated every word out of Comey's mouth, beginning with his heartfelt statement directed at the FBI agents whom he had not been allowed to thank in person. Comey now had a public platform to describe each of Trump's transgressions, and describe them he did. In riveting detail, he recounted for his inquisitors the alleged efforts by Trump to improperly influence the FBI's work. He also laid into the president's integrity, repeatedly describing him as a liar. He was asked in detail about his memos, including whether he had shared the contents of them with anyone, and he replied that he had asked a friend to share the contents of one of the memos with a reporter after Trump's threat that he may have recorded the conversation. He also indicated that he had turned over copies of his memos to Special Counsel Robert Mueller.

Comey's testimony was not only helping the public understand the origins of Trump's war on the FBI, but, from his demeanor, I could tell that it was also a relief to him to unburden himself of everything he had been carrying around privately since his first meeting with the president.

After Comey finished his remarks, he tossed his binder to me as he stood up to exit. Perhaps it was his muscle memory, from having done this so many times before, but I no longer worked for him, so I wouldn't be taking his briefing material with me back to headquarters. I followed him and the security entourage out and reunited him with his notebook.

"Forget something?" I asked.

ALONE, I SLOWLY walked back to FBI headquarters, still processing the magnitude of what was unfolding. Although Comey's performance during the hearing had reminded the world that his had been a career dedicated to upholding the rule of law, it also marked the beginning of something much more important: exposing the truth. According to many critics, Donald Trump had worked to obstruct justice, and the American people were now beginning to learn exactly what had allegedly transpired: their president had threatened the FBI's effectiveness by removing its leader.

But the consequences went beyond the impact on any one person. As in any workplace, no one at the FBI is indispensable; people come and go. What matters most is that the institution is able to endure. Although the bureau had been thrown into a state of turmoil following Comey's dismissal, as I turned down Constitution Avenue and again past the grandiose Capitol dome still glistening in the sunlight, I still fervently believed that, in the end, Donald Trump's efforts would be no match for the truth. He might inflict temporary pain on the men and women of the FBI, but he would ultimately fail. *The world breaks everyone*, I thought, *and afterward many are strong at the broken places.*

WHILE COMEY WAS busy testifying, President Trump was across town quoting Bible verses to a group gathered to hear him speak at the Omni Shoreham Hotel. Clearly referring to the FBI director and the widespread condemnation the president had received since canning him, Trump wrapped himself in Scripture in order to portray himself a victim. "We recite today the words of Isaiah chapter 1, verse 17: 'Learn to do right; seek justice. Defend the oppressed. Take up the cause of the fatherless; plead the case of the widow,'" Trump told his supporters. "The entrenched interests and failed, bitter voices in Washington will do everything in their power to try and stop us from this righteous cause, to try to stop all of you." Then, seeming to project a bit, he added, "They will lie. They will obstruct."

Despite his attempts at damage control, all hell was about to break loose for Trump in the Russia investigation. One month from the day of the Comey hearing, the *New York Times* ran a story indicating that the president's son Donald Trump Jr. had arranged a meeting at Trump Tower with a Russian lawyer connected to the Kremlin, and that also in attendance at the meeting were the president's campaign chair, Paul Manafort, and his son-in-law, Jared Kushner.

Asked for comment for the story, Trump Jr. issued a statement indicating that the meeting was primarily about an adoption program. In 2012, the United States passed a law called the Magnitsky Act, which permitted the sanctioning of suspected human rights abusers in Russia and infuriated President Vladimir Putin so much that he put the brakes on adoption of Russian children by US families. Trump Jr.'s doozy of a claim that he and top brass from the campaign had met with a Kremlin-linked lawyer to talk about adoptions spawned lots of eye-rolling inside the Justice Department. We weren't casting total judgment on the claim, but it sure seemed like the makings of a cover story. Was this the best they could do?

The next day, the *Times* dropped a follow-up that appeared to torpedo the lamebrained adoption explanation. "President Trump's eldest son, Donald Trump Jr., was promised damaging information about Hillary Clinton before agreeing to meet with a Kremlin-connected Russian lawyer during the 2016 campaign," the story said.

Faced with the new revelations, Trump Jr. offered a new accounting of the reason for the meeting. He said he had taken the meeting at the request of an associate of his father's, and said the Russian lawyer had indicated that she had information that people connected to Russia were funding the Democratic National Committee. He also said she offered no details and he quickly thought the meeting a waste of time. The *Times* also reported that the president's lawyer said Trump Sr. was not aware of the meeting.

Public knowledge of the meeting came to light only after Kushner revised his background information as part of his attempts to gain a security clearance. Previously, he had omitted foreign contacts on records he'd provided to government investigators under penalty of perjury, but his lawyers had then gone back to the FBI in order to update his file.

July was a banner month for investigative journalists. Intrepid reporters prying into Trump-Russia connections unearthed more evidence of possible collusion with a hostile foreign government by those working on the president's campaign. On July 11, Trump Jr.'s allegiance to the United States was called into question when he was cornered by the *Times*. Reporters had obtained damning emails documenting his actual role in the Trump Tower meeting and were seeking comment for the story. Rather than responding to the reporters, Trump Jr. published several emails himself on Twitter. Although he may have been attempting to get out in front of the story, the facts were the facts, and his preemptive strike fell like a dud once the seriousness of the issue came into view.

In an email exchange the president's son had had with one of his father's business partners in advance of the Trump Tower meeting with the Russians, the business associate signaled that a senior Russian official wanted to provide the Trump campaign with dirt on Hillary Clinton. "This is obviously very high level and sensitive information," the email continued, "but is part of Russia and its government's support for Mr. Trump."

*Part of Russia and its government's support for Mr. Trump!* For anyone who had closely tracked the Kremlin's foreign-influence operations, this appeared to be an unambiguous indication that a hostile foreign government was trying to help throw the election for Donald Trump. And what did Trump Jr. do with this information? Did he pick up the phone and call the FBI in order to report a serious counterintelligence threat and an effort to subvert US democracy? Of course not. In his now-famous reply, Trump Jr. gushed, in part, "If it's what you say I love it."

After the *Times* story was published, Trump Jr. went on Sean Hannity's show on the Fox News Channel in an attempt to play cleanup. He insisted that nothing ever came from the meeting and said that, in retrospect, he "probably would have done things a little differently." But the softball interview did not get at the heart of the larger scandal: Trump Jr. was *willing* to meet with a foreign government official to obtain material about an opponent.

For his part, President Trump would work to defend his son while also continuing his attack on efforts to uncover the truth about his campaign. "My son Donald did a good job last night," Trump tweeted after the Hannity interview. "He was open, transparent and innocent. This is the greatest Witch Hunt in political history. Sad!" Once again, he would play the victim card, acting as if he just continued to deny, deny, deny and to counterattack in his war against those working to find the truth, he might succeed in rewriting what the truth had actually been.

Things would get worse for Team Trump. Later that month, it was reported that President Trump himself had dictated the original misleading statement about the purpose of the Trump Tower meeting with Russians being primarily about adoptions. Asked about it the next day, Sarah Sanders denied it. She suggested that the president had merely weighed in "like any father would do." She then went on to attack the Mueller investigation and the media. "The only thing I see misleading is a year's worth of stories that have been fueling a false narrative about this Russia collusion . . . ," she said from the White House press briefing room. "That's the only thing misleading I see in this entire process."

But, as with many things involving Trump and Russia, sunshine would eventually offer much-needed disinfectant to all the lies. Sarah Sanders's heated claims of "fake news" surrounding the adoption statement were themselves false. In June 2018, it was reported that the president's lawyers had admitted as much to Special Counsel Robert Mueller, by informing him that the president had indeed dictated the statement about the Trump Tower meeting. However, rather than simply correcting the record, Sanders grew defensive, saying that she tried to provide the best information available. Had she left it at that, she may have received sympathy from the media and the public. But she took it a step further and decided again to attack the press, saying that her "credibility is probably higher than the media's." Her statement implied that she wasn't lying but that journalists were, and that there was no distinction between news that was uncomfortable and news that might be inaccurate.

But if this truly were a witch hunt and Donald Trump and his campaign lieutenants were completely innocent, why all the lies? And why would so many people be indicted?

APPROXIMATELY HALFWAY BETWEEN the US Capitol and the J. Edgar Hoover Building, near Judiciary Square, is an institution that has destroyed the lives of dirty politicians, lobbyists, and corporate executives. More aptly put, it has held these people accountable for their misdeeds and, in the process, has affixed the title of "felon" to once-vaunted reputations. Named for a federal circuit judge who sat on the bench for a quarter of a century, the E. Barrett Prettyman Federal Courthouse is home to the US District Court for District of Columbia. Within its walls walk judges, attorneys, and paralegal staff, as well as FBI agents, who routinely pay visits to swear out search warrants and testify in criminal proceedings.

When I served in the FBI, this building was my home away from home—a place I frequented so much I got to know the security officers and court staff by name. Since so many of my cases involved national security matters overseas, federal jurisdiction in these cases would often default to the District of Columbia. This meant I got to spend quality time wandering the halls while I waited for judges to read through and process my search and arrest warrants. I also spent plenty of time appearing before judges in person, raising my right hand and swearing to the accuracy of the information I'd given them.

Although I worked for the government, I never actually felt comfortable in federal court. It is neither a warm nor inviting place, and it is not meant to be, for this is the place where justice is ultimately served and punishment handed down. After the painstaking work by FBI agents and prosecutors to gather evidence and attempt to prove beyond a reasonable doubt that a specific individual has violated the laws of the United States, it is here where the ultimate arbiters render their verdict.

In addition to court staff, this is also the place where ordinary citizens—grand jurors summoned and empaneled to do their civic duty—meet to hear evidence from prosecutors and hand down indictments against fellow citizens charged with crimes. Their responsibility is great; their power, unparalleled.

And so it was that on October 27, 2017, a group of these citizen servants gathered at the Prettyman Federal Courthouse to hear evidence from prosecutors regarding an investigation garnering international attention. The Mueller probe was about to take a dramatic turn as prosecutors sought indictments from the grand jury for former Trump campaign manager Paul Manafort and his aide Rick Gates. Although the proposed charges were not directly related to the topic of Russian collusion, they were nevertheless extremely serious—money laundering, lying to the FBI, and "conspiracy against the United States." During the course of conducting his investigation into whether the Trump campaign was illegally working with Moscow, Mueller had found serious violations of federal law. In addition to rendering justice against these alleged felons, he would have known that bringing charges might also provide the leverage investigators needed to secure their cooperation in the Russia probe. After surrendering to authorities, both Manafort and Gates stood before US Magistrate Judge Deborah Robinson—a firm but fair jurist, before whom I had appeared many times in swearing out warrants—and entered pleas of not guilty.

Upon hearing the news that his campaign manager was now in serious legal jeopardy, Trump immediately attempted to distance himself from his radioactive former aide. "Sorry, but this is years ago, before Paul Manafort was part of the Trump campaign," the president tweeted. This was a continuation of a narrative he had tested earlier that summer, when he'd worked to cast Manafort as someone who wasn't really around that long. He was with the campaign only "for a very short period of time," Trump said. Seeking to put a fine point on his view of the Russia investigation, Trump followed up with another tweet when the news of Manafort and Gates broke, stating, "Also, there is NO COLLUSION!"

But Mueller wasn't finished. That same day, he shocked everyone by dropping another surprise: former Trump campaign foreign-policy adviser George Papadopoulos had also been arrested, charged with lying to the FBI about his interactions with people close to the Kremlin.

While the White House was able to accurately state that Manafort and Gates were in trouble for crimes unrelated to Russian collusion, this wasn't the case with Papadopoulos. For him, it was all about Russia and reported attempts to gather dirt on candidate Hillary Clinton. He admitted to lying to federal agents about his communications with others he thought were connected to the Russian government.

His admission raised an obvious question: Why would someone lie to the FBI if they were innocent? Trump backers rushed in to distance the president, with one former campaign aide describing Papadopoulos as nothing more than a "coffee boy," despite having been mentioned by name by Trump in 2016 when asked about the makeup of his foreign-policy team.

Trump would face yet another blow one month later when former national security adviser Michael Flynn, who had been fired in disgrace, became the next domino to fall in Mueller's investigation. In a filing in federal court, the special counsel indicated that Flynn had accepted a plea deal—admitting to one count of lying to the FBI—and was now cooperating with the investigation. This was someone who had been a key associate of Trump's during the campaign and, of course, one of the primary targets of the original Crossfire Hurricane investigation.

Prosecutors don't typically hand out plea deals in order to target lower-level conspirators. The goal is almost always to go after the big fish. Many legal experts believed there was likely only one direction in which this investigation was headed: all the way to the top—to the president and his family.

As the charges unrolled, the president became increasingly frantic. Two days after the Flynn announcement, Trump made a decision that would cost him dearly in law enforcement circles. Whether he was stirring and unable to sleep or simply rose early that day, at precisely 5:00 a.m. on December 3, he launched an invective-filled tweet that had phones blowing up inside the FBI from coast to coast. After slamming the bureau's former director and ravaging the FBI for its "phony and dishonest Clinton investigation," Trump angered many by publicly claiming that the FBI's "reputation is in Tatters - worst in History!"

At work that morning, I spent nearly an hour trying to convince one dear friend to stay off social media and delete the open letter to the president he was planning to post on Twitter. It just wasn't what FBI employees did; it would only play into Trump's hand if we all started firing off missives criticizing the commander in chief. Surely, many of us thought, the leaders of the Department of Justice would finally step up and defend their people from these vicious and dangerous attacks.

But Attorney General Jeff Sessions and Deputy Attorney General Rod Rosenstein remained silent. Despite running an institution centered on fairness, these two people were willing to let the organization absorb the blows rather than step up, put their own necks on the line, and signal that enough was enough.

"Have you noticed that the only time Sessions or Rosenstein appear to push back is when they are attacked personally?" one FBI colleague wisely observed.

It was the truth—and it was a pattern that would continue well into the next year. It was daily becoming clearer to many of us inside the FBI that Sessions and Rosenstein remained focused on holding on to their own power, rather than correcting the record for the American people. And their silence helped convince segments of the president's base that the deck had been stacked against Trump from the start—that he was being persecuted by dark forces inside government who had been working toward his demise since before he even got elected.

# CHAPTER 11

# Deep State

DONALD TRUMP'S STRATEGY for his assault on FBI leadership sounds as if it were borrowed in part from *The Art of War*, but even more so from his own *The Art of the Deal*. Centuries ago, the Chinese military strategist Sun Tzu famously wrote, "All warfare is based on deception" and "Attack [an enemy] where he is unprepared." The president's efforts would involve both deceit and surprise against government institutions that didn't even know they were his enemy.

But while Trump had famously written that confrontation with others is sometimes the only choice, he most often used his keen understanding of public relations, rather than any great sparring abilities, to face others down. "One thing I've learned about the press is that they're always hungry for a good story," he wrote in his book, "and the more sensational the better." Using the media as a vehicle to reach his base, he concocted a line of attack that publicly portrayed him as the victim of government abuse by unaccountable forces working to bring him down.

The target of his wrath was the so-called deep state—a mythical collection of unelected career officials inside the intelligence community actively plotting against him. The term has been around for close to a century, and was originally used to describe factions inside weak foreign regimes that secretly exercised real control over policy decisions. Its use in the age of Trump is meant to evoke a sense of conspiracy and subversion inside the ranks of the national security establishment, and to convince the president's base that the will of the voters (who elected him) was being threatened.

The administration insisted that leaks to the media about topics unfavorable to Trump—such as Michael Flynn's intercepted phone calls and various contacts between campaign officials and Russians—were all a result of the deep state. As Press Secretary Sean Spicer wildly insisted in March 2017, these nefarious actors, all loyal to Barack Obama, had "burrowed into government" and "continue to espouse the agenda of the previous administration." After the appointment of Robert Mueller as special counsel in May of that year, those in Trumpworld not only blamed government leaks on the "deep state," but labeled the entire investigation a "witch hunt" by those loyal to Democrats. In December 2017, following revelations that the FBI had opened an investigation into Trump, Fox News claimed the bureau was attempting to stage an illegal coup.

THOUGH I ALREADY know from the inside that no such thing as a deep state exists, I asked another former senior national security official what he thought, and he laughed in my face. In his mind, the whole notion was ridiculous. "I'm sorry," he said, "but when I was in government I was more worried about going after bad guys than I was about how I was going to overthrow the government. People in government don't have time for that. They're too busy doing their jobs."

Of course he was correct that, while sensational and provocative, the very idea of a deep state is ludicrous. For one, there are simply too many checks and balances in place for some coordinated mob to be festering inside government. Inside the FBI, there are precisely two levels in the hierarchy of leadership that are held in equal regard. One includes the FBI director—the agency's CEO, who leads thousands of people around the globe—and other managers. The second level—held in equal regard as the director's—consists of the field agents and analysts who work every day on complex investigations. Whereas some institutions, such as corporations or the US military, expect employees to continue moving up a ladder to positions of leadership, the FBI is different. The case agents and intelligence analysts who decide they are going to spend their entire career working investigations are respected as much as, if not more than, the person who leads the entire bureau. This is important to know because if any of the line-level agents or analysts working either the Clinton or Trump investigation thought for a moment that some high-level official was inappropriately meddling in their case, they would be screaming from the rooftops, sounding the alarm with Congress, the courts, or the press.

In addition, no one does anything alone inside the intelligence community. So-called "insider threat" programs actively surveil employees in order to ensure that they are not passing information to foreign governments, journalists, or anyone else without authorization. When dealing with highly sensitive information, everyone watches over everyone else. Computer systems are monitored, and FBI employees with access to classified information are polygraphed every five years. Employees in agencies like the FBI also sign certifications on a routine basis attesting that they have reported any intelligence abuses observed during the course of their work. These civil servants know there are repercussions to turning a blind eye to possible malfeasance happening in their midst.

Still skeptical? Understanding that my denying the existence of a deep state might itself be seen in some fringe circles as being part of the supposed conspiracy, I consulted with someone whose relationship with the government has at times been less than cordial. Mark Zaid is a national security attorney whose entire professional life is oriented around sussing out misbehavior and protecting whistleblowers in US federal agencies. Even he thinks the notion of a deep state is laughable. "I simply don't believe there is this abstract monolithic creature engaged in wrongdoing for political purposes," he told me.

Zaid believes that conspiracy theorists give the government too much credit. His experience working with bureaucracies prevents him from accepting that agencies could actually form an anti-Trump cabal, even if they wanted to. "I just don't think most people inside the agencies have the competency to pull this stuff off," he said with a laugh. "The FBI and CIA do great things, but effectively plotting against the president? No way."

Although it may be difficult to fully understand the mind-set of someone who would actually buy into Trump's deep-state narrative, it is certainly a topic worth exploring. So I contacted David Priess, a former CIA officer and the author of two books on the presidency. An expert in US national security and political history, he has also written about conspiracy theories. "All of the grand conspiracy theories in history seem to share a common psychological, perhaps sociological, trait: the belief that big events must have big causes," he told me. Some people find it difficult to believe that something as significant as President John F. Kennedy's assassination, for example, could have been the work of a lone gunman.

Priess says the search for a cause as monumental as the result leads some to a more expansive explanation. This dynamic applies to President Trump, because rather than accepting the fact that many people around him have been indicted and prosecuted for individual crimes, he claims there must be something larger afoot.

Unfortunately, those who are predisposed to believe conspiracy theories are prime targets for manipulation by unscrupulous politicians. Journalist Carl Bernstein has covered numerous presidents and has seen up close how politicians attempt to handle negative news about their actions. I asked Bernstein for his thoughts on whether Donald Trump might actually believe there is a deep state working against him, or whether perpetuating this myth is part of a campaign of public manipulation.

"The last place I want to be is in Donald Trump's head," said Bernstein, but he added that the way Trump has approached Robert Mueller's investigation "is totally consistent with the way he has conducted his life and his presidency, which is to deny facts and lie. He is a grifter, a con man, and a flimflam artist. Part of the con and the flimflam is to attack the investigators, which also poses deep national security concerns."

Of course, the intelligence community's historical record is not entirely pure, and neither I nor Bernstein give the FBI a full pass. As noted in chapter 2, before the government reforms of the 1970s, the security state engaged in gross abuses and dirty tricks in the name of national security. However, as presidential historian Timothy Naftali says, rather than deep-state government officials running rogue, most historical abuses involved orders from the top. "It's worth noting that the vast majority of intelligence abuses unearthed by the Watergate and Church investigations and by investigations after 9/11 were not the product of an unelected state," wrote Naftali in a commentary for CNN. "They were the product of secret activities ordered by elected officials, namely our presidents."

Although, as described in chapter 12, a small number of FBI employees were indeed exposed for verbalizing their unbridled disgust for candidate Donald Trump, there is no evidence that they actually violated their oaths of office by actively working to undermine him. And while there have been serious leaks of sensitive information during the Trump presidency (and other presidencies—think of the 2013 document dump by former government contractor Edward Snowden, for instance), there is no evidence that such information has come from a cabal of bureaucrats plotting to bring down the president. Rather, as noted by Marc Ambinder, an adjunct professor and my colleague at the University of Southern California, who has long studied the intelligence community, "The knowledge we have about the inner workings of Trump's White House appears to be coming from his own top aides."

Despite all this, many in Trump's orbit have used the deep-state claim as a bludgeon against the career public servants working in the intelligence community and at the Department of Justice. They've concocted lie after lie in order to discredit anyone who might be justifiably investigating the president. "Spin for the sake of presidential reputation is a normal part of political life," Timothy Naftali wrote in his CNN commentary. "But there is spin and then there is spreading poison." Naftali has long studied presidential trickery, having previously served as director of the Richard Nixon Presidential Library and Museum. As he sees it, the Trump administration's public suggestion of "a super-secret, unelected 'Deep State' supposedly intent upon sabotaging the new president was poisonous."

The truth about whether the president actually believed all of the conspiracy theories he promoted will likely remain unknowable. It is also unclear if Trump was ever made aware of the critical institutional norms he was so busy demolishing.

"I think he doesn't know and he doesn't care," former Nixon White

House counsel John Dean told me. "I think one of the reasons he violates so many norms is that he didn't know they even existed. He's about as incompetent a human as we've ever had in this office. He just wants to do his own thing. A lot of it is blunderbuss and just breaking the china because he doesn't even realize it's important not to."

Unfortunately, the FBI was wholly unprepared for the onslaught, not only because the agency had never experienced such maliciousness directed at it from a president, but also because it was in the unenviable position of proving a negative. How could any intelligence agency effectively prove something did *not* exist? It was impossible. And rather than being able to look to other parts of government, such as Congress, to help refute Trump's unfounded accusations, the bureau would find itself taking fire from both ends of Pennsylvania Avenue. President Donald Trump was about to get reinforcements.

THE SENIOR GOVERNMENT official needed to make a quick getaway. It was March 2017 in Washington and his Tuesday evening drive with a staff member was quickly interrupted by an incoming message from a source. It was time to meet. The circumstances of the meeting appeared sensitive enough that the official chose not to brief his associate on what he was up to or where he was going. This operation apparently required extreme secrecy. He changed cars, hopping into an Uber and heading off toward the meeting location, where highly classified information would be divulged.

At first glance, the incident above describes the type of rendezvous that happens daily in the nation's capital. FBI agents and CIA officers (and foreign spies, for that matter) routinely cast off into the night, liaising with sources and obtaining critical intelligence. An evening drive across town along Connecticut Avenue will more likely than not bring one unsuspectingly within the vicinity of a source meet in progress.

But this was no ordinary source meet. In fact, the official at the center of it all wasn't even a spy. He was an elected Republican member of Congress from California who chaired the powerful House Intelligence Committee. He was also an acolyte of the president who had spent time helping Trump's transition team, and someone many in the intelligence community believed was auditioning for the role of director of national intelligence. In what would later be billed as his infamous "midnight run," Rep. Devin Nunes set off that evening to 1600 Pennsylvania Avenue to meet a "source" about possible impropriety on the part of the US intelligence community. This covert meeting would set in motion an extraordinary chain of events that would destroy any notion of impartiality by the person leading an independent investigation into Russian interference while also politicizing the House Intelligence Committee in a destructive manner unseen since its founding.

The day after this run to the White House, Nunes held a press conference to announce that then candidate Donald Trump and his associates may have been swept up in "incidental collection" during surveillance by the US intelligence community. This was apparently what he had been briefed on during his late-night source meet. At the time of the press conference, no one knew where the information Nunes was announcing had originated, but to some of us in the bureau, his goal could not have been more clear: he was now running interference for Trump and working to further the myth that the president was the victim of an out-of-control intelligence establishment, or deep state.

These allegations came on the heels of Trump's nonsensical claim that he had been the target of illegal wiretapping, and after James Comey's public testimony announcing that the FBI was investigating the Trump campaign. Nothing Nunes was describing was illegal—something he himself acknowledged—but by dramatically making a connection between Trump and electronic surveillance conducted by the intelligence community, he was assisting efforts to either confuse or manipulate the public into believing something sinister was afoot.

"This is about to get really bad," a senior FBI official remarked at the time, during one of our regular morning meetings. "We've done nothing wrong, but this is not a space in which we can adequately defend ourselves, because we are talking about highly classified sources and methods."

Generally speaking, what Nunes was describing is something that happens every single day in the intelligence business. While many of our nation's human and technical resources are geared toward stopping threats from abroad, global targets routinely come in contact with US citizens. "Incidental collection" is what happens when a foreign subject of electronic surveillance communicates with or about a US citizen. What readers should understand is the length to which the intelligence community goes to ensure the privacy of people who may be incidentally caught up in authorized intelligence collection. Despite concerns about surveillance, there has not been a single instance in the modern era where the FBI has been found to have abused its intelligence-collection authorities to target an American. It would be unrealistic and, indeed, unsafe for our national security professionals to simply ignore a piece of intelligence that just happens to involve a US citizen. However, intelligence analysts will redact the actual names and simply list those individuals or entities as "U.S. Person 1" or "U.S. Company 1" in reports disseminated across the community. The goal is to balance the need to collect and share critical threat information with an individual's or a company's right to privacy.

Sometimes, it is important for agents and analysts working a particular target to know the identity of a US citizen with whom a foreign target has been in contact. This might stem from a duty to warn that person they are the target of foreign-intelligence recruitment, for example, or perhaps from the need to determine whether that person is in fact complicit in the commission of a crime. Knowing the identity of US citizens in contact with hostile foreign intelligence services, for example, would also fall under the purview of the president, in order to help him or her protect the nation from intelligence threats. In these cases, officials can submit a request to the specific agency responsible for obtaining the original intelligence to "unmask" the name of the person or entity cited in reporting. The requesting party has to articulate the reason for their unmasking submission—one can't simply gather information on somebody out of sheer curiosity—and these requests are all logged.

Having taken on the role of the president's congressional protector by suggesting that the intelligence community had somehow done something wrong in collecting information on Trump and his associates, Devin

Nunes was now offering Trump justification for his false claims that he had been illegally wiretapped by Obama. Nunes said that it was easy to ascertain the identities of Trump's associates, and that some were even listed by name—with the implication being the names of US citizens had either been unmasked or improperly redacted at the outset. He told reporters, "What I have read bothers me, and I think it should bother the president himself and his team, because I think some of it seems to be inappropriate." He refused to indicate where he'd received the information—ironically, citing the need to protect sources and methods—saying later only that it had come from a "whistleblower type," a grave bastardization of the sacrosanct whistleblower role. After his press conference, Nunes went back to the White House to brief Trump in more detail on what he found.

As with most scandals in Washington, it is usually only a matter of time before conspiracies are laid bare. It would soon be reported that Nunes's sources were likely two officials working at the White House—one a senior official on Trump's National Security Council and the other a lawyer in the White House counsel's office.

The entire operation leaves many in national security circles scratching their heads to this day. Why would Nunes race to the White House in the middle of the night, get briefed on intelligence reporting, announce it the next day, and then go back to the White House to brief the very same administration from which he had received the intelligence to begin with? If Nunes's White House sources had discovered that surveillance containing the names of Trump officials had been obtained illegally, why not bring this directly to the attention of the president? Many experts with whom I spoke said it was possible the administration feared that people wouldn't believe Trump, and they suggested that the White House would instead require another party in a different branch of government to be the front man.

The stunt would cost Nunes his position as committee chair for about eight months; he stepped down from his role in overseeing the Russia investigation while the House Ethics Committee investigated his actions. Ultimately, although Nunes had destroyed the House Intelligence Committee's bipartisan spirit by freelancing for Trump, he would be cleared by the Ethics

Committee of wrongdoing, because he had not technically improperly divulged any classified information. To the astonishment of many, he would resume his role as Intelligence Committee chair by year's end.

But the damage had already been done, both to his reputation and to that of the US intelligence community. His public questioning of the actions of the Obama team and our intelligence professionals had provided Trump with ammunition to continue his assault on those upholding the rule of law. It fueled Trump's narrative that he was a victim. By the time Nunes was given the gavel back, the president would need him more than ever before. As pressure from the Mueller investigation grew, few Republicans were as keen as Nunes to play the role of human shield for a president many were unsure was actually innocent.

As one senior FBI official later told me, Nunes's inappropriate relationship with the administration greatly concerned leaders inside the bureau. The operating theory was that anything provided to Congress on the FBI's investigation into Russia and the Trump campaign would immediately be briefed to Trump. "There were times we really wanted to brief congressional overseers on something we were specifically doing," said the official, "but we opted not to because Nunes had demolished that critical divide between politics and oversight. We suspected he would immediately leak to the White House any sensitive information we provided him."

BY THE BEGINNING of 2018, Nunes was as determined as ever to uncover alleged corruption on the part of the FBI. Although the House Intelligence Committee had been publicly working on its high-profile review of Russia's interference in the 2016 election, a group of Republicans had also been secretly working on a parallel investigation geared toward exposing alleged misdeeds by the FBI in targeting Trump. This would be the group that would help Trump continue his deep-state and witch-hunt narratives, and, in doing so, politicize the Intelligence Committee in a way that would ultimately drive it into the ground.

Originally at issue was whether the Steele dossier—intelligence reports that had been done on behalf of a Democratic-funded opposition research project—had been used as the basis for the FBI to investigate Trump. Nunes and his Republican colleagues suspected that an anti-Trump faction inside the intelligence community was so determined to take down Trump it would use faulty and misleading tactics in order to conduct its investigation. The group also seized on the FBI's original electronic surveillance of Trump campaign adviser Carter Page, who at the time was being investigated in the Crossfire Hurricane case as a possible agent of the Russian government. Nunes and his crew set out to draft a memo citing multiple abuses of power by the FBI, which they hoped to release to the public in order to further the false narrative that the bureau had acted in a corrupt fashion.

Inside the FBI, officials were growing concerned with the dangerous waters Nunes had entered. We knew that he was acting recklessly, making serious allegations based on cherry-picked fragments of highly classified information. Certain contents of the draft Nunes memo were starting to leak from Congress, indicating that Nunes was using snippets from the top-secret Carter Page FISA application as its basis and claiming specifically that the FBI had abused its surveillance authority. By suggesting malfeasance on the part of the bureau but withholding the actual details, Nunes was allowing a corrosive picture of the bureau to form in the minds of the American people.

For his part, Trump reportedly thought the memo might make it easier for him to discredit Mueller's ongoing work. The remaining question was whether Nunes would be able to release the memo containing highly classified information, or if that decision would ultimately rest with the president, who had the power to declassify any piece of intelligence in the US government's holdings with the stroke of a pen.

As public release of the memo appeared imminent, the FBI and Justice Department went through the roof. The entire debacle had placed the bureau in an untenable position. Our leadership team knew from leaks that the details and conclusions in the memo were misleading, and they also had to weigh the potential harm that might occur from releasing information about sensitive sources and methods. Not only could some of the bureau's investigations be hindered by the memo, but it would set a dangerous precedent for future acts of politicization by lawmakers.

Most of us inside the FBI had never seen this kind of showdown with Congress or the White House. Everything about it was unprecedented. On one end of Pennsylvania Avenue, you had unscrupulous members of the House Intelligence Committee attempting to manipulate the public into believing distortions of the truth; on the other end of the street, an administration benefiting from all the chaos and the dishonest portrayal of the FBI as crooks; and caught literally and figuratively in the middle of it all, the bureau.

On January 30, Deputy Attorney General Rod Rosenstein and James Comey's replacement as FBI director, Christopher Wray, appealed to John Kelly, now White House chief of staff, insisting that publication of the Nunes memo would compromise classified information. The next day, underscoring the untold harm that might be done here, the FBI issued a stunning rebuke of the planned release, describing the bureau's "grave concerns" with the memo and its omission of key facts.

They were overruled. On February 2, over the strenuous objections of those charged with protecting the nation, President Trump signed off on the Nunes memo's release, and it was made public.

THIS WOULD ALSO be my last day at the FBI, a culmination of weeks of anger and frustration at the unending lies told about the organization I love—by President Trump, his congressional allies, and far-right media enablers. I had recently been promoted from FBI headquarters to a field supervisor position in Los Angeles, but I was now preparing to make a transition of an entirely different kind. After over a decade of working behind the scenes, I had decided to step out into a public role in order to help the public discern fact from fiction.

My final day at the bureau was surreal in a number of ways. Leaving was an incredibly painful experience, but the abuse of power in Washington that was playing out in the very moments I was packing up my office bolstered my resolve. I remember staring up at the TV in my office as I filled boxes with pictures and mementos, watching the breaking news about the highly distorted Nunes memo.

Leaving the FBI isn't as simple as flipping a switch. There are many steps involved. For one, during my nearly thirteen years in the organization, I had acquired some equipment—okay, *a lot* of equipment—that I now had to turn in. From weapons to computers, my official government passports (one for use in visiting Israel; another, free of that immigration stamp, to be used in certain other Middle Eastern nations) to credit cards—all of it had to be logged back in. There was also an issue involving my FBI vehicle that I had to resolve. In the field, all agents are assigned a bureau car—a "bucar," for short—which they use to conduct official investigative business and then take home each night, since they are always in a 24/7 emergency response status. The FBI maintains a large fleet of vehicles, and I had just been assigned one of the sleek sedans delivered to our field office. I wanted it to go to one of my squad's field agents, so I had to do a bit of a two-step shuffle.

I walked into the auto garage and said, "Hi, I want to switch my car with one of the agents on my squad." The nice woman on duty processed the paperwork, reassigning the older vehicle to me, and gave me the forms to sign. I then handed them back to her and said, "Hi, I'm leaving the FBI and want to turn in my car." She looked at me like I was crazy, but processed the paperwork for my departure.

The next step involved a security exit interview. Although I was a reservist in the military and would therefore maintain a government security clearance, I still had to be "read out" of the various compartments of my FBI Top Secret clearance and then sign an agreement to never talk about the classified information I'd learned while inside the bureau, and to permit the bureau the opportunity to review any future books I might write (like this one) in order to ensure that there was no inadvertent disclosure of the classified information I'd learned while inside the bureau.

I joked with the security officer that since I was now going into journalism, I would still be free to discuss sensitive information I learned *after* leaving government.

"Yeah, we can't stop you there," he said with a laugh and a firm handshake as I stood to leave his office.

THE NUNES MEMO was every bit the pile of propaganda many of us were expecting. It stated that, in seeking the FISA court's approval to surveil Trump aide Carter Page, the FBI had failed to disclose the partisan origins of the Steele dossier. The insinuation was that a cabal of deep-state FBI officials sympathetic to the Democratic Party and out to get Trump was attempting to pull a fast one on the federal judges. However, this was a distortion. As Republicans would later admit when pressed, the bureau had included a footnote in the FISA application indicating that the dossier was indeed funded by people seeking to discredit Trump. This footnote ran over one page in length, making it impossible that it would have escaped the attention of the authorizing judge. The footnote then went on to discredit Steele, describing his antipathy for Trump and the fact that Steele had provided information to a Department of Justice attorney whose wife had worked for Fusion GPS, the company on whose behalf Steele was working.

Although the holes in the Nunes memo were large enough to drive a presidential limousine through, in true Trumpian fashion the president moved to convince the public into believing not only that the FBI had operated with corrupt intent, but that the memo had actually proved his innocence. "This memo totally vindicates 'Trump' in probe," the president falsely claimed in a tweet the morning after the memo's release.

In fact, the Nunes memo did nothing of the sort. But all Trump had to do was keep proclaiming his innocence and perhaps folks would start to believe it. And this strategy—deny, distort, and make counteraccusations— would undermine the justice system.

THERE IS A saying in law enforcement circles that "action beats reaction." It is an oft-repeated line during tactical training at the FBI Academy in Quantico and police training facilities across the nation. The underlying premise is that law enforcement officers must always be cognizant of the fact that, in dealing with a potentially dangerous criminal, the officer faces the reality that a person attempting to harm someone has the luxury of making the first move. When facing down a threatening individual, it is that individual who typically sets the stage for what comes next. With this in mind, officers are reminded that maintaining stellar tactical proficiency is not optional but could be the key to survival. They must constantly be on alert, cautiously reading every encounter with another person and mentally preparing to respond rapidly to the actions of others.

The "action beats reaction" mantra also applies to politics, as House Democrats discovered after finding themselves in the unenviable position of having to correct the record—and fast—after the Nunes memo threatened to deceive the American people. A group of Republicans had made the first move; Democrats would now have to play defense in order to salvage public confidence in our institutions of justice and cut through the ever-expanding web of lies.

One of the Democrats leading the charge was Rep. Eric Swalwell, a thirty-seven-year-old former prosecutor from California whose positions on both the House Intelligence and Judiciary Committees had provided him insight into the inner workings of the FBI. He said he knew full well that Nunes and his colleagues were working to pull a fast one on the American people, and was further concerned that Nunes's antics were threatening the historical bipartisan basis on which intelligence oversight rested.

"Traditionally, we never talked about what went on belowground," Swalwell told me, referring to the underground secured meeting room where the House Intelligence Committee did its work.

When he'd first joined the committee, he said, one of his colleagues described the important divide between politics and intelligence: Members were never to mix the Washington political machinations that went on aboveground with the critical national security function of intelligence oversight. But Nunes had shattered the nonpartisan protective shield that had historically set the Intelligence Committee apart from other political bodies. It was up to Swalwell and the then ranking member of the committee, Adam Schiff, also a California Democrat, to sensitize the American people to the fact that Nunes and his Republican colleagues "had taken out shovels to bury the truth about the Russia investigation," as Swalwell put it.

Swalwell had personally witnessed the evolution of Nunes's behavior and the souring relationship between the chairman and the ranking member. Nunes and Schiff had once worked closely together on issues such as cybersecurity reform, intelligence reauthorization, and bulk intelligence collection. But with the arrival of Trump, Swalwell said, something changed; Nunes managed to co-opt otherwise decent Republican officials into sacrificing the intelligence community to benefit a president facing a serious counterintelligence investigation.

As someone who once worked for elected Republicans—previously serving as legislative aide to a state representative and on the staff of the local Republican Party while in college—I was stunned to hear how quickly the party had become Trump's lapdog.

"The only X factor that can really explain the shift is that Donald Trump was elected president, and Devin Nunes had gotten close to Trump during the campaign," Swalwell said. "In the fog of the election's aftermath, as we were starting to understand what the Russians had done, most of us believed that, despite all the politics going on aboveground, the committee would be able to do its work and follow the evidence. But time after time, in hearing after hearing, we saw that Nunes was not working to protect our democracy, but the president."

The environment had grown so toxic Nunes essentially shut out Democrats, refusing to discuss the issues surrounding the ongoing Russia investigation. On Capitol Hill, much of the business of congressional oversight happens not in the actual committee hearings, but in informal exchanges and meetings that occur throughout the building each day. But Nunes wouldn't face his Democratic colleagues and key them in on his operation. This left Democrats with only the option of using the proceedings of formal hearings to appeal to Nunes for cooperation.

Representative Schiff would use his proximity to Nunes at committee hearings—they were seated next to each other—as his opportunity to ask the chair for a modicum of collegiality.

"Schiff would say, 'Mr. Chairman, we have these outstanding issues with the Russia investigation,'" said Swalwell. "'My hope is that we can meet offline and have an informal meeting to air our concerns and try to find a path to do this together.' He did that so many times, and in each instance Nunes would sit there with a blank stare and wouldn't even respond."

I asked Swalwell about reports that the committee hearings often became contentious.

"I wish," he said, "because that would have meant that Nunes and the Republicans were engaging with us. But they never engaged. They would just look at us with blank stares on their faces as we expressed our concern and outrage. There was never a discussion, and there was never an opportunity to meet, despite our many attempts to do so." (I attempted to get former chair Nunes's perspective on all that had transpired; however, two requests to interview him for this book were not returned by his office. A similar request to the White House went unanswered.)

With House Republicans stonewalling any discussion between the two parties, and with Nunes's memo now out in the public ether, Democrats on the committee set out to draft their own rebuttal memo that would highlight the omissions and distortions. But they first had to clear the hurdle of White House authorization. Whereas the president quickly moved to release the Nunes memo over the objections of the Justice Department, the White House initially blocked Schiff's memo, insisting that the point-by-point rebuttal document contained "numerous properly classified and especially sensitive passages." The hypocrisy was laughable.

For our part, many inside the FBI welcomed the delay. Even though we thought the Nunes memo was garbage, that did not change our view that sources and methods should be appropriately protected, despite the fact that their release might lead to vindication. "This is like a bad TV drama," one senior FBI official lamented to me at the time. "One group is lying about us, another group is trying to refute the lies, and we're sitting here caught up in the middle of it, wishing the whole thing would go away."

At the risk of sounding too sanctimonious, it is this important difference in orientation that sets national security professionals apart from many political operatives in Washington. Those who work to collect sensitive intelligence from sources understand that protecting the ability to collect national security secrets in the future is more important than putting points up on the political scoreboard.

On February 24, following negotiations between the bureau and House
Democrats on the contents of the rebuttal memo, the White House finally
signed off on its release. Its ten-page refutation of the Nunes memo systematically dismantled the Republican claims of abuse. As Schiff wrote in a
statement, his review "failed to uncover any evidence of illegal, unethical,
or unprofessional behavior" by the FBI.

While action may beat reaction, Schiff, Swalwell, and their colleagues
had done a yeoman's job in reacting to correct the record and defend the
men and women of the FBI against unfair and untrue political attacks.
When I stopped for a moment to think about their efforts, I came to the
conclusion that Democrats on the House Intelligence Committee were
the only real leaders in government who attempted to defend institutional
norms. Although the Justice Department had thrown a flag on the release
of either memo, neither Sessions nor Rosenstein were vocally speaking out
against calls from Republicans labeling the FBI corrupt.

"I know they were in a tough spot," said Representative Swalwell.
"Because if they spoke out, they would probably reaffirm Trump's accusation of a deep state, but by not speaking out, Trump's blows went unanswered, and the American people were only offered one version of the story.
DOJ should have recognized that these were extraordinary times, and they
were on the ropes and had to punch back."

Swalwell's observation tracks precisely with the way many inside the FBI
felt at the time. Even after leaving the bureau, I would continue to get calls
and emails from former colleagues who were incensed: The FBI was under
siege. President Trump was at war with an institution that was investigating him, and he was playing dirty. And his own party was complicit in its
silence. And the Justice Department leadership was silent.

# CHAPTER 12

# Standard Operating Procedure

CONTRARY TO POPULAR belief, FBI agents do not treat white-collar criminals differently than other criminals. The truth is that white-collar criminals can be even more dangerous than your run-of-the-mill crook. This fact became clear to me during a training scenario I still recall vividly from my days at the FBI Academy. In an exercise testing our ability to execute an arrest warrant on the president of a fictitious bank, my partner and I strode into a mock bank branch and located the subject of our arrest. In a perfect illustration of the action-beats-reaction rule, the "banker" pulled out a Simunition gun (which shoots paint pellets in place of real bullets) and drilled me and my partner in our chests. The exercise was over. We were notionally deceased.

In our after-action interview with the instructor, he asked us what was going through our minds as we approached the bank. We explained that it hadn't seemed like a particularly violent scenario because the subject was a businessman.

"Wrong," the instructor declared. An encounter with a white-collar criminal, he explained, can actually be even riskier than the arrest of an ordinary street criminal, because, my instructor warned, they often "have the most to lose."

With this basic principle in mind, FBI agents in Manhattan set out to seize control of property occupied by Michael Cohen, longtime personal lawyer and fixer for the Donald Trump. On the morning of April 9, 2018, special agents in New York City donned their bureau raid jackets and fanned out to simultaneously execute a search warrant that had been obtained for three properties associated with Cohen—his home, his office, and a hotel room. I knew that such an effort would have been massive, requiring dozens of personnel to secure each scene and then methodically search them for evidence.

THE PRESIDENT ERUPTED. Sitting before reporters in a meeting with military leaders at the White House that day, he doubled down on his continued attacks on the justice system. "So I just heard that they broke into the office of one of my personal attorneys—a good man," Trump said. "And it's a disgraceful situation. It's a total witch hunt." And it wasn't just terrible for Cohen, he went on: the arrest was somehow a threat to the United States. "It's an attack on our country, in a true sense. It's an attack on what we all stand for."

I believe that the president knew exactly what he was doing here in attempting to portray law enforcement as jackbooted thugs. Crooks break into places. By contrast, although FBI special agents may break down doors when necessary (by the way, there's no indication that they did so here), doing so requires lawful authority. Up to this point, Trump and many of his apologists—including some former federal agents—were trying to explain away his disdain for law enforcement by suggesting that he meant to disparage only the leadership at the FBI, but here he was clearly going after regular folks doing their jobs the way they had been instructed. And his new attorney would soon peddle another vicious line that would make Trump's comments look like child's play.

THE MAN WHO took over for Cohen as the president's bulldog defender was someone I'd once admired. In fact, he was one of the reasons I had pursued an FBI career in the first place. This former lawman had once been heralded as a national hero for his steady leadership and calm response to unspeakable tragedy. When I unexpectedly found myself standing before him in late 2014, I was awestruck.

The venue was Shelly's Back Room, a dark but raucous cigar bar in downtown Washington where politicians, bureaucrats, and federal agents often gather to socialize at the end of a long day. Television screens were tuned to various sporting events; beer and cocktails were served up at the oak-paneled bar against the far wall; and a ceiling ventilation system worked hard to keep pace with the rings of cigar smoke filling the air.

I had arrived ahead of my friends. As I made the approach to an open table, another patron was zeroing in on the same location. We arrived at the table at the same time and did the typical awkward dance one does when vying for an open seat or parking space.

"You take the table," he said with a chuckle.

"No, you take it," I replied. We were both opting for a display of chivalry, not wanting to sour an evening of fun with a fight over a bar table. As our reverse duel continued, the people next to us stood to put on their coats before heading for the exit.

"You take this one," I said, pointing to our original joint conquest, "and my friends and I will sit over here."

Finally relenting, he stuck out his hand to introduce himself. "I'm Rudy Giuliani," he said with a smile.

"I know, sir," I replied. "Josh Campbell, FBI."

"Thanks for what you do," he said. Pointing his index finger into my chest, he offered, "I did a lot of work with the FBI."

"I know that too, sir," I said. The man I stood chatting with was the former US attorney for the Southern District of New York, who had once worked closely with the bureau as a criminal prosecutor. "Thank you for all you've done."

We retired to our tables and were both soon joined by our respective parties—mine consisting of two special-agent friends from another part of the country, who had come to visit headquarters and finalize logistics for a major counterintelligence operation being planned, and Giuliani's consisting of two rotund men in expensive-looking three-piece suits.

"Do you know who that is?" I asked incredulously when one of my colleagues remarked that the guys looked like "mob bosses."

He glanced over at the table once again, eyes squinting as he tried to make out their faces through the haze of smoke.

"That's Rudy Giuliani," I said. "America's mayor."

"I'll be damned," he replied.

I went on to explain how Giuliani's handling of the tragic attacks of 9/11 had inspired me to go into public service. As a college freshman in September 2001, I was still trying to figure out my career trajectory when the Twin Towers were attacked. Giuliani's grace under pressure and service over self during the aftermath contributed to my decision to pursue a career with the FBI. He was named *Time* magazine's "Person of the Year 2001." I was excited when he later decided to seek the 2008 presidential nomination.

Little did I know at the time that he would one day sign up to become Donald Trump's chief propagandist, in the process going from celebrated law enforcer to a spin doctor working to undermine the very institution he once nobly served.

Now, WITH HIS former attorney a prime target of investigators, Trump desperately needed help; it would likely be only a matter of time before Cohen agreed to cooperate with the government. The president already had a large legal team, but he needed someone who could help with the public relations side of the effort—someone who could command attention on the national stage, but also someone with enough cunning to denigrate the law enforcement investigators working the case. For those qualities, he turned to none other than former New York City mayor and federal prosecutor Rudy Giuliani. By this point, Giuliani had become close friends with Trump and was rumored to be in the running for the position of secretary of state early on in the administration.

In theory, Giuliani offered the president the credentials of a distinguished lawyer and former politician who could use that reputation to go on the attack against Trump's perceived enemies. But when he went on TV to defend his client, he often offered up some new "revelation," including information that countered things the president had previously said. In one instance, he dropped a bombshell by indicating that Trump had in fact reimbursed Michael Cohen for hush money paid to the adult film actress

Stormy Daniels, although the president had previously told reporters that he didn't know about the payment. In another instance, Giuliani stated that past claims by one of Trump's lawyers that the president had not dictated his son Donald Trump Jr.'s misleading letter about the meeting with Russians in Trump Tower were "a mistake" and not meant to deceive. He even announced that the president could have actually shot Comey, instead of firing him, and he wouldn't be indicted (an echo of Trump's own comments during the campaign that he could shoot someone on Fifth Avenue and not lose any voters).

"What happened to this guy?" one of my former FBI colleagues texted one night after a Giuliani TV spinfest. "He's gone from statesman to circus clown."

For many of my national security colleagues and friends in the DC political world, some of whom have traveled in Republican circles, the nadir came when Giuliani called the FBI agents who searched the office of Michael Cohen "big storm troopers coming in and breaking down his apartment and breaking down his office." The insult was beyond grave. These were line-level employees simply doing their jobs. And the president's lawyer was comparing them to murderous Nazis. He had once been a federal prosecutor—someone who supervised the execution of countless search warrants. He should have known better.

Remarkably, when pressed on his incendiary comments, Giuliani did not apologize. Quite the opposite. Asked again about his comparison of the FBI to Hitler's private army, Giuliani doubled down. "They are," he said. "You don't go into a man's house in the morning for a case that's ten years old." And then, apparently directly addressing any FBI employees who may have been watching, he added, "You are storm troopers."

While some in the public now largely think of Giuliani as a caricature, his stinging assault on our national security institutions infuriated current and former public servants.

Samantha Vinograd is a former National Security Council official who worked under Presidents George W. Bush and Barack Obama. "While the special counsel was investigating a complex attack by a hostile foreign power, President Trump and Giuliani were making myriad moves that aided and abetted that attack," she told me. "They spread misinformation, sowed divisions, and undermined democratic institutions like our independent law enforcement system. This is exactly what our intelligence community accused Russia of doing."

TRUMP AND HIS associates weren't finished with their efforts to twist standard operating procedures by the FBI into something more sinister. And again he turned to House Intelligence Committee Chair Devin Nunes to take another crack at manufacturing a scandal.

"We now call it Spygate!" the president told a group of assembled reporters on the South Lawn of the White House. The reality-TV host turned president was clearly pleased with his pitchman skills; he had landed on a new phrase he was sure would catch fire. On Twitter, he would insist, "SPYGATE could be one of the biggest political scandals in history!"

The word "Spygate" (which no serious journalist would adopt) pertained to the claim that the US intelligence community had planted a spy— or "implanted," as Trump would tweet—in his 2016 campaign for political purposes, in order to hurt his chances of winning. The claim was ludicrous on its face, but that did not stop Trump from going full bore.

The notion of a "spy"—or, more aptly put, "confidential human source," in FBI parlance—being used as part of the investigation into the Trump campaign first surfaced in January 2018. Congress released a transcript of testimony from Glenn Simpson, the cofounder of Fusion GPS, the Democratic-linked firm that had hired former British spy Christopher Steele to gather opposition research on Trump. In discussing the veracity of the Steele dossier, Simpson testified that Steele had told him that FBI agents with whom he was in contact had indicated Steele's information might be credible because they had similar reporting coming to them from "a human source from inside the Trump organization."

Devin Nunes later issued a subpoena to the Justice Department for information about this supposed human source. Although Nunes declared he was not interested in any one individual, the *Washington Post* was able to review a copy of the subpoena, which commanded the release of "all documents referring or related to the individual" referenced in an earlier letter from Nunes to the attorney general. Nunes had been caught in a lie, but that was the least of the Justice Department's worries. The larger issue was whether Nunes was again destroying institutional norms by attempting to go after sensitive sources and methods.

Alarmed by his subpoena, intelligence officials thought the matter so serious they decided to appeal to the White House for top cover, and Chief of Staff John Kelly sided with DOJ over Nunes. House Republicans then threatened to hold Attorney General Jeff Sessions in contempt and impeach Deputy Attorney General Rod Rosenstein if the source information wasn't turned over.

A chronological dissection of news segments from this time appears to lay out the path the issue took from initial reporting to Trump's ears. After the *Washington Post* revealed news of the subpoena showdown, a firebrand opinion writer at the *Wall Street Journal* took a more conspiratorial view of the matter, writing that the whole episode might mean "the FBI secretly had a person on the payroll who used his or her non-FBI credentials to interact in some capacity with the Trump campaign," adding "This would amount to spying, and it is hugely disconcerting." From there, the story hopped over to Trump's favorite spin-machine provocateurs—namely, Sean Hannity and the crew at *Fox & Friends*, who amplified the original *Wall Street Journal* opinion piece, followed by a segment on the conservative talk radio show hosted by Rush Limbaugh.

"When I say 'the FBI,' I mean the Obama administration," Limbaugh warned. "They infiltrated the Trump campaign with a spy, and while they had that spy implanted, they were unmasking and leaking and obtaining FISA spying warrants and conducting criminal investigations of Trump advisers. This is a big deal. It is a gigantic, big deal."

Not wanting to miss out on the action, Fox News Channel's Tucker Carlson invited to his show a fire-breathing former Secret Service agent who regularly joins the network. Asked if this had ever happened before, the agent said, "Not in the United States." And then the former agent went on to insist without evidence that there was actually *more than one* source that the FBI had used. "It would be a crime," Carlson declared.

I am here to explain why this was not, in fact, a "big deal." Or even, to the average FBI agent, very exciting. The *Washington Post* reported that instead of using some deep-state Democratic plant inserted into the Trump campaign for political purposes, the FBI enlisted a confidential human source to gather information as part of its lawful Crossfire Hurricane investigation. The use of a source is one of the most basic investigative techniques in any FBI investigation. Since FBI agents can't typically sidle up to possible criminals and covertly gather evidence to prove a possible crime, they routinely use paid and unpaid sources working on their behalf.

Although routine, the use of a human source is also highly scrutinized. A source being used to gather information on a political candidate would require especially strict high-level approvals. In this case, the source—a veteran staffer in Republican administrations—was tasked by the government to meet with Trump campaign aides George Papadopoulos and Carter Page once they became people of interest in the FBI's Russia investigation.

In other words, the bureau was using a lawful investigative tool in an attempt to identify and mitigate a potential threat to US national security. Nevertheless, Trump was going to ride this scandal as far as it would take him. The next step was to order an investigation, which he would do so via Twitter.

"I hereby demand, and will do so officially tomorrow," the president tweeted, "that the Department of Justice look into whether or not the FBI/DOJ infiltrated or surveilled the Trump Campaign for Political Purposes - and if any such demands or requests were made by people within the Obama Administration!"

Setting aside the fact that the president of the United States cannot actually order the opening of a criminal investigation, this was perhaps the first time such an attempt had ever been made via social media. The charade underscored the belief of many people in the intelligence community that this entire sad episode was all about a PR campaign to destroy the credibility of the Mueller investigation, rather than an honest attempt to ferret out malfeasance. The president is surrounded by some of the most sophisticated telephonic technology on the planet. If he wanted, he could have picked up the phone to the attorney general or the FBI director to express his concerns. Yet he chose Twitter.

The decision on how to respond to the presidential Twitter tantrum was a dicey one for Rod Rosenstein, who was the Justice Department official in charge of all things related to Russia and the campaign, since Sessions had recused himself. Ordering the FBI to open an inquiry into the matter would have threatened the independence of DOJ and perhaps set a precedent that would allow Trump to meddle further in the work of the department. But refusing to do anything might get Rosenstein fired. So Rosenstein chose a third way and punted the issue to the DOJ's inspector general.

After lawmakers were finally permitted to review classified information regarding the source, Rep. Trey Gowdy (R-SC) threw a giant bucket of cold water on the "Spygate" nonsense by explaining to Fox News, "I am even more convinced that the FBI did exactly what my fellow citizens would want them to do when they got the information they got, and that it has nothing to do with Donald Trump."

Unable to grasp this reality, Nunes said in response that we "have to remember that Mr. Gowdy loves the FBI and the Department of Justice," as though that were clouding his judgment. Like many houses of cards that had been built by Trump and Nunes, this one came crashing to the table.

WITH TIME, MOST would begin to see the "Spygate" sham for what it was—public manipulation and nothing more. As the *Washington Post's* Aaron Blake so aptly described, none of what Trump was peddling actually made any sense. "If Trump is to be believed," Blake wrote, "the FBI decided to spy on Trump's campaign 'for political purposes' during the 2016 election. But then it didn't use the information it had collected to actually prevent Trump from becoming president? That seems to be a rather poorly executed conspiracy."

"Spygate" was more than a farce, however; by politicizing intelligence collection and threatening the identity of a confidential human source, it also likely caused grave and lasting damage to US national security. I know from recruiting and handling human sources that the entire relationship between a source and his or her government handler is one based on trust. The handler trusts that the information provided will be accurate, and the source trusts that his or her identity will be protected from disclosure. Trust is the bedrock on which human intelligence collection rests. By working so eagerly to out the FBI's source, Trump and Nunes were sending a signal to other sources around the world that they could no longer be confident that the US government would protect them. Even if an FBI agent or CIA officer promised anonymity, sources might understand that even the most trustworthy government officer was powerless so long as politicians back home had no qualms about outing them purely for partisan gain.

It is impossible to quantify the damage this manufactured scandal has done to US national security, especially as it relates to all of the potential sources who perhaps thought of volunteering their services to the government but then decided against it. However, the impact is clearly being felt by the FBI's rank and file. I spoke with one field agent working counterintelligence cases who described the cloud of suspicion "Spygate" had cast upon his work. After the "Spygate" source was publicly named, this agent found himself being grilled by a source of his own during a routine debriefing. The source demanded the agent promise this person's own identity would never be made public. It was a promise the agent could not make. As he explained to me, he knew full well that the bureau was on dangerous new ground. With elected leaders now politicizing the intelligence collection process, any promise of anonymity would be a lie.

Although most of the allegations of government corruption being peddled by Trump's robust spin machine of Giuliani, congressional Republicans, and far-right pundits were bogus, there was one area in particular where they had good cause for alarm. In a development none of them could have expected in the wildest of dreams, they would soon be handed a great big gift-wrapped scandal, which they would use to bludgeon the Mueller team for months on end.

# CHAPTER 13

# "Don't Embarrass the Bureau"

"THINK OF THE worst possible scenario, and then multiply it by a factor of a thousand," a senior FBI agent told me as he began to describe the details of a scandal that was about to engulf the bureau. The FBI was in damage-control mode—bracing for the fallout of a man-made disaster. As an institution made up of human beings, the bureau was no stranger to the occasional misbehavior and punishment of employees who had exercised poor judgment, but we knew the public scorn on the horizon would be unlike anything we had ever seen.

In January 2017, the Justice Department's inspector general—the independent watchdog that oversees the conduct of DOJ employees—announced that he was launching a review of the FBI's actions during the Clinton email server investigation, including Comey's decision to reopen the case just prior to the election. Comey welcomed the IG's decision, because, in his view, an outside look at his actions would not only vindicate him but would also ensure public confidence in the agency. Although IG investigations can be disconcerting for those under the microscope, most of us just shrugged it off and went about our business.

Michael Horowitz, the former federal prosecutor leading the charge, was widely known as a thorough but fair inspector general. Folks on our side of Pennsylvania Avenue knew full well that he did not suffer fools and would not hesitate to hold the FBI to account if he discovered wrongdoing, but most of us on the executive corridor were confident that the bureau had acted properly vis-à-vis the Clinton investigation during an unprecedented time of chaos for the country. My colleagues and I figured that the worst

thing the IG might eventually say was that James Comey had been insubordinate in not informing Attorney General Loretta Lynch that he was about
to announce the FBI's conclusion in the case, but seeing how these were
extraordinary times, this would be an admonishment Comey could live
with. But this was not the worst of what the IG would eventually uncover.
Far from it. What none of us in the director's office could have expected at
the time was that the IG would unearth a deep and embarrassing secret that
was hiding in our midst.

MUELLER REMOVED TOP AGENT IN RUSSIA INQUIRY OVER POSSIBLE
ANTI-TRUMP TEXTS read the *New York Times* headline on December 2, 2017.
The story the FBI had been bracing for was now going live. Peter Strzok,
the FBI's deputy assistant director for counterintelligence, who was instrumental in the Clinton email server investigation, Crossfire Hurricane, and
the interview that led to the criminal charge against Michael Flynn, had
been detailed to the Mueller investigation following its formation. During
the course of the DOJ inspector general's review into the FBI's handling
of the Clinton case, investigators discovered that Strzok, a seasoned agent
who had been elevated to a senior position, had been engaged in thousands
of text message discussions with an FBI attorney named Lisa Page, during
which both officials repeatedly expressed contempt for Donald Trump and
other politicians.

It would later be revealed that the two were also hiding an extramarital
affair, but the most acute issue facing the FBI at the time was whether these
senior officials had allowed their personal beliefs about Trump to influence their work. For Mueller, this was a no-brainer. After learning of the
messages from investigators, he quickly booted Strzok off his team, and
the agent was assigned to administrative work at FBI headquarters while
the bureau's leadership contemplated what other punitive action might be
required.

To describe the Strzok-Page text messages as damning would be a colos-
sal understatement. They were disastrous. "God, Trump is a loathsome
human," Page wrote. He's an "idiot," Strzok said. "This man cannot be president," Page would add. Hillary Clinton "just has to win now," Page would

also opine. And on and on it went. In vulgar and insulting exchanges, the two laid bare their views of the candidate whose campaign they were investigating. In one of the most controversial cryptic exchanges, Strzok wrote: "I want to believe the path you threw out for consideration in [Deputy Director Andrew McCabe's] office—that there's no way he gets elected—but I'm afraid we can't take that risk. It's like an insurance policy in the unlikely event you die before you're 40."

This "insurance policy" would instantly become red meat for Trump, congressional Republicans, conspiracy theorists, and right-wing pundits, who were now certain that a secret cabal working at FBI headquarters had schemed to undermine Trump during the election and were now actively working to bring down his administration. Although the messages had been devoid of context, the president wasted no time in pouncing. "Tainted (no, very dishonest?) FBI 'agent's role in Clinton probe under review,'" he tweeted the day after news of the Strzok-Page texts surfaced. "Report: 'ANTI-TRUMP FBI AGENT LED CLINTON EMAIL PROBE' Now it all starts to make sense!" he continued. Probably hoping to manipulate his supporters into believing there was some coordinated Democratic plot within the FBI, Trump also returned to attacking McCabe, whose wife had run for a Democratic state senate seat in Virginia and had received a large political donation during the effort from a group run by Clinton friend Terry McAuliffe. "How can FBI Deputy Director Andrew McCabe, the man in charge, along with leakin' James Comey, of the Phony Hillary Clinton investigation (including her 33,000 illegally deleted emails) be given $700,000 for wife's campaign by Clinton Puppets during investigation?" Trump tweeted. To me, the effort was clear: it was time to start throwing anything and everything against the wall to distract from his own team's wrongdoing.

As thousands of Strzok-Page texts began to seep out into public view, distraction became easier. Venting on her evening opinion show, Fox's Jeanine Pirro said, "Members of the FBI and the Department of Justice—some of whom ended up on Bob Mueller's team to prosecute Donald Trump—did everything they could to exonerate Hillary Clinton for her crimes and incriminate Donald Trump with a nonexistent crime," adding that they should be "led out in cuffs."

Rep. Jim Jordan (R-OH), someone who later faced his own scandal when he was accused of turning a blind eye to the alleged sexual molestation of athletes during his tenure as an assistant coach at Ohio State, was all too happy to amplify the Strzok-Page conversations and formulate a conclusion about what it all meant. (An investigation into the Ohio State matter would later conclude there was no hard evidence Jordan had committed wrongdoing.) Appearing on Pirro's show, Jordan claimed that Trump was the victim of dark forces who could not accept the fact that Trump was the duly elected president, insisting that Trump had prevailed "in spite of the Republican establishment being against him, the Democrats being against him, the elite media being against him, and the FBI and Justice Department being against him."

The problem was, this was all nonsense. Although Pirro billed herself as a judge, she was certainly not going to wait for the IG to finish its investigation before rendering a verdict. Yes, the FBI had declined to recommend prosecuting Clinton and was actively working to investigate Trump, but there was no indication that either action was politically motivated. The Page-Strzok text messages were awful from a public relations standpoint, but the independent inspector general (who saw the entire body of evidence, not just select text messages) had not yet concluded that there was any wrongdoing by FBI officials based on their personal political beliefs.

Trump's enablers were so singularly focused on portraying the president as a victim, few of them paused to focus on the true threat at hand: the government of Russia had worked to interfere in the sacred US democratic system, and members of Trump's campaign may have been witting participants. This was a flashing-red national security issue. However, Trump's team continued to appear less concerned with protecting the nation than they were with protecting their president.

In order to appreciate the assistance Trump received during the Russia scandal from right-wing media outlets like Fox News, one need only look to how Nixon fared during Watergate. Although, like Trump, Nixon had congressional allies, in the early 1970s there was no major media outlet where opinion hosts could verbally assault law enforcement and attempt to manipulate the public into believing the president was a victim of abusive investigators. As Nixon's White House counsel John Dean told me, "I have little doubt in my mind that Watergate might have turned out differently if there had been a Fox News."

The revelation of the Strzok-Page messages created an avalanche of fresh accusations. Leadership on the committees now seemed certain that the Steele dossier, political consulting firm Fusion GPS, and officials inside the Justice Department and the FBI were all part of some enormous government conspiracy to elect Hillary Clinton and hurt Donald Trump. The right-wing spin machine was all too happy to keep fueling the narrative of an out-of-control deep state. For those of us in government, it would have been laughable if it weren't such a serious accusation. We prayed that the inspector general would hurry and complete his work.

JUNE 14, 2018, was judgment day for the FBI—that day of the release of the IG's findings. Since January 2017, my former colleagues and I had been yearning for the inspector general's office to finish its investigation and set the record straight about the work we had done and were attempting to continue to do. There was no question that the report would at times be critical of bureau leadership in its findings, but there was no doubt in my mind that a full review of the FBI's work would help reinstill the public confidence that Trump was working to destroy.

No longer with the FBI, I was now a full-time member of CNN's national security team. I have a dual role at CNN: I serve as an analyst, helping viewers understand complex intelligence issues from the perspective of a former practitioner, and I report on crime-and-justice breaking news stories. We knew release of the report was imminent. As I waited to digest and then help explain its findings to the American people, earpiece lodged in my ear at CNN's DC bureau, political operatives aligned with the president were getting ready to do battle. Regardless of what the report actually said, I knew they would soon fill the airwaves and attempt to portray the FBI as Trump's enemy. At precisely 2:00 p.m. Eastern Daylight Time, the IG's report came out. I quickly climbed into a chair in front of the camera.

One of the key conclusions Inspector General Michael Horowitz made was that, although he had uncovered examples of apparent political bias in the text messages between Strzok and Page, there was no evidence that this bias had actually impacted agents' actions in the Clinton investigation. On the air, I began by offering the few key takeaways I had by then digested, explaining that this was a day of reckoning for the FBI and that it appeared as though investigators had indeed found wrongdoing by some inside the bureau. In order to provide crucial context, I also explained that it was key to distinguish between *criminal* wrongdoing (which the president and his allies had been claiming for quite some time) and violating Justice Department policies, which, although not great, was a far cry from accusing someone of breaking the law. I said that although the report was very critical of certain individuals, the political attacks over the past year from those who were calling the FBI corrupt and criminals were not borne out by the assessments of the IG.

Although I'd expected pushback from Trumpworld, I was wholly unprepared for the collision that followed. I found myself debating a Trump supporter who was calling FBI employees "swamp rats" before he had even had a chance to fully read the report. I held my ground. At the end of the day, I wasn't there simply to defend law enforcement, but to defend the concept of institutions of justice being free from outside political influence. I was there to defend the American public's ability to hear the truth about what their national security agencies were up to—warts and all—without being manipulated by undue propaganda.

To be sure, the IG's report was scathing. The inspector general's office wasn't there to hand out gold stars. It took its mission of uncovering policy violations by employees seriously and came to some uncomfortable conclusions. For one, the IG concluded that Comey was "extraordinary and insubordinate" in his unilateral decision to hold a press conference in July 2016 to announce his conclusion in the Clinton case, and that his decision later that October to inform Congress that the case was being reopened was "a serious error of judgment." However, the IG also found that Comey's decisions weren't motivated by political bias.

The report was also damning in that we all learned that the Strzok-Page text messages were even worse than we'd thought. Strzok was known throughout the organization as a talented investigator, and had become a punching bag for Trump, but there was no question he had also exercised serious lapses in judgment. In a dramatic showdown, one month later, he would testify before Congress in a hearing filled with fiery exchanges with Republican legislators who seemed certain, despite the conclusions of the IG, that Strzok was a deep-state operative. The hearing was a circus act, with Republicans and Democrats yelling at each other and over each other, with the witness sitting mostly calm throughout until he just couldn't take it anymore and lashed out at his inquisitors.

Although I concurred with many of my former colleagues that a good agent had made bad decisions, I found it horrifying to watch House Republicans striving for a sound bite and a pound of flesh. The most embarrassing stunt during this hearing came from Rep. Louie Gohmert (R-TX), who, looking at Strzok, called the FBI agent's behavior a "disgrace." "I've talked to FBI agents around the country," Gohmert continued. "You've embarrassed them. You've embarrassed yourself."

I knew there was no way FBI agents around the country were calling Gohmert to express their dismay. It was reminiscent of the claim White House Press Secretary Sarah Sanders made after Comey's firing, when she'd insisted that FBI employees were reaching out to tell her thank you. These were lies.

But Gohmert wasn't finished. As he scowled at Strzok, he proceeded to ask, "I can't help but wonder when I see you looking there with a little smirk, how many times did you look so innocent into your wife's eye and lie to her about Lisa Page?"

The hearing room erupted in shouting, with members on both sides of the aisle stupefied by Gohmert's low blow.

"You need your medication," Rep. Bonnie Watson (D-NJ) said to her colleague from Texas.

"I have always told the truth," Strzok said with conviction as Gohmert sat glaring at him. "The fact that you would accuse me otherwise, the fact that you would question whether or not that was the sort of look I would engage in with a family member who I have acknowledged hurting, goes more to a discussion about your character and what you stand for and what is going inside you."

"Total sh*t show," a senior FBI agent texted to me as I sat in front of the camera in the CNN newsroom, waiting for the hearing to wrap up. "These people are a complete and total disgrace."

Although Gohmert was widely ridiculed for his theatrics, the congressman would again cause jaws to drop in a later hearing in February 2019 when the successor to Jeff Sessions, Acting Attorney General Matthew Whitaker, sat before him testifying about the Mueller investigation. Again championing the deep-state myth, Gohmert said the Justice Department should look into the personal beliefs of career DOJ employees and determine whether they are loyal to the attorney general and the president. Setting aside the fact that career employees don't pledge fealty to any one person, Gohmert's rhetoric smacked of McCarthyism and the widely detested actions of the House Un-American Activities Committee in the 1950s, which ruined the reputations of career government employees and average citizens by raising the suspicion of whether they were disloyal to the United States.

Gohmert went on to name several people he suspected were plotting against the administration. I personally knew some of the people he referenced. They were my friends and among the most talented and honorable professionals I have ever had the opportunity to serve alongside. This was nothing but political grandstanding.

IN A SURPRISING development, Peter Strzok was fired about a month after his contentious House hearing. The move was stunning both because Strzok was relatively close to being able to retire and draw a pension and also because the punishment meted out by FBI deputy director David Bowdich was more severe than what the bureau's internal affairs team had recommended, that Strzok be demoted and suspended for sixty days. Lisa Page had quietly resigned from the FBI in May 2018.

By this time, Andrew McCabe, who had served as deputy director and acting director of the FBI, had also been fired by the Justice Department, after the DOJ inspector general found that he had lied to investigators when asked about his role in a media leak. The McCabe case was shocking in the haphazard way it was handled—he was fired by Jeff Sessions just hours before he was eligible to retire—but few FBI employees with whom I spoke were able to rationalize keeping him on if he had in fact been untruthful with the IG. All employees, from their first day on the job, are sensitized to the fact that their credibility is their currency in the bureau; if they risk their integrity, they are no longer of value to the organization. McCabe's case had then been referred to prosecutors in Washington for possible criminal charges, making it even more difficult for him to remain in place. I greatly admire McCabe and his decades of service to the FBI. He is a good man and was a fine leader. However, absent some new revelation contradicting the findings of the highly respected inspector general, it is difficult for me to stare at the facts and call his dismissal excessive or unfair.

I have talked quite a bit with former FBI colleagues since the Strzok firing, and most seem to come to the same conclusion when it comes to how strict Bowdich was in his case. It is worth noting that I know Bowdich personally and served under him in a number of positions in Los Angeles and Washington. He is a man of the utmost integrity and is that rare breed that has zero patience for politics, either within the building or without. There are few things I can say for certain in life, but the idea that Bowdich would make a personnel decision due to politics—including one as high-profile as that involving Peter Strzok—is ludicrous. Rather, not only would he have factored in the specific aspects of Strzok's case and the fact that Strzok had acted so recklessly, but Bowdich would also have considered the larger message a lighter punishment would send to the rank and file. How could every other employee be expected to exercise good judgment and act in accordance with the organization's values if bureau leadership had allowed Strzok to keep his job after causing so much damage?

In the end, Strzok was guilty of the cardinal sin all employees know to avoid. As author Ronald Kessler said in his authoritative work *The Bureau: The Secret History of the FBI*, J. Edgar Hoover's mantra was "Don't embarrass the bureau." It is an expression carved into the psyche of every agent who carries the FBI badge. By violating policies and threatening the credibility of the institution, Strzok had rendered himself ineffective. There was no precedent for how FBI leadership should handle such a situation. So they created their own.

EVEN AFTER THEIR professional demise, McCabe, Page, and Strzok would remain key targets of attack by Trumpworld—symbols of law enforcement gone rogue. Although it was a clever PR strategy for the president and his enablers to cherry-pick the inspector general's report and use it to attack Robert Mueller, the Department of Justice, and the FBI, the American public should understand that in the US judicial system, the government has to show its work. If the Mueller investigation were indeed a witch hunt full of people conspiring to illegally bring down Trump, whatever evidence it used to criminally charge people would eventually have to be laid out in a court of law for a jury of our peers to review. The entire line of attack that investigators were somehow going to target Trump and not have to explain in detail everything they found was a sham.

If I haven't already debunked the deep-state anti-Trump conspiracy thoroughly enough, I will make one last key point here. Take yourself back to 2016, when the FBI was quietly investigating members of the Trump campaign without the world knowing. It was Crossfire Hurricane inside the bureau, clear sailing outside. No one knew about it. If Comey, McCabe, Strzok, and Page had intended to hurt Donald Trump and help Hillary Clinton, why did no one reveal that the FBI had an ongoing counterintelligence investigation into the Trump campaign? Such a public revelation would have been a death knell to the Republican nominee. Lights out. Campaign over. Yet none of it was made public. Why not? Because the men and women of the FBI who were conducting and overseeing the investigation understood their professional duty to do their national security work in secret.

## CHAPTER 14

# Felons and Flippers

WHEN I'D GREETED Robert Mueller at FBI headquarters back in May 2017, the newly appointed special counsel was returning to an agency in turmoil: James Comey had been fired in an effort to thwart an active investigation, and the FBI was forced to deal with institutional decapitation while fulfilling its commitment to holding the powerful to account. With so many of us alarmed by Donald Trump's behavior as it related to Russia, the new acting director, Andrew McCabe, quickly launched an investigation to determine whether the president of the United States had obstructed justice and himself posed a threat to national security. The American people may be numb to it now, but it bears repeating: the president of the United States was under investigation for possibly colluding with a hostile government, for perhaps being a Russian asset himself. This was not Tom Clancy; it was the real world.

As Mueller assumed control of an already wide-ranging probe into Trumpworld, he immediately became a target of attack—and an almost mythical creature who some segments of the country hoped would save our democracy.

Mueller's credentials are impeccable: he served and was wounded in Vietnam, spent a career at the highest levels of the Justice Department and FBI under both Republican and Democratic administrations, and answered the call to return to public life in order to help investigate a potential counterintelligence threat. But despite the fact that some looked to Mueller as their savior, I continually cautioned people publicly and privately that Mueller would only go as far as the evidence took him.

During Mueller's tenure as FBI director, I spent plenty of time with him. He was never one to wax poetic about the state of the world, and only rarely did I hear him speak in hypotheticals. He was hardwired to uncovering the truth, not opinions of the truth. "How do we know that?" was a question he asked often when presented with a piece of information. The director received case briefings throughout the day and was known to pry into the tiniest of details, such as the color of a particular car or what a criminal had been wearing when they committed the act. The moment he sensed someone was winging an answer rather than distinguishing between what was known and unknown, he would eat them alive. I was amused later in my career when I was set to brief him on a major counterterrorism investigation I had been working, and one of his assistants (who did not know I had previously worked in the director's office) called to warn me of the danger of offering Mueller anything other than the facts known at the time.

This quality is important to highlight because it shows the inner core of a prosecutor whom the president and his allies have painted as a criminal. They would falsely have the public believe that the special counsel is a conflicted and corrupt partisan who was leading a witch hunt and making things up to destroy the Trump presidency. As we now know, Mueller's report showed the opposite. His ultimate commitment all along was to lead his team in a manner consistent with the rule of law. He did not overstep. He did not overreach. Faced with extraordinary external pressure, he and his team kept their heads down in a way that should make all Americans proud.

On April 18, 2019, the bulk of Mueller's work came to an end and a redacted version of his findings was made public. After nearly two years of investigation, the special counsel was unable to conclude that members of the Trump team willfully colluded with the Russian government, even as the report laid bare numerous questionable actions by those associated with the campaign. In the end, when presented with the opportunity to receive help from a foreign adversary, no one in Trumpworld had picked up the phone to call the FBI.

The issue of whether the president had obstructed justice was also left unsettled by Mueller. Although the new attorney general, William Barr, had done his best to portray Trump as innocent, the matter was actually much more nuanced. Adhering to the Justice Department's long-held norm that a sitting president cannot be indicted, Mueller chose not to pursue whether Trump had actually broken the law. In my view, he was leaving that question up to Congress, which would then have to decide whether the ten instances of presidential interference outlined in the Mueller report constituted impeachable offenses. Although Trump claimed total victory after the report's release, these haunting words will continue to cast a dark cloud over his presidency: "[W]hile this report does not conclude that the president committed a crime, it also does not exonerate him."

One aspect of the Mueller report was quietly celebrated among current and former FBI officials with whom I spoke: the exposure of lies told by White House press secretary Sarah Sanders. After Comey's firing, she had stood in the briefing room and announced that "countless" FBI employees had personally contacted her, expressing their appreciation for Comey's firing. This was no slip of the tongue. When pressed by reporters, she had doubled and tripled down on the lie, insisting that there were even text messages and emails between her and FBI personnel. Those of us who had watched her remarks live knew this was nonsense. No bureau employee— Republican or Democrat—would engage in such a blatantly political act. When finally questioned by Mueller, under the penalty of perjury, Sanders admitted her original comments were baseless. In other words, she had lied.

As we look back upon Donald Trump's assault on Mueller, DOJ, and the FBI, there is one central question that ties everything together: Why all the lies? The president and spokespeople such as Rudy Giuliani and Sarah Sanders lied repeatedly to the American people. Many Trump-connected associates found themselves under arrest for lying to the FBI. People went to prison! Although Mueller's work is now finished, we cannot lose sight of the unprecedented corruption and deceit his investigators unearthed while simply working to protect the nation. When I served as a special agent, I never encountered a subject who actively worked to obstruct an investigation that would have proven them innocent. Lying to the FBI was one crime that suggested the existence of other crimes. People in Trumpworld have lied at every turn. The president's allies have tried to minimize all the deception as "process crimes." But process crimes are still crimes. What were they hiding? And by "they," I mean the seven (as of this writing) Trump associates convicted of criminal activity.

IT WAS EARLY August 2018, and the first trial stemming from Robert Mueller's special counsel probe was now underway. Christopher Flood was growing increasingly impatient with the gathering gaggle of mischief-makers. As the lanky sentry paraded down the hallway inside the federal courthouse in Alexandria, Virginia, he stared at the throng of reporters and bystanders who had assembled for the trial of former Trump campaign manager Paul Manafort. As Flood strode past me, I stood in line next to my CNN colleague Marshall Cohen and a friend, Carrie Johnson from National Public Radio. Together, we marveled at the magnitude of the moment: one of the president's key aides facing prosecution on corruption charges.

As more and more people showed up, all hoping to gain entry and watch history in the making, the volume of chatter had grown to a roar in the narrow, echoing passageway outside the courtroom. The chaos was pierced by a bellow from the frustrated court security officer.

"Folks!" Flood thundered. "Keep it down, please. The judge is right on the other side of this door trying to prepare. He doesn't need any of this!"

For me, his words brought home the gravity of what was about to transpire. We were now on the judge's turf: in the middle of President Trump's endless efforts to undermine his own administration's law enforcement agencies, we had entered a territory that might be safe from Trump's bluster.

As we filed into the courtroom and took our seats, I looked to my left and saw a group of FBI agents gathering, including some familiar faces. A pair of agents were dragging in two carts containing boxes of documents and evidence. In those boxes lay many of the goods Mueller's team had collected during months of work, including records seized from Manafort's home.

As the lead prosecutor stood in silence in a dark-blue suit, hands resting on the table in front of him, Manafort's defense team sat nearby whispering to each other. In walked the barrel-chested former Trump campaign chair, who smiled and offered a two-finger salute to his team of lawyers before taking his seat in front of me. It was amazing how carefree he seemed.

I was always curious to witness the body language of defendants. When facing serious federal charges, people typically have a hard time hiding their discomfort. Manafort seemed unfazed. Although he had been sitting in jail before his trial, he appeared no worse for wear.

This trial would be a key test for Mueller's ability to follow the facts and ferret out alleged corruption. It would also be a reminder of what was at stake in Trump's war on law enforcement. As I looked at the sober expressions on the faces of the six men and six women on the jury, I knew that each of these citizens had come into court that day with a predetermined opinion of the FBI, and this view would dictate, at least in part, whether they believed the government's case. If Trump succeeded in damaging the credibility of the bureau, the repercussions might be felt in jury boxes around the country.

"Oyez, oyez, oyez!" a court staffer declared, offering the traditional opening phrase for federal proceedings, adding, "God save this court." *God save this country*, I thought.

The trial of Paul Manafort was unlike anything I had ever seen. The presiding judge, T. S. Ellis, a cantankerous man in his late seventies, ran roughshod over the prosecution. He frequently demanded that government lawyers pick up the pace. When prosecutors asked a witness to read a particular invoice or tax document aloud, Judge Ellis would balk and insist that the jury could read it for themselves. "Let's move on" became his go-to phrase. At one point, I found myself laughing along with the rest of those in attendance as the curmudgeonly jurist finally demonstrated he was at wits' end with the thoroughness of the federal prosecutors. "You know, the more I can do to shorten this thing, the better," Ellis said in exasperation. "You get to go home, and I get to go home!"

The judge's behavior was clearly annoying the prosecutors, who made the mistake of allowing their facial expressions to betray them. Noting the periodic eye-rolling from the attorneys, the judge said such disrespectful behavior was akin to saying, *Why do we have to put up with this idiot judge?* "Don't do that," he said. "Rein in your facial expressions and proceed." The aggressive way the judge treated prosecutors is important to note, because it made clear to all of us watching that Manafort's prosecution would not be a slam dunk.

After three weeks of hearing from witnesses and reviewing mountains of evidence, it was finally time for the jury to render a verdict. Reading the decision aloud, the court clerk announced the word "guilty" a total of eight times—on charges of tax evasion, hiding bank accounts, and bank fraud. Although members of the jury would be unable to reach a verdict on ten other charges, they were fundamentally convinced by the Mueller team's presentation that the former Trump aide had defrauded the government of millions of dollars. And as the trial had moved forward, the American people were reminded that the man Trump had chosen to run his campaign was also someone who had sidled up to dictators around the world in order to make a buck. His résumé read like a who's who of despots, with clients including shady characters in Ukraine, the Philippines, Angola, and Zaire. The millions of dollars he had attempted to hide had finally been exposed.

Following the verdict, the president opted to slam his own Justice Department. Speaking just hours after the announcement in court, Trump lashed out. "Paul Manafort's a good man," he insisted. "It's a witch hunt, and it's a disgrace. But this has nothing to do [with] what they started out looking for Russians involved in our campaign—there were none."

That night, at a rally in West Virginia, he continued the attack. "Where is the collusion?" Trump asked the crowd. "You know they're still looking for collusion."

Although the Manafort criminal activity exposed by Mueller was unrelated to Russia, it did fall within the larger purview of his mandate to also pursue other federal crimes unearthed in his collusion investigation. As a top official who had been a subject in the original Crossfire Hurricane investigation, Manafort had potentially stood to serve as an important cooperator for the government if he'd chosen to play ball. But he had not, so Mueller's team moved forward with a full prosecution.

The proceedings in Virginia represented only the first of Manafort's criminal trials. Prosecutors in the District of Columbia were beginning their own case against the former Trump aide on other charges. Less than a month after his first trial, Manafort told prosecutors that he was now willing to assist them in the Russia investigation and signed a plea deal agreeing to assist the government "fully, truthfully, completely, and forthrightly."

However, as convicted criminals are wont to do, Manafort continued his pattern of deception, even after he'd agreed to cooperate. Two and a half months after signing the plea deal, Mueller abruptly terminated it, saying that the former campaign chair had breached his plea agreement and committed additional federal crimes "by lying to the Federal Bureau of Investigation and the Special Counsel's Office on a variety of subject matters," Mueller's team told the court.

A day later, the *New York Times* reported that Manafort's team had also been double-dealing—pretending to cooperate with Mueller while also briefing the White House on details of what the defendant had been telling the special counsel team. Although not technically illegal, it did appear highly deceptive.

Mueller was now ready to wash his hands of Manafort. A federal judge confirmed the breach of the plea agreement, and the case was referred back to court for sentencing. In March 2019, Manafort was sentenced to seven and a half years in prison.

THE CASE OF George Papadopoulos also took a bizarre twist, which I would experience firsthand when the former foreign-policy adviser to the Trump campaign mistakenly decided I might be a sympathetic ear to his conspiratorial rantings. Although he'd pleaded guilty to lying to the FBI about his involvement with Josef Mifsud, the Russia-linked academic who had suggested to him that Moscow might have dirt on Hillary Clinton,

Papadopoulos changed course and apparently decided the victim card might instead be the ticket to both image rehabilitation and fortune. About a year after he expressed remorse for deceiving investigators attempting to probe the Trump campaign's ties to Russia, he became a proponent of the idea that the entire operation was a setup. He claimed that Mifsud had been working for Western intelligence agencies the whole time and had actually been sent after him in an effort to entrap a Trump aide. Possibly attempting to get in on the "witch hunt" act, he would embrace the idea of a rogue deep state and launch a TV and social media PR campaign to attack the intelligence community.

When Papadopoulos was sentenced to two weeks in prison for lying to investigators, he petitioned the court to delay going to prison, pending the decision in a separate lawsuit by a person linked to longtime Trump confidant Roger Stone. That case was seeking to question the legitimacy of the entire Mueller investigation. Faced with a defendant who had expressed remorse before a federal judge but who was now busy spreading conspiracy theories that ran counter to his original admission in court, Mueller worked to defeat Papadopoulos's request, citing some of Papadopoulos's incendiary tweets in the process. A federal judge was unmoved by the former Trump campaign aide's claim and refused the delay.

On November 26, Papadopoulos reported to federal prison to begin serving his short sentence. But just beforehand, he reached out to me, after reading my analysis of his case. Our conversation began on Twitter and continued via private messaging. Papadopoulos wanted to make sure that I, now a member of the media, knew how badly he believed he had been treated by the FBI.

"America is waking up to this fake Russia narrative," he said. "When the FBI fails to disclose to a Federal Court that Joseph Mifsud was western intelligence, not Russian, then you see how corrupt this is. The narrative is upended."

I could not help but be curious about whether he was a nut, a liar, or maybe a little of both. What I couldn't make out was how a corrupt FBI leadership team, the false notion that he was suggesting, could convince line-level agents working the investigation to go along with their sinister plan. I posed this question to Papadopoulos.

He was "just laying out the facts," he told me in a private direct message on Twitter. "I love the FBI and our intel agencies," he insisted, "but the way they were weaponized along with the British and Australians for political purposes . . . can never be repeated."

Trying to drill down on the bizarre claim that rank-and-file FBI agents would go along with a mysterious plot by senior FBI leaders, I pressed him on his experience with the agents who had arrested and interviewed him. He simply insisted that he was "violently arrested at an airport," adding, "unless people get arrested all the time with no arrest warrants and their bags searched without approval in this country then there's nothing to investigate. But that's not how things happen at the federal level, and you know that as a former agent."

He had completely lost me. I think what he was trying to say was that he was illegally arrested and had his bags searched without his authorization. Unfortunately for Papadopoulos, his own lawyer refuted this claim, insisting that agents "had probable cause" to arrest the former Trump aide when he stepped off an airplane in Washington. "What they did was absolutely lawful," his lawyer said.

And there was another aspect of the investigation that was being covered up, Papadopoulos told me. "I was never really under investigation for Russia," he said. "It was all about Israel. Why? I have no idea. Seems all very political."

I pressed him on the new angle. He claimed that his first interview with the FBI was all about Israel until he brought up Mifsud. "And then all hell breaks loose," he said. "So lots about my case people have no idea about."

It was difficult to assess all that Papadopoulos was claiming, and whether he actually believed it. I was also agnostic on his claims that he had been targeted by Western intelligence agencies. *So what?* was my initial thought. US and foreign law enforcement counterparts liaise all the time in order to share intelligence and plan joint operations. I've coordinated a multitude of operations with international partners, which are not inherently sinister.

If the FBI was working to determine whether the Trump team was in bed with the Russians and had enlisted the help of international partners to that end, it seemed the system was working as it should.

I came to believe that Papadopoulos's end goal was probably to become a cause célèbre of fringe segments of the far right, who had, sadly, been manipulated before by Team Trump. What else would there be for him to do? He was a convicted felon whose reputation had been stained by his association with Trump.

"THAT'S RIGHT. LOCK her up!" Michael Flynn famously yelled onstage in Cleveland at the 2016 Republican National Convention. The retired Army lieutenant general was calling for the extralegal violation of Hillary Clinton's right to due process and the imprisonment of a political opponent. However, it was he who would find himself looking at the possibility of staring through the bars of a prison cell, a convicted felon who would join the large club of Trump associates who had run afoul of the law.

On at least ten occasions throughout his accomplished career, as he rose from junior Army officer to national security adviser, Flynn would have pledged an oath to support and defend the US Constitution. Explicit in that oath was a commitment to "bear true faith and allegiance" to the rule of law. He failed to do both. Flynn's case was interesting, not just because he had pleaded guilty to lying to the FBI but because, like Papadopoulos, he would take a page from Trump's playbook and depict himself as an unfortunate victim of criminals inside the FBI.

In a December 2018 defense memo presented to the courts, Flynn's lawyers attempted to convince a federal judge to spare the disgraced former Trump official from serving jail time, citing his personal contrition and ongoing cooperation with Special Counsel Robert Mueller's Russia investigation. While it was standard practice for defendants to seek reduced sentences in exchange for cooperation, Flynn went a step further, insinuating that his legal troubles were all the FBI's fault, using a three-pronged approach: suggesting impropriety because FBI agents who interviewed him didn't tell him that lying was wrong; manipulating the public into believing that investigators had originally believed Flynn was innocent; and, claiming that because Flynn wasn't offered a lawyer, the bureau was breaking the law.

Using a tactic that surely made members of the armed forces around the world shudder in disbelief, Flynn's lawyers and his supporters insinuated wrongdoing on the part of the FBI because the agents conducting his interview reportedly did not warn him that making false statements to government agents was punishable by up to five years in federal prison. As a senior intelligence official who no doubt signed countless forms under penalty of perjury throughout his career, no one needed to tell Michael Flynn that lying to the FBI was illegal. And putting legalities aside for a moment, it is simply abhorrent for anyone who once wore the uniform to suggest that they needed to be reminded of the importance of candor, honor, and integrity. Or, as Mueller unleashed in a scathing rebuttal memo: "A sitting National Security Advisor, former head of an intelligence agency, retired Lieutenant General, and 33-year veteran of the armed forces knows he should not lie to federal agents. He does not need to be warned it is a crime to lie to federal agents to know the importance of telling them the truth."

Four days after Mueller's scolding, Flynn appeared back inside the Prettyman Federal Courthouse for his sentencing hearing, to finally learn the judgment of the court about whether he would serve prison time or simply receive probation. The hearing did not go as Flynn might have hoped. Federal Judge Emmett Sullivan blasted Flynn and his illegal actions. "I want to be frank with you, this crime is very serious," said the judge. "I am not hiding my disgust, my disdain for your criminal offense," he added. He then launched into a serious line of questioning that directly refuted Flynn's original attack on the FBI.

The judged asked Flynn's attorney if his client believed he had been entrapped by the FBI. "No, Your Honor" came his reply.

Did Flynn know at the time of his interview that lying to the FBI was a crime? "I was aware," said the former lieutenant general.

Did Flynn wish to challenge the circumstances surrounding his interview? "No, Your Honor," he said.

At this point, the hearing took a strange turn as the judge wondered why a low-level person like George Papadopoulos would have to serve time in jail while Flynn, a former high-ranking government official, would be able to skate away without incarceration. Prosecutors had recommended little to no jail time, citing Flynn's extensive cooperation with government investigators, but the judge wasn't so sure. He asked if the defense would like to recess the hearing and think it over—perhaps search for additional areas of cooperation where Flynn might be helpful. Understanding that the judge was almost certainly about to send Flynn to jail, his lawyers concurred, and the hearing was recessed for three months.

On the morning of Flynn's original sentencing hearing, White House Press Secretary Sarah Sanders stood in front of the White House and attacked FBI agents. She said that Flynn had been "ambushed." Her attempt to paint Flynn as a victim and the FBI as the real criminals appeared to be a last-ditch effort to undermine the ongoing investigation into her boss.

At the hearing later that day, Flynn and his attorney refuted this line of attack, but that wasn't stopping Sanders. Standing in the White House press briefing room after the hearing was recessed, Sanders doubled down. With news that Flynn's lawyer had said Flynn was *not* entrapped by the FBI, a reporter asked if Sanders would like to revisit her early statements attacking the FBI.

"No," she said. "We don't have any reason to walk that back."

She was also asked whether the president had any concern that Flynn had lied to administration officials about his communications with the Kremlin. Incredibly, Sanders insisted that the matter had nothing to do with the president.

I was livid, not only at the attacks on the FBI from the White House, but also because Sanders was lying. I use that term advisedly because often-times I believe Sanders merely parroted lies told to her by other people—without knowing whether they are true or not—but in this instance she *knew* that what she was saying was untrue. Flynn and his lawyers had just contradicted her, yet she continued the line of attack on the bureau.

The next morning, I joined Joe Lockhart, White House press secretary during the Clinton administration, on the CNN set in New York to break down all of the lies from Sarah Sanders. Lockhart didn't hold back. This is someone who had been in the spotlight, speaking on behalf of a president who had faced impeachment. He said that the job was hard but added, "You have to adhere to the truth, and she has stopped doing this."

Lockhart then made a point that I had not fully appreciated until that moment. The job wasn't just to represent the White House, but to represent the United States to the entire world. He explained how the international community had historically looked upon the White House press secretary with respect—as a vessel to truthfully explain the actions of the United States. But Sanders had consistently failed in that endeavor by peddling lies. "We don't send out 'Baghdad Bob' or 'Tokyo Rose,'" he said, referring to the famous dishonest propagandists of foreign-policy lore. "We send out people the rest of the world can count on."

Another key player in the Russia investigation was Roger Stone, the self-described "dirty trickster" who had been involved in shady political operations for decades. He was also a longtime friend of Donald Trump. The pinstripe-wearing staple of DC's political swamp—who sports a tattoo of Richard Nixon across his back—came under scrutiny for his suspected role in helping to disseminate the stolen Democratic emails that had been hacked by Russian intelligence during the 2016 presidential campaign. Investigators worked to determine whether Stone and Jerome Corsi—a lesser-known peddler of conspiracy theories, ranging from questioning Obama's place of birth to suggesting that the Twin Towers collapsed in part due to explosives detonated from within—had been in contact with WikiLeaks founder Julian Assange in an effort to prompt the release of the emails. Stone was also an associate of Trump campaign aide Michael Caputo, who had previously worked for Russian president Boris Yeltsin. After both men had insisted they never had contacts with Russians about the 2016 campaign, the *Washington Post* later exposed an effort by the two men to meet with a suspected Russian national to gather dirt on Hillary Clinton, although the meeting didn't appear to be fruitful.

In January 25, 2019, Roger Stone was indicted by a federal grand jury on charges of lying to Congress, witness tampering, and obstruction, igniting a fresh round of attacks against Robert Mueller by Donald Trump and his allies. Early that morning, a large team of FBI agents had descended on Stone's home in Fort Lauderdale, taking the Trump associate into custody, followed by a search of his home for evidence. Caught on video by reporters from CNN, the arrest caused many on the far right to cry foul and suggest that the FBI was being heavy-handed in its show of force. Trump himself would balk at the way the arrest went down and help portray Stone as a victim.

The Stone arrest was, in fact, textbook. Agents brought with them enough personnel to surround his home and safely take the indicted subject into custody. Although Stone insisted he would have willingly turned himself in, the Mueller team thought otherwise and convinced a federal judge that Stone should not be given advance warning that he was under indictment because they feared he would flee and destroy evidence.

In addition to triggering the anti-FBI factions inside Trumpworld—who couldn't resist slamming the bureau and labeling its agents out of control—there was another aspect of the Stone arrest that was especially enlightening. At issue was how CNN, the lone network to obtain footage of the arrest, had been able to position a team of journalists at Stone's house before the FBI arrived. Trump and his acolytes smelled a rat, and claimed Mueller or the FBI had tipped off CNN in order to put on a show. The conspiracy theorists went absolutely berserk. In reality, the reason producer David Shortell had been in place was because our team had noticed unusual grand jury activity and suspected Stone's arrest might be imminent.

Then I got dragged into the affair personally. Right-wing trolls on social media had been suggesting that, since I worked at CNN, someone inside the FBI must have tipped *me* off to the arrest. This morphed into a narrative that it was actually me staking out Stone's home rather than my colleague. I sort of laughed off the conspiracy until former Arkansas governor Mike Huckabee threw gasoline on the situation by blasting the conspiracy and my photo out to his one million Twitter followers. All hell broke loose. I received all kinds of threats, including messages from people wanting to harm my dog. Huckabee eventually took down his tweet, but not before it had been retweeted and likely viewed thousands and thousands of times. Roger Stone then went on Infowars and called me out by name, spreading the lie that I had been outside his house when he was arrested.

This one event was symbolic of much of what the FBI and Mueller had suffered over the past two years: fearmongers making things up, which in turn get picked up, repeated, and amplified. The truth is, I had been sleeping soundly at my home in Los Angeles when the Stone arrest went down, and didn't learn about it until my producer, Mary Kay Mallonee, called to pass along the news. But that inconvenient truth didn't stop Mike Huckabee and Roger Stone from shamelessly peddling lies that risked my personal safety.

Although Michael Caputo would escape any criminal charges, life for Roger Stone and Jerome Corsi could turn out very differently.

WITHOUT QUESTION, THE person in the Justice Department's crosshairs who poses the single greatest risk to the president is the man who had stood by his side for years, overseeing nearly every aspect of Trump's business ventures—a man who had once insisted that he would take a bullet for the president. After being targeted by Robert Mueller and the US Attorney's Office for the Southern District of New York, Michael Cohen made the fateful decision to become a cooperator and assist investigators.

In August 2018, Cohen admitted in federal court that Trump had directed him to pay two women hush money in exchange for their silence about affairs with the real estate mogul. His admission came as he pleaded guilty to violating campaign laws and a slew of other charges. Up to this point, many Americans suspected that Trump had lied when he told the press he didn't know anything about the payments, but it was not specifically clear that Trump himself had ordered the payment. Trump lashed out at Cohen's claims. "If anyone is looking for a good lawyer, I would strongly suggest that you don't retain the services of Michael Cohen!" the president tweeted.

Trump blasted people who decide to cooperate with authorities. "It's called 'flipping,' and it almost ought to be illegal," he said on Fox News. "I know all about flipping—thirty, forty years I have been watching flippers. Everything is wonderful, and then they get ten years in jail and they flip on whoever the next highest one is or as high as you can go."

The president was right about one thing here: investigators have long relied on government witnesses to help move investigations up the food chain to criminals in charge of conspiracies. However, his use of the term "flipper," and the disdain he was relaying about the basic mechanics of law enforcement investigations made him sound like a crook. Indeed, he was using the same terminology Mafia kingpins had used for decades in ridiculing those fighting crime.

As a former law enforcement officer, I was simply stunned at how much like a crime boss he was sounding. In my career, I had worked to recruit numerous sources and witnesses, and one of the biggest hurdles I would often have to overcome was convincing someone who knew about criminal activity that helping the government was actually a noble feat, helping to ensure public safety and maintain the rule of law. Here, we had a president trying to undermine it. Rather than sounding like an innocent man, he was sounding like a Mafia don.

On December 12, an emotional Michael Cohen was sentenced to three years in prison for his role in what the presiding judge labeled a "veritable smorgasbord" of criminal activity.

One of the major crimes that Cohen had admitted to was lying to Congress about potential business dealings between Trump's company and Russia during the 2016 campaign. Not only did this claim run counter to what Trump had previously stated—he had consistently insisted he had no business dealings with Russia, apart from his work running a beauty pageant in Moscow—but it also signaled something more sinister about Trump. During the campaign, he had publicly called for closer relations between the United States and Russia and an end to economic sanctions. What he failed to disclose to the public was that he was at that very same time working to build a Trump Tower in Moscow. His public statements about needing friendlier ties to Russia appeared to stem not from his desire to improve US foreign policy, but because he was secretly trying to persuade the Russian government to approve his building project.

Following the plea deal, Donald Trump had stood before the cameras on the South Lawn and called Michael Cohen "weak," while at the same time describing Paul Manafort as "brave." (Many saw this as a signal to Manafort to continue to hold out and a pardon might be forthcoming.) And then, using typical Trumpian verbal jujitsu, the president publicly claimed not only that Cohen was a liar, but also that the activities he was lying about were not actually illegal. Everyone knew about the Trump Tower dealings, he lied. This display in front of the White House smacked of the linguistic leaps in logic Trump had become famous for—rationalizing his behavior while minimizing its impact.

In the end, Trump's former fixer was sentenced to three years in federal prison.

PERHAPS THE MOST significant aspect of Mueller's work—overshadowed by all the White House palace intrigue—was the effort by his team to identify and help neutralize a hostile foreign power that was undermining US national security. While the president continually made everything about himself, the special counsel understood that the threat posed by Russia went far beyond anything related specifically to Trump. Not only was Mueller a veteran of the FBI but he had once overseen the bureau's counterintelligence operations, so he knew the threat and he was no stranger to Russia's intelligence services. As his investigation would find, Kremlin operatives had successfully interfered in the 2016 presidential election using an arsenal of tactics that included cyber intrusions, identity theft, and sophisticated influence operations.

It was difficult to predict when Mueller would make a move—his operation was airtight, with no leaks—but when he struck, he often did so in dramatic fashion. His targeting of Russian actors came in two major waves. The first occurred on February 16, 2018, when, out of the blue, the Justice

Department announced the indictment of thirteen Russian nationals and three companies for their alleged involvement in election interference. The group was associated with the innocuously named Internet Research Agency—a Kremlin operation with the "strategic goal to sow discord in the US political system," according to the indictment.

Since 2014, the organization had been creating false online personas and social media accounts with the goal of spreading disinformation and chaos in the United States. Taking advantage of the ubiquitous nature of platforms like Facebook and Twitter, the group preyed on average voters and attempted to sway their voting decisions by disseminating false information harmful to Hillary Clinton and beneficial to Donald Trump. The document says that staff members working for the group's troll farms— banks of desks and computers where employees would manage multiple false aliases—were told to "use any opportunity to criticize Hillary and the rest (except Sanders and Trump—we support them)."

The Mueller indictment was stunning in the amount of detail it included about the systematic effort of Russian operatives to manipulate public opinion in the United States. Although not a shot was fired, many deemed this covert psychological influence operation to be information warfare.

The Russian troll farms were not the only enterprise Mueller sought to unravel. He also pointed the finger directly at Russia's military intelligence service—the GRU—in a criminal indictment he unsealed in July 2018 against twelve GRU officers charged with managing a sustained effort to hack the Democratic National Committee and other party affiliates. This was the group that had stolen Democratic emails and worked to release them to the public under the online pseudonym Guccifer 2.0, and later through WikiLeaks. Although experts largely believed it unlikely the US government would ever get its hands on the indicted conspirators, Mueller's surprising court filing did three things: publicized and boxed in the foreign intelligence operatives, making it highly unlikely they'll ever be able to travel again to any place in the world that enjoys an extradition treaty with the United States; unearthed the sheer scale of the Kremlin's efforts to attack the US electoral process; and provided much-needed confidence

to the American public that the US national security community continued efforts to bring the perpetrators to justice, even if the president of the
United States was at the same time actively working to thwart the effort.

This indictment's release could not have come at a worse time for
Trump. The president was embarking on an international trip, which
included a much-anticipated meeting with Russian president Vladimir
Putin. Deputy Attorney General Rod Rosenstein had given the president a
heads-up about the coming indictments, which allowed Trump to launch
a preemptive strike and attempt to make news of his own by focusing on
the misdeeds of Peter Strzok and Lisa Page. "Public opinion has turned
strongly against the Rigged Witch Hunt and the 'Special' Counsel because
the public understands that there was no Collusion with Russia (so ridiculous)," Trump wrote during one of his tweetstorms, adding "The two FBI
lovers were a fraud against our Nation & that the only Collusion was with
the Dems!"

For me, this chapter was a turning point. Although many of us may
have become numb to these tirades, we cannot lose sight of what Trump
was trying to do. The president of the United States was working to con-
flate the failed judgment of two employees in their personal decisions with
the ongoing investigation into foreign interference. He *knew* the Justice
Department was about to announce serious charges against Russian intelligence operatives. An ordinary president would have chosen this moment to
sensitize the public to the grave threat posed by foreign intelligence officers.
Despite all the evidence and mounting indictments against Russia, Trump
remarkably chose to publicly doubt the assessments of the US intelligence
community.

It got worse. In a terrifying episode in Helsinki shortly after Mueller
had laid out in court filings the malicious efforts of Russia's intelligence
operatives, Trump stood next to Putin on the global stage and in effect
legitimized Russia's regime at the expense of the United States' own standing in the world. Thumbing his nose at the US intelligence community,
Trump sided with Putin over the assessments of our intelligence and law
enforcement professionals. "President Putin says it's not Russia," Trump

said, parroting the Kremlin's vacuous denials about the covert campaign our own government had unearthed.

Until this point, I had never really bought into the long-running narrative among current and former intelligence professionals that perhaps Trump's unwillingness to say nary a cross word about Putin stemmed from some type of leverage the Kremlin asserted over Trump. I'd assumed he was surrounded by corrupt actors who would sidle up to anyone to make a buck, including foreign spies, but I didn't actually believe he had been compromised by a foreign regime. It wasn't until that day in Helsinki that I finally became a believer. At every turn, Trump had rationalized, minimized, and excused atrocious actions by the Russians. His capitulation included issues involving election interference, Moscow's backing of the brutal regime in Syria, and Russia's attempts to murder defectors around the world. For many national security experts, President Trump had simply exhausted all reasonable explanation for behavior that consistently put the interests of Russia over those of the United States.

This was almost certainly a key reason behind his full-scale assault on Mueller and the FBI: he was afraid of what Mueller might find. A president with nothing to hide would have worked to help investigators in any way possible. He would have voluntarily submitted to a full interview and ordered everyone under him to do the same. He would have moved heaven and earth to ensure that the special counsel had whatever information was needed to ferret out threats from a hostile foreign government. But Trump chose to attack.

## CHAPTER 15

# Taken for Granted

DONALD TRUMP'S CAMPAIGN against those working to uphold the rule of law has been vicious. The president's supporters insist he is a "fighter" who never fails to punch back, but his efforts to subvert justice go far beyond mere self-defense. They are destructive. He has defiled the FBI when investigators have targeted him, and has sought to use the bureau to his advantage when politically convenient. His tactics have risked damaging public confidence in law enforcement in ways that may take a generation to repair. They have overshadowed *actual* challenges law enforcement agencies face, such as the serious mistrust of police in some minority communities that has resulted from instances of the improper use of force.

Since the intelligence abuses unearthed by Congress in the 1970s, our law enforcement and national security agencies have spent decades trying to reassure the public that these institutions have learned from the lessons of the past. Put simply, law and order breaks down when the public begins to question whether the system is rigged. And although our society is far from perfect, we have made great strides when it comes to increasing the mutual respect between citizens and those who enforce the law. That balance in trust is a very fragile thing.

To understand just how fragile, it helps to look to other places around the world where corruption and authoritarianism have caused populations to doubt whether law enforcement is truly on their side. While working overseas as an FBI agent, I experienced firsthand instances where law enforcement was largely seen as under the thumb of unscrupulous politicians. The resulting effect was a lack of public engagement—who would willingly help the police solve crime when the cops themselves might be crooks?—and an overall lack of respect for those who wear the badge.

This dynamic was on full display in one harrowing episode in 2011, when citizens in a tiny village in Southeast Asia had grown so distrustful of the police that not only would they resist helping investigators solve crime, but some would even turn their backs on an officer who lay bleeding in the street. My partner, Special Agent David Winsett, and I were conducting an overseas counterterrorism investigation, and we drove from our encampment inside a military base into town to see the local police chief. Suddenly, a man on a motorbike pulled alongside a police officer several cars in front of us, brandished a handgun, and opened fire. It happened in the blink of an eye, and the perpetrator sped off through heavy traffic and escaped. The officer stepped outside the car and slumped over. I lay on the horn, trying to get around the stopped traffic and closer to the incident.

Perhaps even worse than seeing a cop shot in front of us was observing that almost no one near the police vehicle rushed to render aid to the officer. Most bystanders averted their eyes and continued on their way. Fortunately, the incident happened near a hospital, so the cop's partner and another man dragged the wounded man back inside the vehicle and hit the gas, barreling over the median and into the hospital driveway, where medical personnel rushed him inside.

After determining there was nothing we could do, my partner and I continued on to the local police station. We weren't exactly shocked by what we had just witnessed, because murders and bombings happened in the area nearly every day, but it was depressing to witness up close the consequences of public resentment of law enforcement. I can still remember the police chief's face when I told him, "We're sorry to inform you, sir, but one of your men was just shot."

He snatched up the cell phone on his desk and dialed the hospital. In a couple of minutes, the news came, and he slowly set down the phone.

"He didn't make it," he said somberly.

FOR ME, IMPROVING the standing of law enforcement among various populations was not just a by-product of my specific investigations but came to be a mission in and of itself. As I progressed in my FBI career, I was tapped not only to work cases, but I was assigned to various embassies around the world as the bureau's acting representative to foreign governments. The role included liaising with foreign law enforcement, intelligence, and military personnel, as well as with my fellow US diplomatic representatives overseas. In my role, I helped embassy leadership coordinate new "rule of law" strategies, which would ensure that local investigations important to US interests were conducted not only rigorously but fairly. Our goal was to sensitize local authorities to the fact that it was not enough to solve a crime; they also had to conduct their investigations professionally and in a manner that engendered respect from the citizens they were sworn to serve.

In one country (which shall go unnamed, because it has progressed light-years ahead of where it was when I served on the ground), my FBI partner and I were given a tour of a local police facility and shown to an "interview room." The only fixture in sight was something akin to a dental chair in the middle of the room, with metal loops to secure foot shackles protruding from the floor. The place looked like a torture chamber.

"What the hell is this?" I asked my police counterpart, enunciating each word in the question to express my disgust.

"This is where we conduct our interrogations," he said.

I shook my head, pausing to collect my thoughts. Our team was strictly forbidden from conducting joint operations with any foreign entity that engaged in human rights abuses. But stomping out of the room and swiftly ending the relationship would have been a missed opportunity.

Over the course of the next few months, my colleagues and I secured US funding to build the foreign police agency an *actual* interview room and trained the local police force on how to conduct lawful and humane interviews. We knew that helping professionalize the police would also help instill public confidence in their efforts. By equipping our foreign partners and helping them improve their own standing among their constituents, we would in effect be safeguarding the United States from threats as well. The project was among the proudest accomplishments of my career.

IT IS VITAL that we study the detrimental effects of political interference and the lack of public faith in law enforcement, because much more than the reputation of cops is at stake. The safety of entire communities is on the line. This is what has made Donald Trump's war on our institutions of justice so alarming. By eroding public confidence, he is simultaneously making Americans less safe. I doubt his intention is to cause a more dangerous United States—he appears to be single-mindedly focused on keeping himself safe—but he must know by now that a by-product of his war is a corrosion of our justice system. Nevertheless, he persists. His tactics have been nothing short of authoritarian: bringing law enforcement to heel, discrediting an adversarial press, and manipulating public opinion. That is the authoritarian's script. And we have seen this movie before in other parts of the world.

During 2003, after the US military toppled Saddam Hussein, our country undertook the monumental task of helping Iraq to reestablish the rule of law in a society that for decades had only known life under the ironfisted reign of a dictator. One man central to that effort was Lieutenant General Mark Hertling, who retired later as a thirty-seven-year veteran of the US Army, whose career had culminated in the prestigious assignment of commanding general of US Army Europe. His experiences abroad help illustrate what is at stake here at home in the age of President Trump. Hertling served in Baghdad as assistant division commander of the 1st Armored Division, managing combat operations while also helping with rebuilding efforts. "We were not only fighting the fight," he told me, "but we were trying to establish the rule of law, the court systems."

Working with FBI agents and other experts assigned to the Coalition Provisional Authority, Hertling and his colleagues were trying to establish institutions of justice from the ground up. "As a brand-new one-star, this was my first taste of how countries that don't have those systems can be terrorized by autocratic rulers," he said. "We saw the results of what Saddam had done in order to establish a dictatorial rule with an authoritarian system."

Under Hussein, law enforcement, military, and intelligence professionals were extensions of the ruling regime. There was no transparency. It was not unusual for perceived enemies of the state to be thrown in jail, never to be seen again. With thirty thousand US troops and sixty thousand Iraqi troops under Hertling's command, one of his priorities was to build a police force that would not only be effective, but would garner confidence from a public that had lived in fear of law enforcement for generations.

"I was told to establish about ninety thousand Iraqi police officers," he said, a tremendous undertaking. "We built police academies in Mosul, Kirkuk, and Diyala, and started cranking out police officers in two-week courses, because we just needed that beat cop on the streets."

Hertling and his team knew that they would have only one opportunity to get it right. "It was a continual attempt to break down the lack of trust in the system, but also to build up the confidence in the societal norms we were trying to establish," he said. "It wasn't easy. One thing I'm sure you've heard some former military officials say is, 'We need to win their hearts and minds.' Well, I banned that expression from our division. I couldn't give a sh*t less about their hearts and minds. I'm talking about their trust and confidence."

Later in his career, he would witness the rebuilding of another society that had been ravaged not by war, but by a different kind of dictatorial regime. After being assigned to Europe in March 2011, Hertling was responsible for engaging with some forty-nine nations. One of those countries— the former Soviet republic of Georgia—was attempting to reestablish a new government following the bloodless "Rose Revolution," which saw the ouster of the Soviet-era president and the installation of the reform-minded Mikheil Saakashvili. Widespread corruption remained from the days of the USSR, when people were accustomed to kickbacks and political meddling by government oligarchs. Saakashvili was determined to use sunshine and transparency to disinfect the system. "When Saakashvili came in," Hertling told me, "one of the fascinating things he did was to renovate the police stations with glass fronts. As you drove through a town, you would easily identify the police stations, because they all had huge glass windows."

Hertling wondered whether the new architecture was merely a form of refurbishment, or if there was more to it. He had occasion to ask the Georgian president during one of his official engagements. "I pulled him aside and asked why he had built all the police stations with these glass frontages. He just looked at me and smiled," Hertling recalled.

Then Saakashvili responded. "So people can see what's going on inside," he'd said. "We could never do that during the old Soviet days."

Bringing the discussion back to the current state of affairs in the United States, Hertling described his concerns about the reign of Donald Trump. "It all goes back to the element of building trust," the retired lieutenant general said. "This is what we are losing in the United States. We are losing trust in our officials, and we risk losing trust in our institutions. Nobody can trust President Trump right now. We're questioning everything. That is exactly what was happening in all of these authoritarian governments, because there was always that question mark of what's real and what's not."

The problem with would-be authoritarians is that there is typically no one in their orbit who will actually point out the dangerous consequences of their actions. Trump is no exception. By now, a chorus of national security and political experts (including some from his own party) have warned of the deleterious effects of his treatment of law enforcement. Sadly, he appears not to know the limitations of his own expertise. In his mind, he is "an extremely stable genius."

INTERESTINGLY, WHEN AN iron-fisted leader like Trump also happens to have the qualities of a TV pitchman, his relationship with entities like the FBI can become fair-weathered and transactional. When they are investigating him, they are crooks. When they can be helpful, they are the gold standard.

One of the most glaring examples of this behavior could be seen during the 2018 confirmation of Supreme Court Justice Brett Kavanaugh. In that case, the nominee was facing serious allegations of past instances of sexual assault, and the White House was all but pressured into ordering an FBI investigation to uncover any wrongdoing. Trump claimed that the FBI was free to investigate whatever they wanted, but the truth was much different. In fact, the president was once again lying to the American people. As I learned from FBI insiders during the course of reporting this story, far from having wide latitude, the bureau was limited in what it could review.

In background investigations, the FBI merely acts on behalf of its client agency—in this case, the White House—and cannot go beyond the scope of what the client requests. The White House controlled the scope of the investigation, which resulted in only a handful of Kavanaugh witnesses being interviewed, not the full sweeping review the president claimed. On top of that, the White House gave the FBI a deadline of one week to complete its supplemental review of Kavanaugh's past, setting an arbitrary deadline on investigative activity that might have taken weeks. When the bureau had found nothing by week's end, Trump declared victory and attempted to use the FBI's brand for his own political purposes. Referencing the bureau's background investigation, Trump turned to Kavanaugh at the judge's swearing-in ceremony and declared, "I must state that, you, sir, under historic scrutiny, were proven innocent." This was, of course, a complete distortion of the FBI's work.

It is vital to revisit the Kavanaugh affair because it was yet another instance of Trump playing politics with the FBI. It shows that he looks at every person and entity through the lens of how it impacts him personally.

For its part, the FBI remained silent during the controversy, failing to go on the record and correct the president's and Senate Republicans' claim that the bureau had free rein. By staying quiet and allowing the lie to persist about what the agency was or was not able to investigate, the FBI took yet another reputational hit.

Although the comparison to past cases is imperfect, it illustrates the benefit of an independent FBI that is not afraid to step out and distance itself from politicians who are politicizing the organization. With the Russia investigation lies, the bureau took heat from the right. With the Kavanaugh lies, it lost trust with progressives, who suspected the bureau was either placating the president or inherently in the tank for Kavanaugh. With a new normal that involves politicians not being afraid to use the FBI as a political pawn, it is incumbent upon law enforcement to ensure that the public is always told the truth.

LIKE MANY EXPERTS, Lieutenant General Hertling told me he worries about Trump's approach to the instruments of national power—military, law enforcement, etc.—and how, like many authoritarians, the president sees them as tools that belong to him. Trump has frequently talked about "my generals" and has sought to use law enforcement to investigate his own political enemies.

"They're not doing it for you," Hertling said, "They're doing it for the country. Whether it's the FBI, the CIA, or the military, these institutions risk degradation as Trump continues to treat them as his own belongings. That's what you see in dictatorial regimes."

Largely ignored until the election of Trump was the appreciation by many that federal law enforcement—charged with enforcing criminal statutes and holding accountable those who violate the law—is not an arm of the executive branch. One of the many things that makes the United States special is how those serving the nation pledge fealty to the supreme law of the land rather to any one individual.

"One of the things that I made a habit of when I went around to the forty-nine different countries in Europe was to ask soldiers what they vowed their allegiance to," said Hertling. "I would get all kinds of interesting responses—they'd vow to defend the motherland, or the fatherland, or the president. We are the only country that vows to defend a piece of paper—the Constitution. That makes us distinctly different from any other country in the world."

The awesomeness of our system of justice is so easy to take for granted, until you see firsthand what happens elsewhere when corruption is rampant and laws are applied unequally. While traveling the globe working with our foreign partners, never did I think I would someday witness my own country's legal system begin to atrophy due to the relentless efforts of a US president. Although we are far from regressing into a state of affairs akin to Iraq or the former Soviet bloc, any amount of backsliding that results from the actions of our own president is un-American.

# CHAPTER 16

# Hotwash

WE WERE PROUD to report we had just saved the United States from annihilation. Well, at least theoretically. Deep underground in a facility outside Washington, I had spent the past forty-eight hours without sleep, running on caffeine and adrenaline, as I, along with dozens of colleagues from nearly every federal agency, conducted an exercise to test our ability to respond to a catastrophic bombing of our nation's capital. The goal was to ensure that the national command authority would be ready to absorb an attack by whatever aggressor triggered the doomsday scenario, respond appropriately, and then reconstitute the US government after the attempted destruction.

We hadn't done half bad. We had spent the past two days racing back and forth through dark World War II–era tunnels to share critical information. The place smelled of mold and hissed with the echoing sounds of dripping water leaking through rocks that had been carved out to make room for makeshift workspaces.

"Exercise, exercise, exercise," came the muffled voice across the loudspeaker. While clunky, every phone call, email, and announcement during the drill had started with this same word repeated three times. Although the scenario was fake, the national assets we were working with were very real. Someone calling the North American Aerospace Defense Command (NORAD), for example, would want to sound off to alert them the call was part of an exercise before reporting that a mushroom cloud had just enveloped Washington.

"ENDEX!" the voice thundered, signaling the end of the days-long exercise. The drill was over. Humanity had been saved from total apocalypse.

As I packed up my things in the FBI's section of the facility, I walked through a small conference room and into tiny quarters with the sign FBI DIRECTOR affixed to the door. This was 2006, and Robert Mueller was still at the helm. Curious what the director's digs looked like and where he would spend his time during a global calamity, I peered inside and saw a small bed next to a large black leather electronic massage chair. *A massage chair?* I thought. I sat down in it and pressed one of the buttons, thoroughly enjoying the lumbar feature. I was exhausted, so this was the perfect way to relax before heading back to DC.

"Not bad, huh?" said one of my colleagues as he walked into the room.

"Not at all," I said. "But I still find it strange Director Mueller has a massage chair."

"We took the liberty of getting it for him," he said. "We figure if the boss is one day actually busy saving the country from annihilation, he's probably going to be under a little stress."

"Fair enough," I said, switching the chair off and rising to my feet.

"Let's go," he said. "Time for the hotwash."

THE "HOTWASH," AS it's known in military and other government circles, is the critical period after an exercise, event, or operation when key stakeholders gather together to discuss everything that just transpired. The term comes from the historical practice of soldiers dousing their rifles in hot water in order to help remove residue and grit. The goal of these sessions is to provide each other with candid feedback—both positive and negative—in order to gauge how personnel responded to a particular situation.

I had been through untold numbers of these during my FBI career, following arrests, interrogations, responses to major incidents, and the like. They typically started diplomatically; we'd shower each other with praise about what had gone well before the inevitable pivot to what, if anything, had gone off the rails. FBI employees are known for their bluntness—their mission often involves matters of life and death, which is one good reason we don't call this kind of analysis a postmortem—and it was important to speak frankly.

Put simply, these sessions are critical. It is human nature after a major event that taxes the mind and body to want to relax, unwind, and think about anything else, but it is important to allocate the space and time to look back and review your work promptly. Doing so allows team members to improve by hearing ideas from peers they may not have originally considered. The hotwash also helps to identify blunders that can be avoided the next time. Equally important, these sessions can allow one to home in on outside malevolent factors that might present a challenge to one's effectiveness.

IN LOOKING BACK from the 2016 presidential campaign to the present, one of my goals has been for this book to serve as the hotwash for that time period—the national pause we all need to reflect and understand what really transpired inside the FBI as it took on two politically charged investigations. Although it may *seem* easier to let bygones be bygones and simply move on, doing so would be a recipe for national and institutional disaster. With a frenetic news cycle made more intense by a president who is adept at making news dozens of times per day, it is hard enough to keep tabs on current events, much less carve out time to look in the rearview mirror. However, as for major government operations, a retrospective review is essential for all Americans, lest we continue to make the same mistakes and fail to identify and address glaring problems in our midst.

So how then are we to assess the FBI's performance over the past three years and that of our elected leaders? How do we allocate the degree to which different parties are responsible for the bureau's modern reputational challenges? I think an honest assessment begins by divorcing the Clinton and Trump investigations—something President Donald Trump and his allies have sought to blur at every turn—and look independently at critical decisions that were made along the way by those in positions of leadership.

The most obvious place to start in the Clinton case is with FBI director James Comey's July 2016 press conference announcing that the bureau
would not be recommending prosecution, followed by his October decision
to reopen the investigation—and to announce that reopening—just before
election. Both decisions were instrumental in shaping public opinion of
the bureau across the political spectrum, with Republicans and Democrats
either loving or hating Comey depending on how the choices made affected
their side politically.

Setting aside the machinations of political types, whose indignation
rises and falls on any given day based on whose partisan ox is being gored,
among law enforcement experts, a candid hotwash of the way Comey
stepped outside the confines of Justice Department leadership results in
mixed feelings, in particular the language—"extremely careless"—that he
used to describe Hillary Clinton while nevertheless recommending she not
be prosecuted.

"I am understood to be a Comey defender, and in the broad scheme
of things I am," Benjamin Wittes told me. Wittes is cofounder of *Lawfare*,
a blog that breaks down key national issues involving the collision of law,
national security, and politics. "But the irony is that I'm actually one of the
relatively small number of people who in real time said there was a problem
with this. And, by the way, it says a lot about Jim [Comey] that he does not
consider that criticism an act of disloyalty."

"I think Comey was wrong," Wittes's colleague Susan Hennessey, a former attorney at the NSA, told me. "We had an FBI director talking about
the conduct of a US citizen who had not been charged with a crime. It's not
right to talk about a US citizen, whether they're a political figure or not."

I pressed her on whether the need for transparency with the American
people was required in such an unusual situation as having a presidential candidate under investigation, and whether the FBI's reputation would
have been negatively impacted had Comey simply issued a one-line statement indicating that the investigation was being closed.

"I think I understand why Comey did what he did," she said. "I understand the desire and the need to want to preserve the bureau's integrity and

independence—that in an unusual circumstance this is a higher order of value. I think the preservation of that reputation with the public is really important. That said, sometimes there's a clash between the ability of an agency to defend itself and preserve its integrity, and the rights of an individual citizen. In those circumstances, the agency has to take the hit."

Matthew Miller, a former top spokesperson at the Justice Department, was much more blunt. "In several instances, Comey made assertions that are outside the authority of the FBI," he wrote in an opinion piece in the *Washington Post*. In his view, the entire episode represented an abuse of power and risked setting a dangerous precedent for future FBI investigations.

Of all the hard calls Comey had to make in unprecedented times, I concur that the language he used to describe Clinton's actions was, in hindsight, an avoidable error. His goal had been to ensure that the American people fully understood what had transpired. His penchant for candor and transparency is one of Comey's best qualities—especially in a town where it seems so many politicians opt instead to hide and deceive—but it would have been possible to describe the investigative steps taken without labeling the candidate "extremely careless."

For his part, Comey agrees. He has since said that one of the mistakes he made was in the language he used to characterize Clinton's conduct.

"I should've worked harder to find a way to convey that it's more than just the ordinary mistake but it's not criminal behavior," he has said, "and find different words to describe that."

Apart from the language used in the press conference, Comey's decision to make the announcement without coordinating with the Justice Department has also been the subject of intense debate. One person with credibility among current and former bureau employees is Chris Swecker, a retired FBI agent who served as assistant director for the bureau's Criminal Investigative Division. He was a kind leader who was widely respected. I worked for Director Robert Mueller when Swecker was the head of criminal operations, and despite the fact that he was carrying the burden of managing a host of high-profile life-and-death operations, he always had time for mentoring.

Since retirement, Swecker has frequently appeared on both CNN and Fox News, analyzing criminal and national security issues. One thing that sets him apart from other former officials you see on television is that there is no bluster; he is sincere and expresses his views from the place of someone who cares deeply about the FBI's reputation. I disagree with nearly everything he has publicly said and written on the topic of James Comey and the Hillary Clinton email investigation, but since his beliefs match those of some other current and former FBI employees, it is important that they be included here in order to help illuminate the full spectrum of views.

"I watched the whole press conference," Swecker told me, "and I remember thinking it was very unusual. When he went on to exonerate Hillary Clinton and say there was no reason to prosecute her, I just about fell out of my chair. The FBI doesn't get to decide or decline whether someone gets prosecuted."

In Swecker's mind, Comey's decision to weigh in on the outcome of the Clinton case is a key aspect of the politicization that followed. It was the Justice Department's decision to make, not the FBI's.

In my judgment, the decision by Attorney General Loretta Lynch not to recuse herself from the Clinton investigation after that conversation with Bill Clinton on the Arizona tarmac was the key factor that helps explain Comey's decision to act unilaterally. His goal had been to find a way to remove any perception of politics being at play in whether to prosecute Clinton. By remaining in the chain of command for decision-making in the case, DOJ political appointees had, perhaps unknowingly, boxed him in.

"I think that genuinely put Jim [Comey] in a difficult position," Lawfare's Benjamin Wittes told me. "Sally Yates should have gone to Lynch and said, 'You've got to step aside and let me handle this.' Of the three of them, Jim has a tendency to throw himself on top of every grenade, and the other two are people who have a tendency to run away from grenades. In the end, Jim arrogates some authority to himself that really was not his to exercise properly."

We will never know how much the decision to reopen the email case after the Anthony Weiner laptop discovery affected the 2016 presidential election. "We like to believe it [did] because we need a villain, we need a bad guy, and it's possible that it did," said Wittes. "If you're telling me that the optics are terrible, well, yeah, the optics are terrible. If you're telling me that it was one factor among many, yeah, that's probably right. If you're telling me there is but-for causation, you're making that up."

IN THE END, good people of all political stripes will discuss for time immemorial which courses of action were most appropriate. However, there are two things I know for certain. The first is that James Comey is an honorable person. I'm well aware that his critics fault him for being pious and sanctimonious, but in an era when our elected leaders lie to us with reckless abandon about all matters big and small, maybe a little piety isn't such a terrible thing.

The second thing I know is that Comey was dealt an impossible hand. How many FBI directors have found themselves investigating the presidential candidate from one political party and associates of the candidate from the other party, and then facing a president who asked him to pledge loyalty before attempting to obstruct justice?

To those who claim that Comey should have stood up to Trump and started pounding the table and lecturing the president on right and wrong, I say that this is not the way an investigator would handle the situation. By this point, the FBI had been investigating several members of the Trump campaign and wondered if Trump himself was possibly complicit in wrongdoing. Once the president had, in Comey's words, begun speaking like a mob boss and attempting to interfere with the FBI's work, the logical thing to do was to keep him talking—see how far he would be willing to go. Comey acted like the investigator he'd been for so many years. He took notes, filed them away, and waited to see if the president would commit a crime. After Trump took the remarkable step of firing him—thereby sidelining the person leading the investigation—all of those exchanges suddenly became material and Comey became a key witness. In my opinion, those who consider his silence weakness—including former law enforcement types—don't really understand how investigations work.

On Wednesday, November 9, 2016, I accompanied Comey to the head-quarters of the National Geospatial-Intelligence Agency, a mammoth compound outside Washington where professionals from across the intelligence community had gathered for a semiregular conference on leadership in government. Comey was to be one of the keynote speakers.

When we entered the space where hundreds had gathered, the roar of the assembled crowd turned to deafening silence. All eyes were on Comey. Only hours before, Donald Trump had been elected the forty-fifth president of the United States, and the man now standing before them had been at the center of one of the most controversial and stormy election seasons ever.

After Comey finished his leadership talk and headed for the door, we were stopped by a man in his late fifties. His hands were clasped and his head was shaking. He was clearly emotional, but I wasn't sure why.

"Director Comey," he said, clearing his throat. "I don't have a question, but I do have a comment." He paused. The tension was palpable. I thought he was about to blast the FBI director. Then he continued. "You were in an impossible situation, sir. You were in an impossible situation."

Comey and I were both rendered speechless. In a matter of seconds, this stranger had thoughtfully summed up an entire year of chaos.

No review of the FBI's recent reputational challenges would be complete without an honest assessment of the outside forces that have worked so desperately to undermine it. When Donald J. Trump stepped forward to take the oath of office in January 2017, he swore to "preserve, protect, and defend the Constitution of the United States." Many presidential experts believe he has failed.

At every turn, he has sought to throw sand into the gears of justice as career public servants have worked to investigate his campaign and those in his orbit. Special Counsel Robert Mueller unearthed serious corruption and deception by those associated with Trump. Taken off the deck at the time of this writing alone were Trump's former lawyer, campaign manager, foreign-policy adviser, and a half dozen others. His family's charitable foundation stands accused of being nothing less than a money-laundering machine, which personally benefits the Trump family. His inaugural committee is under criminal investigation for the manner in which it has raised and spent money. By 2019, nearly every entity Donald Trump had ever led was under some type of investigation.

Despite the mounting evidence, his only play has been to attack, distort, and discredit. He has called people cooperating with the federal government "rats," has urged police officers to go "rough" on criminal suspects, and has embraced dictators around the world who flout the rule of law.

"Trump is an authoritarian," Benjamin Wittes told me. "He's not very good at it, but he's an authoritarian. If you are an aspiring authoritarian, independent law enforcement is unacceptable, both for self-protective reasons, but also for offensive reasons. You need to be able to go after your political enemies."

In the seminal work *How Democracies Die*, authors Steven Levitsky and Daniel Ziblatt survey the fundamental ingredients of every authoritarian seeking to gain and hold on to power. "It always helps to have the referees on your side," they write. "Modern states possess various agencies with the authority to investigate and punish wrongdoing by both public and private citizens. . . . In democracies, such institutions are designed to serve as neutral arbiters. For would-be authoritarians, therefore, judicial and law enforcement agencies pose both a challenge and an opportunity."

Put simply, the authoritarian understands that independent law enforcement is a threat. It must be brought to heel, which is exactly what Trump has attempted. "Trump and Comey were on a collision course from the beginning," Wittes told me. "It was a clash between their very cores. Trump represented the personalized powers of the presidency, while Comey represented the long American tradition of investigative and prosecutorial independence. Trump was not competent and Comey may have been an imperfect champion, but they were both committed to their roles."

ON THE NIGHT after the release of the Justice Department inspector general's report on the FBI's actions during the 2016 election, I found myself unable to sleep, my mind racing. I had been on television since the early morning hours—first, discussing what the public should expect from the IG, and then, once it had finally dropped, reporting on the findings documented in the 568-page investigative summary, while working to refute the partisan lies painting the entire FBI leadership structure as corrupt. It was exhausting.

Although I had to be up in a few hours to go back on the air, I needed some fresh air. I stepped out of my hotel near DC's Union Station into the pitch-black night and headed west. As I passed the FBI's Washington field office, lights were still glowing on several floors, and I thought about the men and women inside, still hard at work.

A little farther up the street, I stopped at the National Law Enforcement Officers Memorial, a park near the city's center marked by statues of bronze lions standing watch near a wall listing the names of fallen officers. It is a hallowed place that pays tribute to those who made the ultimate sacrifice while wearing the badge. They were moms and dads, brothers and sisters—all taken from the world while serving others.

In an instant, all the machinations of the day fell away. None of it seemed to matter. All that political noise paled in comparison to what this memorial represents. What, I thought, would life in the United States be like if those who backed the badge spent their time honoring the fallen rather than refuting lies? What would it be like if those constantly working to undermine law enforcement would instead spend time reflecting upon what that line of work actually means?

It was now past midnight, but I wasn't ready to call it a day. Anyone who has spent enough time in Washington likely has a favorite spot that means something special to them. For some, it's one of the grand historical monuments; for others, a building or park. Mine has always been that concrete brutalist structure that rises high on Pennsylvania Avenue halfway between the White House and the Capitol. FBI headquarters is merely one of hundreds of buildings the bureau occupies in communities across the nation, but in Washington it serves as a symbol of strength and independence to all who pass by. It is a reminder to the lobbyist, corporate executive, member of Congress, and president of the United States alike that in their midst exists a team some thirty-six thousand strong that is working to hold both ordinary and powerful people to account.

As I walked by, I peered up at my old office—the last window on the building's eastern edge. The lights were off along the entire executive corridor. I saw an employee exit the building and head in my direction. He was about my age, and I had no idea what his role was, but I took the opportunity to ask him about the chaotic day, when the actions of the FBI over the past two years had been dissected for hours on end by pundits and politicians.

He admitted morale had taken a hit and the people on his team had simply switched off their TVs. Then he said something that left me momentarily speechless. "The FBI has been here for a hundred years," he said. "Times are tough, but you just have to ignore it all. We'll still be here tomorrow."

I mean no disrespect, but he was only half-right. The organization simply cannot continue to ignore its critics if it is to maintain public trust. Citizens who sit in jury boxes, and the few who will ever actually meet a special agent on the street asking them for help, all formulate their opinion of the agency based on the information they consume well before these interactions. The bureau must be willing to engage publicly and ensure that it is accurately depicted.

The leaders representing our institutions of justice cannot be afraid to speak up and call out lies when they see them. This isn't to say they should engage in childish tit-for-tat Twitter fights with a president who uses social media as a bludgeon. But they do need to speak out and defend the institutions when they are the subject of blatant lies that seek to manipulate public opinion at the expense of institutional confidence.

"A former member of the FBI senior leadership team made an observation to me," said *Lawfare's* Susan Hennessey. "He was commenting on claims that the FBI simply needs to do things by the book. This person said, 'What book? There is no book!' Everyone keeps acting as though there's an actual book that you can open and there's a rule for this particular situation. There is no book. The book is a myth."

It is true that there is no instruction manual for responding to Trump's war on the FBI—no plans on the shelf they can pull to run a counterplay. Leaders simply must be willing to speak truth to power and not be afraid to correct the record for the constituents they serve. Put simply, they must be willing to lose their jobs in order to do their jobs.

I make it a point to speak with someone in the FBI every single day. It is not just because I have many friends there who remain special to me, but also because I want them to know they are not alone in weathering this storm. There is one constant theme I've noticed when my friends from the bureau describe what angers them the most. "The question that stings to my core," said one former colleague, "is when I'm around family or friends and they ask me, 'What happened to the FBI?' As though the negative perception is all our doing."

"What do you tell them?" I asked.

"I tell them Washington politics happened to the FBI. We are still the same FBI they remember, but we are now being defined by people with political agendas."

# EPILOGUE

BY THE TIME special counsel Robert Mueller finally broke his silence and closed the books on the Crossfire Hurricane investigation, the bell had already been rung. Partisan officials with questionable motives had filled the void that had been left by his lengthy reticence to face the public and explain his work. "Total exoneration," the President and his allies had trumpeted again and again. Two months after Mueller had submitted his final report to the attorney general, the special counsel was forced to play cleanup.

Who was largely responsible for much of the public confusion about Mueller's findings? None other than the man hand-selected by President Donald Trump to lead the Justice Department following the ouster of Attorney General Jeff Sessions: William Barr, a brilliant, barrel-chested former career government lawyer who had previously held the position of AG back in the George H. W. Bush administration.

For many inside DOJ with whom I've spoken, the nomination of Barr—an institutionalist by any measure—at first signaled that perhaps they were on the road to returning to some semblance of normalcy. But that dream was short-lived.

After his nomination, the *Wall Street Journal* reported that Barr, then a private citizen, had submitted unsolicited a memo to DOJ criticizing Robert Mueller's obstruction of justice inquiry as "fatally misconceived." If the memo was meant to be a job application, it certainly worked. Barr was now overseeing the very investigation he had once ridiculed.

In late March, when Robert Mueller ended his investigation and formally submitted his report to Barr, the attorney general was then required to notify Congress that the special counsel's work had been completed.

Pursuant to federal law, however, Barr was afforded wide latitude in determining what, if anything, of substance should be released publicly.

Just two days later, and in a move that would all but destroy any notion Barr was operating in a manner independent of the White House, the attorney general released a document outlining his own principal conclusions of the Russia investigation: that Mueller had not found evidence that members of the Trump campaign had conspired with Russia, and that Mueller had failed to reach a conclusion about whether the president had obstructed justice. He then claimed that that left the decision to the attorney general. After laying out his legal reasoning, Barr wrote, "Deputy Attorney General Rod Rosenstein and I have concluded that the evidence . . . is not sufficient to establish that the president committed an obstruction-of-justice offense."

Barr's letter was a bombshell. After conducting the most high-profile investigation in the modern history of the Justice Department, Mueller had seemingly concluded that Trump and his team had not committed crimes. Trump and his allies quickly declared victory.

"No Collusion, No Obstruction, Complete and Total EXONERATION," the president tweeted immediately in a refrain that would be echoed time and again by his surrogates.

This was the narrative that the attorney general permitted to bake into the national psyche for weeks on end while DOJ and Congress debated how much of the full report should actually be made public.

One person apparently frustrated by Barr's actions was Robert Mueller himself, who quickly fired off a letter to the attorney general complaining that Barr's mischaracterization "did not fully capture the context, nature, and substance" of his work. For a usually calm and collected Robert Mueller, the letter was a shot across the bow. Rather than picking up the phone, the special counsel had opted to memorialize his dismay in a written document that would be an official record.

At long last, on April 18 the public finally got to see the fruits of Mueller's labor. The day began with a press conference at the Justice Department, during which the attorney general fielded questions from reporters as Rod Rosenstein—ever the loyal lieutenant—stood over his left shoulder. The entire press conference was bizarre, most notably because of the manner in which the attorney general went out of his way to describe Trump as a victim. He described the president as frustrated, angered, and sincere.

Former FBI agents like myself watched with alarm as the nation's top cop seemed to run interference for the president, even falsely claiming that the White House "fully cooperated" with Mueller's team. As I have described in these pages, this was the same president who had been engaged in a full-on assault of the very department Barr was now leading.

Asked by CNN's Laura Jarrett why Mueller had not reached a conclusion about obstruction of justice, and if this decision had anything to do with the Justice Department's longstanding policy against indicting a sitting president, Barr insisted that the policy was not a factor and it was not as though Mueller would have found a crime had the policy not existed.

But Barr's answer was highly misleading. In fact, as the full report eventually stated, Mueller was so closely adhering to DOJ's policy against indicting a sitting president, he determined that he could not even *look* for crimes that might implicate Trump. Put simply, Mueller's hands were tied.

On May 29, Mueller finally faced the cameras for the first time since his investigation had begun. Although he did not go beyond the four corners of his original report, it was striking to hear Mueller describe his investigation of the president in his own voice. He made it clear that, although he could not prove beyond a reasonable doubt that the Trump campaign conspired with Russia in a manner that would warrant prosecution, there were numerous interactions that raised eyebrows. Lost on no one was the fact that those close to Donald Trump were at the very least willing to accept help from a hostile foreign adversary. Additionally, Mueller laid out at least ten instances of possible presidential obstruction of justice, before noting the DOJ's policy precluded further action against Trump.

One could conclude that Mueller was subtly insisting that although his own hands were tied, Congress certainly had the power to impeach Trump should they determine his actions met the threshold of high crimes and misdemeanors.

WHILE THE WORLD had been waiting for the public release of the Mueller report, Barr did something else that caused jaws to drop inside the FBI and across the larger intelligence community. In an April 10 hearing on Capitol Hill, Barr publicly suggested that the Trump campaign had been spied on. Adopting the president's own witch hunt lingo, the AG said, "I think spying did occur."

Barr's apparent willingness to throw red meat to the president and his base by describing lawfully predicated surveillance as "spying" was concerning. For one thing, it's simply not a term that's widely employed inside the halls of the FBI and DOJ. When it is used by law enforcement, "spying" almost always refers to the sinister activities undertaken by foreign governments to target us—not to cast suspicion on the work of career government investigators. FBI director Christopher Wray said that "spying" is "not the term I would use," while the former director of national intelligence James Clapper called Barr's performance "both stunning and scary."

The attorney general later doubled down and announced he would be investigating the origins of Crossfire Hurricane. As he told CBS News, Crossfire Hurricane crossed "a serious red line" and was truly unprecedented.

Clearly, Trump's war on the FBI is far from over.

So where does this leave the women and men of the FBI? And how should members of the public handle the president's continual assault on the rule of law? In a word: action. Silence will only further the continued erosion of public confidence in federal law enforcement.

One mistake I made when I was in the bureau was believing I cared more about the FBI than anyone else. It was hard not to feel this way when my self-image was so closely tied to my profession. However, I have since come to realize that the FBI does not belong to any one person. It belongs to us all. As I have argued throughout these pages, if the bureau is to succeed in its mission of protecting the American people and upholding the Constitution of the United States, those who care about the rule of law must be willing to speak up in its defense. We must hold the bureau fully accountable when it strays, but must also not be afraid to go to the mat in its defense when the agency is targeted for purely political gain. Our public safety depends on it. Staying out of the fray is no longer an option.

# ACKNOWLEDGMENTS

THE FIELDS OF law enforcement and journalism are remarkably similar. At their core, both professions center on collecting facts, analyzing them, and piecing together a story. FBI agents and gumshoe reporters pound the pavement, shake the branches, and ask uncomfortable questions in pursuit of the truth, on behalf of the public. Sometimes this pursuit of the facts means the pursuer becomes an enemy in the eyes of the person they are seeking to hold to account. This fact makes public support of law enforcement and journalism all the more important. Thank you, readers, for supporting the rule of law and a free press.

My transition from the FBI to the media was not a happy occasion. As I believe this book has shown, I was content in a career I loved, renewed each and every morning by the privilege of putting on my badge and serving the American people. But outside factors intervened. Politics intervened. After witnessing the organization I'd spent a dozen years serving constantly targeted and attacked by politicians in survival mode, and discovering that the bench of those speaking out against these attacks wasn't that deep, I came to the realization that I could do more to serve my FBI colleagues by stepping out and speaking out than I could by staying in and remaining silent.

After starting in journalism, I was approached by several people inquiring whether I would "naturally" write a book. I told them no; it pained me to even think about the hubris involved in filling the pages of a memoir all about me. In a business where some public personalities can't order breakfast without giving you their résumé, I try to remain at the other end of the spectrum—someone who would much rather spend my time reading about the fascinating lives of others, not writing about my own. But then by chance I met the Javelin literary-agent team of Keith Urbahn, Matt Latimer, and Matt Carlini, who urged me to consider writing something that was not a memoir or the typical Washington tell-all, but more a thoughtful call to action for the American people based on the reason I left the FBI. Betsy Gleick, my remarkable editor at Algonquin Books, was the perfect partner for such an endeavor. I thank my agents and editor for helping arrange my thoughts in a compelling way. And I thank the entire team at Algonquin for helping to get the finished product out into the world.

What nearly kept me from finally accepting the challenge of writing a book was any notion that I would be outlandishly profiting from this story. It's hard to explain, and perhaps will not make total sense to those who have not been privileged to wear the FBI shield, but the idea of voluntarily leaving the agency and then selling a book seemed to me to be cashing in on a great gift I probably didn't deserve in the first place. For many nights, I stared at the ceiling, grappling with this issue.

But then I read an article by my CNN colleague David Shortell documenting recent stories of FBI special agents who continue to tragically die from latent illnesses stemming from their work nearly two decades ago searching through the toxic rubble at Ground Zero in Manhattan. As I researched the issue, I learned of a fund established by the FBI Agents Association that supports the families of agents killed in the line of duty and covers the college expenses of their surviving children. It clicked. I could use this book to help others. Therefore, half of my proceeds from your book purchase will go to support the families of special agents who made the ultimate sacrifice. Whether you agree or disagree with some or all of the words in these pages, you can rest assured your purchase is making a difference.

This book would not be complete without a word of thanks to a number of others who made it possible. In addition to my own firsthand account of living through the turmoil of the 2016 election season, the firing of an FBI director, and the investigation of a president, I relied heavily on the insights of a diverse group of people who served in key positions both in and out of government. I am grateful for the gracious gift of their time amid incredibly demanding schedules. I'm also thankful for the contributions of the brilliant Joey Seymour, a presidential expert who spent countless hours at the Richard Nixon Presidential Library, delving into past instances of administrations colliding with the rule of law. Where the book succeeds in shedding light on important topics in the national interest, I have all of the above to thank. Any failings are mine alone.

In accordance with my obligations as a former FBI employee pursuant to my FBI employment agreement, this book has undergone a prepublication review for the purpose of identifying any potential disclosures of classified or sensitive information, but has not been reviewed for editorial content or accuracy. The FBI does not endorse or validate any information that I have described in this book. The opinions expressed in this book are mine and not those of the FBI or any other federal government agency or department. The factual descriptions of FBI investigations I did not directly work on are based primarily on public news reports, interviews, and other open source reporting, and are not based on information I learned while serving as an FBI special agent. The sources of my information are cited at the end.

To end where I began, a special note of thanks to members of the FBI and CNN families. Both institutions have frequently been targets of attack by elected officials being investigated. Thank you for continuing to ask the hard questions. Democracy demands your dogged pursuit of the truth.

JOSH CAMPBELL
Los Angeles, California

# NOTES

vii     **"When you're attacking FBI agents"**   Sarah Sanders (@SarahHuckabee), Twitter, November 3, 2016, https://twitter.com/sarahhuckabee/status/794255968448020480.

## Prologue

3     **Steele . . . approached the FBI**   "How Ex-Spy Christopher Steele Compiled His Explosive Trump-Russia Dossier," *Vanity Fair*, April 2017, https://www.vanityfair.com /news/2017/03/how-the-explosive-russian-dossier-was-compiled-christopher-steele.

3     **Burr . . . pulled Comey aside**   James Comey (former FBI director), in discussion with the author, July 9, 2018.

3     **"He needed to give it to me"**   Comey, discussion.

10     **"It's a shame"**   "Trump: It's a Shame What Happened to the FBI," CNN, December 15, 2017, https://www.cnn.com/videos/politics/2017/12/15/trump-shame-what-happened-fbi-sot.cnn.

11     **Crossfire Hurricane . . . code name**   "Code Name Crossfire Hurricane: The Secret Origins of the Trump Investigation," *New York Times*, May 16, 2018, https://www.nytimes.com/2018/05/16/us/politics/crossfire-hurricane-trump-russia-fbi-mueller-investigation.html.

## Chapter 1: More Than a Motto

14     FBI DEADLY FORCE POLICY   "What Is the FBI's Policy on the Use of Deadly Force by Its Special Agents?" FBI.gov, https://www.fbi.gov/about/faqs/what-is-the-fbis-policy-on-the-use-of-deadly-force-by-its-special-agents.

15     **CIA personnel . . . killed in Afghanistan**   "Source: Jordanian Double-Agent Killed 7 CIA Officers in Suicide Blast," CNN, January 5, 2010, http://www.cnn.com/2010 /US/01/04/bombing.cia.index.html.

16     **"Fidelity - Bravery - Integrity"**   "Seal & Motto," FBI.gov, https://www.fbi.gov /history/seal-motto.

17     **"More than just a motto"**   Robert Mueller, speech commemorating the 100th anniversary of the FBI (National Building Museum, Washington, DC, July 17, 2008), https://archives.fbi.gov/archives/news/speeches/fbi-commemorates-100-years-of-fidelity-bravery-and-integrity.

18 **Giglio v. United States** "Policy Regarding the Disclosure to Prosecutors of Potential Impeachment Information Concerning Law Enforcement Agency Witnesses ('Giglio Policy')," US Department of Justice Archives, https://www.justice.gov/archives/ag/policy-regarding-disclosure-prosecutors-potential-impeachment-information-concerning-law.

21 **Robert Hanssen** "Robert Hanssen: A Brief History," NPR, February 4, 2007, https://www.npr.org/templates/story/story.php?storyId=7152496.

## Chapter 2: Hands Off

24 **Tidbits of information** "FBI Director Hoover's Dirty Files: Excerpt from Ronald Kessler's 'The Secrets of the FBI,'" *Daily Beast*, August 2, 2011, https://www.thedailybeast.com/fbi-director-hoovers-dirty-files-excerpt-from-ronald-kesslers-the-secrets-of-the-fbi.

24 **"Don't make any calls"** Anthony Summers, *Official and Confidential: The Secret Life of J. Edgar Hoover* (New York: Open Road, 1993), 441.

24 **His political enemies** *The Nixon Tapes: 1973*, edited and annotated by Douglas Brinkley and Luke A. Nichter (New York: Houghton Mifflin, 2015), 83.

25 **"Goddamn bugging crap"** Stephen E. Ambrose, *Nixon: The Triumph of a Politician 1962–1972* (New York: Simon & Schuster, 1989).

25 **Lording embarrassing material** "Trump Thinks Comey Was Trying to Blackmail Him," *Vanity Fair*, July 20, 2017, https://www.vanityfair.com/news/2017/07/trump-thinks-comey-was-trying-to-blackmail-him.

25 **Close personal relationship** "Deep Throat, Watergate, and the Bureaucratic Politics of the FBI," *Journal of Policy History* 24, no. 2 (April 2012): 157–83, https://doi.org/10.1017/S0898030612000012.

25 **Nixon . . . acting as defender** "Deep Throat," *Journal of Policy History*.

26 **"Putting congressmen on notice"** "FBI Director Hoover's Dirty Files," *Daily Beast*.

26 **"A sufficient threat"** Ambrose, *Nixon: The Triumph of a Politician 1962–1972*.

26 **"Outside the tent pissing in"** "FBI Director Hoover's Dirty Files," *Daily Beast*.

26 **"He was not a monster"** "Tim Weiner: Getting Inside the Bureau," *Barnes & Noble Review*, February 20, 2012, https://www.barnesandnoble.com/review/tim-weiner-getting-inside-the-bureau.

27 **"The tactics of totalitarian regimes"** *Intelligence Activities and the Rights of Americans, Book II*, final report of the Select Committee to Study Governmental Operations with Respect to Intelligence Activities, US Senate, April 26, 1976, https://web.archive.org/web/20061019170937/http://www.icdc.com/~paulwolf/cointelpro/churchfinalreportIIa.htm.

27 **Five hundred thousand domestic intelligence files** "Intelligence Activities," Select Committee to Study Governmental Operations. Summers, *Official and Confidential*, 238.

27 **Containing damning information** "Like Trump, Nixon Was Obsessed with Leaks. It Led to Watergate—and Ruin," *Washington Post*, July 22, 2017, https://www.washingtonpost.com/news/retropolis/wp/2017/06/22/like-trump-nixon-was-obsessed-with-leaks-it-led-to-watergate-and-ruin/.

27 **"It would have destroyed everything"** "Tim Weiner," *Barnes & Noble Review*.

28 **A highly inappropriate conversation** "Dick and J. Edgar Diss Kay Graham," *Slate*, September 26, 2007, https://slate.com/news-and-politics/2007/09/listening-to-richard-nixon-and-j-edgar-hoover-diss-katharine-graham.html.

28 **Single ten-year term** "FBI Director: Appointment and Tenure," Congressional Research Service, February 19, 2014, https://fas.org/sgp/crs/misc/R41850.pdf.

29 **"A criminal president"** Carl Bernstein (journalist), in discussion with the author, January 3, 2019.

29 **Dozens of . . . charged with crimes** "48 Are Involved," *New York Times*, September 11, 1974, https://www.nytimes.com/1974/09/11/archives/48-are-involved-aides-wont-say-how-serious-president-is-on-clemency.html.

30 **"He's complicated"** "FBI Oversight," C-SPAN, December 7, 2017, https://www.c-span.org/video/?438042-1/fbi-director-responds-president-trumps-attacks-agency&start=7891.

30 **His family's peanut business** "Inquiry Clears Carter Family's Peanut Business," *Washington Post*, October 17, 1979, https://www.washingtonpost.com/archive/politics/1979/10/17/inquiry-clears-carter-familys-peanut-business/ca5371c9-f0a7-4809-9b7d-7a57e78b76b0/.

30 **The Iran-Contra affair** *Final Report of the Independent Counsel for Iran/Contra Matters, Vol. 1: Investigations and Prosecutions*, Lawrence E. Walsh, independent counsel, August 4, 1993, Washington, DC., https://fas.org/irp/offdocs/walsh/.

30 **Banking scandal** "Figure in Bank Scandal Links Bush to Iraqi Loans," *New York Times*, November 10, 1993, https://www.nytimes.com/1993/11/10/us/figure-in-bank-scandal-links-bush-to-iraqi-loans.html.

30 **"Filegate," "Travelgate," "Whitewater"** "Clinton Scandals: A Guide from Whitewater to the Clinton Foundation," NPR, June 21, 2016, https://www.npr.org/2016/06/12/481718785/clinton-scandals-a-guide-from-whitewater-to-the-clinton-foundation.

31 **A political fishing expedition** "Trashing Kenneth Starr," *Weekly Standard*, June 29, 1998, https://www.weeklystandard.com/tucker-carlson/trashing-kenneth-starr.

31 **"A late-night call from the president"** Interview with confidant of former president Bill Clinton, September 4, 2018.

31 **"I wanted all my visits to be official"** "Ex-FBI Chief on Clinton's Scandals," *60 Minutes*, October 6, 2005, https://www.cbsnews.com/news/ex-fbi-chief-on-clintons-scandals/.

32 **In a dramatic scene** Comey, discussion.

32 **Hospitalized for acute pancreatitis** James Comey, *A Higher Loyalty* (New York: Flatiron Books, 2018), 75.

32 **CIA officer Valerie Plame** "Transcript of Special Counsel Fitzgerald's Press Conference," *Washington Post*, October 28, 2005, http://www.washingtonpost.com/wp-dyn/content/article/2005/10/28/AR2005102801340.html.

32 **Trump pardoned Libby** "Trump Pardons Scooter Libby in a Case That Mirrors His Own," *New York Times*, April 13, 2018, https://www.nytimes.com/2018/04/13/us/politics/trump-pardon-scooter-libby.html.

33      **Criminals and even Nazis**   "Rudy Giuliani's Most Despicable Comment," *Washington Post*, May 3, 2018, https://www.washingtonpost.com/blogs/right-turn/wp/2018/05/03 /rudy-giulianis-most-despicable-comment/?utm_term=.ec6522b779c6.

33      **A twelve-point drop**   "Republican Confidence in the FBI Has Dropped Since 2015," *HuffPost*, January 31, 2018, https://www.huffingtonpost.com/entry/republican- confidence-in-the-fbi-has-dropped-since-2015_us_5a721bbbe4b09a544b5616a7.

## Chapter 3: The Never-Ending Election

36      **"No political influence whatsoever"**   Comey, discussion.

36      **"I want to be kept up on it regularly"**   Comey, discussion.

36      **Turning the compound into an inferno**   Jack Murphy and Brandon Webb, *Benghazi: The Definitive Report* (New York: HarperCollins, 2014), 25–58.

36      **Result in the deaths of**   "Clinton: 7 Benghazi Probes So Far," PolitiFact, October 12, 2015, https://www.politifact.com/truth-o-meter/statements/2015/oct/12/hillary-clinton/clinton- there-have-been-7-benghazi-probes-so-far/.

37      **Gowdy requested . . . documents**   "How Clinton's Email Scandal Took Root," *Washington Post*, March 27, 2016, https://www.washingtonpost.com/investigations /how-clintons-email-scandal-took-root/2016/03/27/ee301168-e162-11e5-846c- 10191d1fc4ec_story.html.

37      **Asking the State Department**   "State Department: We Need until January 2016 to Release Clinton Emails," CNN, May 19, 2015, https://www.cnn.com/2015/05/19 /politics/hillary-clinton-emails-state-department/.

37      **Private email accounts**   "Breaking Down Hillary Clinton's Private Email Scandal," *Forbes*, June 19, 2016, https://www.forbes.com/sites/ivonaiacob/2016/06/19 /breaking-down-hillary-clintons-private-email-scandal/#2132b09d5290.

37      **The fight turned vicious**   "Is Donald Trump Right When He Says Hillary Clinton Deleted 33,000 Emails? Yes and No," *Vox*, October 10, 2016, https://www.vox.com /2016/10/10/13222360/trump-emails-clinton.

38      **A handful were classified**   "Official: Clinton Emails Included Classified Information," CNN, July 24, 2015, https://www.cnn.com/2015/07/24/politics/hillary-clinton-email- justice-department/index.html.

38      **Referred the matter to the Justice Department**   "Inquiry Sought in Hillary Clinton's Use of Email," *New York Times*, July 23, 2015, https://www.nytimes.com/2015/07/24/us /politics/inquiry-is-sought-in-hillary-clinton-email-account.html.

39      **"Comment publicly on leaked information"**   Robby Mook (campaign manager for Hillary Clinton), in discussion with the author, August 16, 2018.

39      **The Clintons and the bureau had crossed swords**   "Ex-FBI Chief on Clinton's Scandals," *60 Minutes*.

40      **"It's a criminal problem"**   "Trump: Hillary Has Got 'a Big Problem,'" CNN, August 15, 2015, https://www.cnn.com/videos/politics/2015/08/15/donald-trump-hillary- clinton-emails-question-iowa-state-fair-jeff-zeleny.cnn.

41    **Wrestled with two important aspects**    Comey, discussion.

41    **Should transparency . . . outweigh secrecy**    Comey, *A Higher Loyalty*, 167.

41    **Clinton's own lawyers were publicly talking**    "Investigators Find Emails Hillary Clinton Said Were Erased," *New York Times*, September 22, 2015, https://www.nytimes.com /2015/09/23/us/politics/investigators-find-emails-hillary-clinton-said-were-erased.html.

41    **Foolish to continue playing coy**    Comey, discussion.

41    **Investigating the Clinton server issue**    "FBI Director Confirming Inquiry into Clinton Email Setup," Associated Press, October 1, 2015, https://www.businessinsider .com/fbi-director-confirming-inquiry-into-clinton-email-setup-2015-10.

41    **Counter homegrown violent extremists**    "FBI Chief on Clinton Investigation: My People 'Don't Give a Rip about Politics,'" CNN, October 1, 2015, https://www.cnn.com /2015/10/01/politics/james-comey-fbi-hillary-clinton/index.html.

42    **Comey was asked about the case**    "FBI Fiscal Year 2017 Budget Report," C-SPAN, February 25, 2016, https://www.c-span.org/video/?405327-1/fbi-director-james-comey-testimony-fiscal-year-2017-budget&start=5385.

44    **"As professionally and promptly as we can"**    Comey, discussion.

44    **Bill Clinton walked onto the plane**    "Documents Discussing the Meeting Between Former Attorney General Loretta Lynch and Former President Bill Clinton," FBI.gov, June 27, 2016, https://vault.fbi.gov/documents-discussing-the-meeting-between-former-attorney-general-loretta-lynch-and-former-president-bill-clinton-june-27-2016/.

44    **Golf and their grandchildren**    "Bill Clinton Meeting Causes Headaches for Hillary," CNN, June 30, 2016, https://www.cnn.com/2016/06/29/politics/bill-clinton-loretta-lynch /index.html.

44    **"It was really a sneak"**    https://www.cnn.com/2016/06/29/politics/bill-clinton-loretta-lynch/index.html.

44    **The topic of Hillary Clinton's emails**    "Loretta Lynch to Accept F.B.I. Recommendations in Clinton Email Inquiry," *New York Times*, July 1, 2016, https://www.nytimes.com/2016/07/02/us/politics/loretta-lynch-hillary-clinton-email-server.html.

46    **Three and a half hours of questioning**    "F.B.I. Interviews Hillary Clinton Over Private Email Server," *New York Times*, July 2, 2016, https://www.nytimes.com /2016/07/03/us/politics/hillary-clinton-fbi-emails.html.

48    **"I'm not going to tell you what that decision is"**    Comey, discussion.

48    **Comey stepped out to the cameras**    "Statement by FBI Director James B. Comey on the Investigation of Secretary Hillary Clinton's Use of a Personal E-Mail System," FBI.gov, July 5, 2016, https://www.fbi.gov/news/pressrel/press-releases/statement-by-fbi-director-james-b-comey-on-the-investigation-of-secretary-hillary-clinton2019s-use-of-a-personal-e-mail-system.

48    **Recommendation that Clinton not be prosecuted**    "F.B.I. Director James Comey Recommends No Charges for Hillary Clinton on Email," *New York Times*, July 5, 2016, https://www.nytimes.com/2016/07/06/us/politics/hillary-clinton-fbi-email-comey.html.

49    **"It was highly climactic"**    Mook, discussion.

50   **Two difficult decision points**   Comey, discussion.

51   **"Case reopened"**   "FBI Reviewing More Emails Related to Clinton Case," *Roll Call*, October 28, 2016, https://www.rollcall.com/news/politics/fbi-re-open-clinton-email-investigation.

51   **"Hillary Clinton is guilty"**   "Trump: 'Now It's Up to the American People to Deliver Justice,'" CNN, November 6, 2016, https://www.cnn.com/2016/11/06/politics/trump-now-its-up-to-the-american-people-to-deliver-justice/index.html.

52   **"IMPOSSIBLE"**   "'It's Not a Complicated or Improvised Process': How It's Possible to Examine 650,000 Emails in 8 days," *Business Insider*, November 7, 2016, https://www.businessinsider.com/how-did-fbi-go-through-650000-clinton-emails-in-8-days-2016-11.

52   **"Six hundred fifty thousand new emails"**   "Trump: 'You Can't Review 650,000 New Emails in 8 Days,'" *Business Insider*, November 7, 2016, https://www.business insider.com/donald-trump-hillary-clinton-fbi-james-comey-650000-politics-2016-11.

## Chapter 4: Espionage to Sabotage

53   **Designated a "prohibited place"**   "Contact," General Intelligence and Security Service, Ministry of the Interior and Kingdom Relations, https://english.aivd.nl/contact.

56   **Beat the Russians at their own game**   "Dutch Agencies Provide Crucial Intel about Russia's Interference in US-Elections," *de Volkskrant*, January 25, 2018, https://www.volkskrant.nl/wetenschap/dutch-agencies-provide-crucial-intel-about-russia-s-interference-in-us-elections~b4f8111b/.

57   **"Hand-to-hand combat"**   "New Details Emerge about 2014 Russian Hack of the State Department: It Was 'Hand to Hand Combat,'" *Washington Post*, April 3, 2017, https://www.washingtonpost.com/world/national-security/new-details-emerge-about-2014-russian-hack-of-the-state-department-it-was-hand-to-hand-combat/2017/04/03/d89168e0-124c-11e7-833c-503e1f6394c9_story.html.

57   **"Activity of concern"**   "State Department Shuts Down Its E-mail System Amid Concerns about Hacking," *Washington Post*, November 16, 2014, https://www.washingtonpost.com/world/national-security/state-department-shuts-down-its-e-mail-system-amid-concerns-about-hacking/2014/11/16/92cf0722-4815-41ca-b602-9bfe8ecdb256_story.html.

57   **Opened an investigation**   "FBI Confirms Investigation of State Department Hacking," Bloomberg News, November 17, 2014, https://www.dailyherald.com/article/20141117/news/141118603.

58   **Access to the unclassified network**   "How the U.S. Thinks Russians Hacked the White House," CNN, April 8, 2015, https://www.cnn.com/2015/04/07/politics/how-russians-hacked-the-wh/index.html.

58   **The Dutch . . . picking up the phone**   "Dutch Agencies," *de Volkskrant*.

59   **FBI cyber agent**   "The Perfect Weapon: How Russian Cyberpower Invaded the U.S.," *New York Times*, December 13, 2016, https://www.nytimes.com/2016/12/13/us/politics/russia-hack-election-dnc.html.

59   **AIVD . . . notified the United States**   "Dutch Agencies," *de Volkskrant*.

59 **The in-house help desk** "The Perfect Weapon," *New York Times.*

60 **Only a cursory search** "The Perfect Weapon," *New York Times.*

60 **"I did not return his calls"** "The Perfect Weapon," *New York Times.*

60 **"Calling home"** "The Perfect Weapon," *New York Times.*

60 **John Podesta's Gmail account** "The Perfect Weapon," *New York Times.*

60 **Neither group of Russian hackers** "The Perfect Weapon," *New York Times.*

61 **A packed conference room** "Inside Story: How Russians Hacked the Democrats' Emails," Associated Press, November 4, 2017, https://www.apnews.com/dea73efc0159 4839957c3c9a6c962b8a.

61 **"Don't even talk to your dog"** "Inside Story," Associated Press.

61 **"Okay with it going to the press"** Mook, discussion.

62 **"Hackers Penetrated DNC"** "Russian Government Hackers Penetrated DNC, Stole Opposition Research on Trump," *Washington Post,* June 14, 2016, https://www.washingtonpost.com/world/national-security/russian-government-hackers-penetrated-dnc-stole-opposition-research-on-trump/2016/06/14/cf006cb4-316e-11e6-8ff7-7b6c1998b7a0_story.html.

62 **Opened fire at Pulse** "Orlando Shooting: 49 Killed, Shooter Pledged ISIS Allegiance," CNN, June 13, 2016, https://www.cnn.com/2016/06/12/us/orlando-nightclub-shooting /index.html.

63 **A WordPress blog post** "Guccifer's 2.0 DNC's Servers Hacked by a Lone Hacker," https://guccifer2.wordpress.com/2016/06/15/dnc/.

63 **Stolen material to WikiLeaks** "'Lone Hacker' Claims Responsibility for Cyber Attack on Democrats," Reuters, June 16, 2016, https://www.nbcnews.com/tech/tech-news /lone-hacker-claims-responsibility-cyber-attack-democrats-n593491.

63 **Tie . . . to the GRU hacker group** *United States v. Netyksho et al.*, US District Court for the District of Columbia, July 12, 2018, https://www.justice.gov/file/1080281/download.

63 **"Steal information"** Interview with former intelligence officer, July 11, 2018.

64 **Opposition research file** "A Chaotic Whodunnit Follows the DNC's Trump Research Hack," *Wired,* June 15, 2016, https://www.wired.com/2016/06/chaotic-whodunnit-follows-dncs-trump-research-hack/.

64 **"Hillary Leaks series"** "WikiLeaks Releases Thousands of Documents about Clinton and Internal Deliberations," *Washington Post,* July 22, 2016, https://www.washingtonpost .com/news/post-politics/wp/2016/07/22/on-eve-of-democratic-convention-wikileaks-releases-thousands-of-documents-about-clinton-the-campaign-and-internal-deliberations/.

65 **"Damn liar" and "particularly scummy"** "Emails Offer Insights into Wasserman Schultz at DNC," *Sun Sentinel,* July 24, 2016, https://www.sun-sentinel.com/news /politics/sfl-emails-offer-insights-into-wasserman-schultz-at-dnc-20160724-story.html.

65 **Wasserman Schultz to resign** "Debbie Wasserman Schultz to Resign D.N.C. Post," July 24, 2016, *New York Times,* https://www.nytimes.com/2016/07/25/us/politics /debbie-wasserman-schultz-dnc-wikileaks-emails.html.

65    **Clinton's terrible instincts**   "18 Revelations from Wikileaks' Hacked Clinton Emails," BBC News, October 27, 2016, https://www.bbc.com/news/world-us-canada-37639370.

65    **"Russia, if you're listening"**   "Donald Trump Calls on Russia to Find Hillary Clinton's Missing Emails," *Vox*, July 27, 2016, https://www.vox.com/2016/7/27/12297304/donald-trump-russia-hack-hillary-clinton-email-dnc.

65    **"A national security issue"**   "Donald Trump Calls on Russia," *Vox*.

66    **"It could also be China"**   "Some of the People Trump Has Blamed for Russia's 2016 Election Hack," *Atlantic*, July 18, 2018, https://www.theatlantic.com/international/archive/2018/07/trump-russia-hack/565445/.

66    **"You don't know who broke in"**   "First Presidential Debate," CNN, September 26, 2016, http://www.cnn.com/TRANSCRIPTS/1609/26/se.01.html.

## Chapter 5: Crossfire

67    **"Incredibly stupid ideas"**   Matt Tait (former analyst with GCHQ), in discussion with the author, July 28, 2018.

68    **Flynn was a senior adviser**   "Michael Flynn, the Retired General on Donald Trump's VP Shortlist, Explained," *Vox*, July 9, 2016, https://www.vox.com/2016/7/9/12129202/michael-flynn-vice-president-donald-trump.

68    **Five groups of hackers**   "GOP Operative Sought Clinton Emails From Hackers, Implied a Connection to Flynn," *Wall Street Journal*, June 29, 2017, https://www.wsj.com/articles/gop-operative-sought-clinton-emails-from-hackers-implied-a-connection-to-flynn-1498770851.

72    **Accidentally received an email**   "The Time I Got Recruited to Collude with the Russians," *Lawfare*, June 30, 2017, https://www.lawfareblog.com/time-i-got-recruited-collude-russians.

72    **Smith . . . killed himself**   "GOP Activist Who Sought Hillary Clinton Emails Killed Himself," *Wall Street Journal*, July 14, 2017, https://www.wsj.com/articles/gop-activist-who-sought-clinton-emails-killed-self-1500002994.

72    **Left behind a suicide note**   "Peter W. Smith's Final Day: 'It seemed like he had a lot on his mind,'" *Chicago Tribune*, July 14, 2017, http://www.chicagotribune.com/news/local/politics/ct-peter-w-smith-death-met-0716-20170714-story.html.

74    **Alexander Downer**   "How the Russia Inquiry Began: A Campaign Aide, Drinks and Talk of Political Dirt," *New York Times*, December 20, 2017, https://www.nytimes.com/2017/12/30/us/politics/how-fbi-russia-investigation-began-george-papadopoulos.html.

74    **Aussies were curious**   "Downer, Papadopoulos, Gin and the File," Australian Associated Press, September 12, 2018, https://www.sbs.com.au/news/downer-papadopoulos-gin-and-the-file.

75    **A sinister motive**   "Downer, Papadopoulos," Australian Associated Press. "How the Russia Inquiry Began," *New York Times*.

75    **A meeting . . . with Joseph Mifsud**   "How the Russia Inquiry Began," *New York Times*.

75   **Shrouded in secrecy**   "How We Got Here: A Timeline of Events Leading Up to the Charges," *New York Times*, October 30, 2017, https://www.nytimes.com/2017/10/30/us/politics/timeline-charges-special-counsel-mueller.html.

76   **Notify their US counterparts**   "Alexander Downer's Secret Meeting with FBI Led to Trump-Russia Inquiry—Report," *Guardian*, May 16, 2018, https://www.theguardian.com/us-news/2018/may/17/alexander-downers-secret-meeting-with-fbi-led-to-trump-russia-inquiry-report.

77   **"What to make of these four"**   Interview with former official, July 12, 2018.

77   **Russian state oil company Gazprom**   "Trump's New Russia Adviser Has Deep Ties to Kremlin's Gazprom," Bloomberg, March 30, 2016, https://www.bloomberg.com/news/articles/2016-03-30/trump-russia-adviser-carter-page-interview.

77   **A useful "idiot"**   "Russian Spies Tried to Recruit Carter Page Before He Advised Trump," *New York Times*, April 4, 2017, https://www.nytimes.com/2017/04/04/us/politics/carter-page-trump-russia.html.

77   **"Impeded potential progress"**   "Trump Adviser's Visit to Moscow Got the F.B.I.'s Attention," *New York Times*, April 19, 2017, https://www.nytimes.com/2017/04/19/us/politics/carter-page-russia-trump.html.

78   **"Sort of a screwed-up dude"**   Interview with former official, July 12, 2018.

78   **In Republican political circles**   "Paul Manafort, Donald Trump's Top Adviser, and His Ties to Pro-Russian Politicians in Ukraine," PolitiFact, May 2, 2016, https://www.politifact.com/global-news/article/2016/may/02/paul-manafort-donald-trumps-top-adviser-and-his-ti/.

78   **Governments widely deemed repressive**   "Paul Manafort," PolitiFact.

78   **Subject of FBI investigation and surveillance**   "Exclusive: US Government Wiretapped Former Trump Campaign Chairman," CNN, September 19, 2017, https://edition.cnn.com/2017/09/18/politics/paul-manafort-government-wiretapped-fisa-russians/.

78   **Stepped down from the campaign**   "Paul Manafort Resigns from Trump Campaign," *Politico*, August 19, 2016, https://www.politico.com/story/2016/08/paul-manafort-resigns-from-trump-campaign-227197.

78   **Flynn Intel Group**   "Michael Flynn Was Paid to Represent Turkey's Interests During Trump Campaign," *New York Times*, March 10, 2017, https://www.nytimes.com/2017/03/10/us/politics/michael-flynn-turkey.html.

78   **The Kremlin-backed television network RT**   "How Michael Flynn's Disdain for Limits Led to a Legal Quagmire," *New York Times*, June 18, 2017, https://www.nytimes.com/2017/06/18/us/politics/michael-flynn-intel-group-trump.html.

79   **Investigation by the Department of Defense**   "Pentagon Inquiry Seeks to Learn if Flynn Hid Foreign Payment," *New York Times*, April 27, 2017, https://www.nytimes.com/2017/04/27/us/politics/michael-flynn-trump-investigation-defense-department.html.

79   **Harry Reid wrote a letter to James Comey**   "Harry Reid's Letter to James Comey," *New York Times*, August 29, 2016, https://www.nytimes.com/interactive/2016/08/29/us/politics/document-Reid-Letter-to-Comey.html.

80 **Accusing Comey of breaking the law** "Harry Reid's Incendiary Claim about 'Coordination' between Donald Trump and Russia," *Washington Post*, October 31, 2016, https://www.washingtonpost.com/news/the-fix/wp/2016/10/31/harry-reid-just-made-a-huge-incendiary-evidence-free-claim-about-trump-and-russia/.

80 **Glenn Simpson of Fusion GPS** David Corn and Michael Isikoff, *Russian Roulette: The Inside Story of Putin's War on America and the Election of Donald Trump* (New York: Twelve, 2018), 281.

80 *Mother Jones* **article** "A Veteran Spy Has Given the FBI Information Alleging a Russian Operation to Cultivate Donald Trump," *Mother Jones*, October 31, 2016, https://www.motherjones.com/politics/2016/10/veteran-spy-gave-fbi-info-alleging-russian-operation-cultivate-donald-trump/.

81 **Article in the** *New York Times* "Investigating Donald Trump, F.B.I. Sees No Clear Link to Russia," *New York Times*, October 31, 2016, https://www.nytimes.com/2016 /11/01/us/politics/fbi-russia-election-donald-trump.html.

81 **"To maintain success"** Interview with former FBI special agent, August 24, 2018.

81 **"With the Trump campaign investigation"** Comey, discussion.

## Chapter 6: Collusion

83 **"Impose costs on an adversary"** Interview with former Obama administration official, January 7, 2019.

83 **Executive order imposing economic sanctions** "Taking Additional Steps to Address the National Emergency with Respect to Significant Malicious Cyber-Enabled Activities," Executive Order 13757 of December 28, 2016, *Federal Register*, January 3, 2017, https://www.treasury.gov/resource-center/sanctions/Programs/Documents/cyber2_eo.pdf.

83 **Suspected Russian intelligence operatives** "Obama Strikes Back at Russia for Election Hacking," *New York Times*, December 29, 2016, https://www.nytimes.com /2016/12/29/us/politics/russia-election-hacking-sanctions.html.

83 **One of the most serious diplomatic confrontations** "U.S. Sanctions Russia over Election Hacking; Moscow Threatens to Retaliate," *Wall Street Journal*, December 29, 2016, https://www.wsj.com/articles/u-s-punishes-russia-over-election-hacking-with-sanctions-1483039178.

84 **Obama team readied itself** Interview with former Obama administration official, July 19, 2018.

84 **"You eject our spies"** Interview with former Obama administration official, July 19, 2018.

84 **"Official statements, countermeasures"** "Kremlin Says Russia Plans Retaliation Following New U.S. Sanctions," *Wall Street Journal*, December 29, 2016, https://www.wsj .com/articles/kremlin-criticizes-new-u-s-sanctions-1483046159.

84 **"The principle of reciprocity"** "U.S. Sanctions Russia," *Wall Street Journal*, https://www.wsj.com/articles/u-s-punishes-russia-over-election-hacking-with-sanctions-1483039178.

84    **"Not going to downgrade ourselves"**    "Vladimir Putin Won't Expel U.S.
Diplomats as Russian Foreign Minister Urged," *New York Times*, December 30, 2016,
https://www.nytimes.com/2016/12/30/world/europe/russia-diplomats-us-hacking.html.

85    **Senior member of the Trump transition team**    *United States v. Flynn*, US District
Court for the District of Columbia, December 1, 2017, https://www.justice.gov/file
/1015126/download.

85    **A column by David Ignatius**    "Why Did Obama Dawdle on Russia's Hacking?"
*Washington Post*, January 12, 2017, https://www.washingtonpost.com/opinions
/why-did-obama-dawdle-on-russias-hacking/2017/01/12/75f878a0-d90c-11e6-9a36-
1d296534b31e_story.html.

85    **Legal experts debated**    "Did Michael Flynn Just Admit to Violating the
Logan Act? And What Is the Logan Act?" *Washington Post*, December 1, 2017,
https://www.washingtonpost.com/news/the-fix/wp/2016/07/28/democrats-think-
donald-trump-just-violated-the-logan-act-what-is-that/.

85    **Flynn called Kislyak**    "Flynn, Kushner Targeted Several States in Failed U.N.
Lobbying: Diplomats," Reuters, December 1, 2017, https://www.reuters.com/article
/us-usa-trump-russia-un/flynn-kushner-targeted-several-states-in-failed-u-n-lobbying-
diplomats-idUSKBN1DW015.

86    **"We protect our intelligence sources."**    Interview with former official, August 9, 2018.

86    **CBS's *Face the Nation***    "Pence: I Knew Flynn Lied to Me about Russian Contacts When
He Was Fired," *Face the Nation*, December 22, 2017, https://www.cbsnews.com/news
/pence-i-knew-flynn-lied-to-me-about-russian-contacts-when-he-was-fired/.

87    **"We were like, wait a minute"**    Interview with former Justice Department official,
August 2, 2018.

87    **The Logan Act**    "Logan Act Lingers for Others in Russia Probe, as All Eyes Look Up
the Trump Ladder," NPR, February 13, 2017, https://www.npr.org/2017/02/14/515279336
/what-is-the-logan-act-and-why-does-it-matter.

88    **Up to three years in prison**    18 U.S. Code § 953, "Private Correspondence
with Foreign Governments," Legal Information Institute, Cornell Law School,
https://www.law.cornell.edu/uscode/text/18/953.

89    **Appreciated the sentiment**    Comey, discussion.

90    **A director could be fired**    "Why President Clinton Fired Then-FBI Director
William Sessions in July 1993," ABC News, May 10, 2017, https://abcnews.go.com
/Politics/president-clinton-fired-fbi-director-william-sessions-july/story?id=47323746.

90    **Felt the most comfortable about**    Interview with former official, July 6, 2018.

91    **The FBI had yet to discover**    "Intelligence Official: Transcripts of Flynn's Calls Don't
Show Criminal Wrongdoing," NPR, February 15, 2017, https://www.npr.org/sections
/thetwo-way/2017/02/15/515437291/intelligence-official-transcripts-of-flynns-calls-dont-
show-criminal-wrongdoing.

91    **"With all the chaos"**    Comey, discussion.

92   **A last-ditch effort**   Comey, discussion.

95   **"Why do I care"**   Comey, discussion.

## Chapter 7: Collision

96   **Sally Yates telephoned**   "Full Transcript: Sally Yates and James Clapper Testify on Russian Election Interference," *Washington Post*, May 8, 2017, https://www.washington post.com/news/post-politics/wp/2017/05/08/full-transcript-sally-yates-and-james-clapper-testify-on-russian-election-interference/.

101   **The continued confidence**   "Exclusive: In Final Interview, Defiant Flynn Insists He Crossed No Lines, Leakers Must Be Prosecuted," *Daily Caller*, February 14, 2017, https://dailycaller.com/2017/02/14/ exclusive-defiant-flynn-insists-he-crossed-no-lines-leakers-must-be-prosecuted/.

101   **"Criminal" media leaks**   "Exclusive," *Daily Caller*.

102   **Flynn had remained on the job**   "How the White House Explains Waiting 18 Days to Fire Michael Flynn," *New York Times*, May 9, 2017, https://www.nytimes .com/2017/05/09/us/politics/michael-flynn-russia.html.

102   **"I just want to talk to Jim"**   Comey, *A Higher Loyalty,* 252.

103   **The *Times* had overstated**   "FBI Refused White House Request to Knock Down Recent Trump-Russia Stories," CNN, February 24, 2017, www.cnn.com/2017/02/23 /politics/fbi-refused-white-house-request-to-knock-down-recent-trump-russia-stories /index.html.

105   **Trump Tower wiretap claims**   "Birth of a Conspiracy Theory: How Trump's Wiretap Claim Got Started," CNN, March 6, 2017, https://money.cnn.com/2017/03/06/media /mark-levin-joel-pollak-breitbart-trump-obama/index.html.

106   **Hold up the confirmation**   "Senate Judiciary Chairman: No Deputy AG Vote until We Get an FBI Briefing on Russia," *Washington Post*, March 14, 2017, https://www.washingtonpost.com/news/powerpost/wp/2017/03/14/senate-judiciary-chairman-no-deputy-ag-vote-until-we-get-an-fbi-briefing-on-russia/.

107   **"I have been authorized"**   "Full Transcript: FBI Director James Comey Testifies on Russian Interference in 2016 Election," *Washington Post*, March 20, 2017, www.washingtonpost.com/news/post-politics/wp/2017/03/20/full-transcript-fbi-director-james-comey-testifies-on-russian-interference-in-2016-election/.

108   **Spicer . . . sought to downplay**   "F.B.I. Is Investigating Trump's Russia Ties, Comey Confirms," *New York Times*, March 20, 2017, https://www.nytimes.com/2017/03/20 /us/politics/fbi-investigation-trump-russia-comey.html.

109   **Trump called in an irritated mood**   Comey, discussion.

109   **Carter Page had been the subject of surveillance**   "FBI Obtained FISA Warrant to Monitor Former Trump Adviser Carter Page," *Washington Post*, April 11, 2017, https://www.washingtonpost.com/world/national-security/fbi-obtained-fisa-warrant-to-monitor-former-trump-adviser-carter-page/2017/04/11/620192ea-1e0e-11e7-ad74-3a742a6e93a7_story.html.

110   **"I have been very loyal to you"**   Comey, discussion.

## Chapter 8: "You're Fired"

111 **"Perhaps Trump just ran a great campaign?"** "Trump Says James Comey Was 'Best Thing That Ever Happened' to Hillary Clinton," *Time*, May 3, 2017, http://time.com/4764639/donald-trump-james-comey-hillary-clinton/.

113 **"Intelligence community . . . concluded it was Russia"** "Read the Full testimony of FBI Director James Comey in Which He Discusses Clinton Email Investigation," *Washington Post*, May 3, 2017, https://www.washingtonpost.com/news/post-politics /wp/2017/05/03/read-the-full-testimony-of-fbi-director-james-comey-in-which-he-discusses-clinton-email-investigation/.

114 **"Sally Yates made the fake media extremely unhappy today"** Donald J. Trump (@realDonaldTrump), Twitter, May 8, 2017, https://twitter.com/realdonaldtrump /status/861713233786404864.

115 **"Why doesn't the media report on this?"** Donald J. Trump (@realDonaldTrump), Twitter, May 8, 2017, https://twitter.com/realdonaldtrump/status/861715019674910721.

122 **"It is essential that we find new leadership"** "Trump's Letter Firing FBI Director James Comey," CNN, May 10, 2017, https://www.cnn.com/2017/05/09/politics/fbi-james-comey-fired-letter/index.html.

122 **That detail was not necessary** "F.B.I. Official Wrote Secret Memo Fearing Trump Got a Cover Story for Comey Firing," *New York Times*, May 30, 2018, https://www.nytimes.com /2018/05/30/us/politics/rosenstein-trump-comey-firing-mccabe-memo.html.

123 **The White House disputed the claim** "James Comey: John Kelly Called Trump 'Dishonorable' for Firing Me," *Daily Beast*, April 12, 2018, https://www.thedailybeast .com/james-comey-john-kelly-called-trump-dishonorable-for-firing-me.

## Chapter 9: Mueller Time

132 **Whether Trump was a counterintelligence threat** "Former Acting FBI Director: Trump's 'Own Words' Prompted Counterintelligence Investigation," CNN, February 18, 2019, https://www.cnn.com/2019/02/17/politics/mccabe-fbi-investigation-russia-trump /index.html.

132 **A major plot** "U.S. Authorities Brief Media on U.K. Plot," NPR, August 10, 2006, https://www.npr.org/templates/story/story.php?storyId=5634298.

137 **Mueller and his longtime aide . . . took notes** Interview with government official, May 2017.

140 **Sessions . . . would recuse himself** "Attorney General Jeff Sessions Will Recuse Himself from Any Probe Related to 2016 Presidential Campaign," *Washington Post*, March 2, 2017, https://www.washingtonpost.com/powerpost/top-gop-lawmaker-calls-on-sessions-to-recuse-himself-from-russia-investigation/2017/03/02/148c07ac-ff46-11e6-8ebe-6e0dbe4f2bca_story.html.

140 **The attorney general's candor** "Sessions Met with Russian Envoy Twice Last Year, Encounters He Later Did Not Disclose," *Washington Post*, March 1, 2017, https://www.washingtonpost.com/world/national-security/sessions-spoke-twice-with-russian-ambassador-during-trumps-presidential-campaign-justice-officials-say/2017/03/01/77205eda-feac-11e6-99b4-9e613afeb09f_story.html.

141  **Talked about campaign matters**  "Sessions Discussed Trump Campaign-Related Matters with Russian Ambassador, U.S. Intelligence Intercepts Show," *Washington Post*, July 21, 2017, https://www.washingtonpost.com/world/national-security/sessions-discussed-trump-campaign-related-matters-with-russian-ambassador-us-intelligence-intercepts-show/2017/07/21/3e704692-6e44-11e7-9c15-177740635e83_story.html.

141  **Russia investigation was on Trump's mind**  "F.B.I. Official Wrote Secret Memo," *New York Times*.

143  **"Countless members of the FBI"**  "Huckabee Sanders Stands By Claim FBI ' Rank and File' Lost Faith in Comey," *Hill*, May 11, 2017, https://thehill.com/homenews/administration/332998-huckabee-sanders-stands-by-claim-fbi-rank-and-file-lost-faith-in.

144  **Three years of these surveys**  "F.B.I. Agents Supported Comey, Surveys Show, Weakening Trump's Claim of Turmoil," *New York Times*, August 16, 2017, https://www.nytimes.com/2017/08/16/us/politics/comey-fbi-agents-confidence-survey.html.

145  **Relieved the "great pressure"**  "Trump Told Russians That Firing 'Nut Job' Comey Eased Pressure From Investigation," *New York Times*, May 19, 2017, https://www.nytimes.com/2017/05/19/us/politics/trump-russia-comey.html.

145  **Trump . . . asked [Comey] for a pledge of loyalty**  "In a Private Dinner, Trump Demanded Loyalty. Comey Demurred," *New York Times*, May 11, 2017, https://www.nytimes.com/2017/05/11/us/politics/trump-comey-firing.html.

146  **"James Comey better hope there are no 'tapes'"**  Donald J. Trump (@realDonaldTrump), Twitter, May 12, 2017, https://twitter.com/realdonaldtrump/status/863007411132649473.

146  **If there *were* tapes**  Comey, discussion.

147  **Didn't want to go to the media himself**  Comey, *A Higher Loyalty*, 270.

147  **Trump's efforts to shut down the Flynn probe**  "Comey Memo Says Trump Asked Him to End Flynn Investigation," *New York Times*, May 16, 2017, https://www.nytimes.com/2017/05/16/us/politics/james-comey-trump-flynn-russia-investigation.html.

147  **Appointed by a Republican president**  "Obama Signs 2-Year Extension to Mueller's FBI Tenure, CNN, July 26, 2011, http://www.cnn.com/2011/POLITICS/07/26/obama.mueller.term/index.html.

148  **"Rod [Rosenstein] is rightly lauded"**  Interview with former senior Department of Justice official, January 12, 2019.

148  **I'm f*cked**  https://www.thedailybeast.com/mueller-report-trump-said-im-fucked-after-special-counsels-appointment.

## Chapter 10: Witch Hunt

149  **"The single greatest witch hunt"**  Donald J. Trump (@realDonaldTrump), Twitter, May 18, 2017, https://twitter.com/realdonaldtrump/status/865173176854204416.

151  **A wide-reaching mandate**  "Special Counsel Appointed in Russia Probe," CNN, May 18, 2017, https://www.cnn.com/2017/05/17/politics/special-counsel-robert-mueller/index.html.

153    **"The world breaks everyone"**   Ernest Hemingway, *A Farewell to Arms: The Hemingway Library Edition* (New York: Scribner, 2012), 317.

153    **"A man of incorruptible integrity"**   "Hart Senate Office Building," United States Senate, https://www.senate.gov/visiting/common/generic/HartBuilding.htm.

156    **Laid into the president's integrity**   "10 Things We Learned from the James Comey Hearing," CNN, June 8, 2017, https://www.cnn.com/2017/06/08/politics/james-comey-hearing-takeaways/index.html.

156    **Turned over copies of his memos**   "Comey Testimony: Highlights of the Hearing," *New York Times*, June 8, 2017, https://www.nytimes.com/2017/06/08/us/politics/james-comey-testimony-hearing.html.

157    **Across town quoting Bible verses**   "Remarks by President Trump at the Faith and Freedom Coalition's Road to Majority Conference," White House, June 8, 2017, https://www.whitehouse.gov/briefings-statements/remarks-president-trump-faith-freedom-coalitions-road-majority-conference/.

157    **A meeting . . . with a Russian lawyer**   "Trump Team Met with Lawyer Linked to Kremlin during Campaign," *New York Times*, July 8, 2017, https://www.nytimes.com/2017/07/08/us/politics/trump-russia-kushner-manafort.html.

158    **Promised damaging information**   "Trump's Son Met with Russian Lawyer after Being Promised Damaging Information on Clinton," *New York Times*, July 9, 2017, https://www.nytimes.com/2017/07/09/us/politics/trump-russia-kushner-manafort.html.

159    **Trump Jr. published several emails**   Donald Trump Jr. (@DonaldTrumpJr), Twitter, July 11, 2017, https://twitter.com/DonaldJTrumpJr/status/884789418455953413.

159    **A senior Russian official**   "Russian Dirt on Clinton? 'I Love It,' Donald Trump Jr. Said," *New York Times*, July 11, 2017, https://www.nytimes.com/2017/07/11/us/politics/trump-russia-email-clinton.html.

159    **"The greatest Witch Hunt in political history"**   Donald J. Trump (@realDonaldTrump), Twitter, July 12, 2017, https://twitter.com/realDonaldTrump/status/885081181980590084.

160    **Dictated the original misleading statement**   "Trump Dictated Son's Misleading Statement on Meeting with Russian Lawyer," *Washington Post*, July 31, 2017, https://www.washingtonpost.com/politics/trump-dictated-sons-misleading-statement-on-meeting-with-russian-lawyer/2017/07/31/04c94f96-73ae-11e7-8f39-eeb7d3a2d304_story.html.

160    **"Like any father would do"**   *8/1/17: White House Press Briefing*, YouTube, August 1, 2017, https://www.youtube.com/watch?v=494FsviSz50&t=4m01s.

160    **The president had indeed dictated**   "Trump Lawyers Say He 'Dictated' Statement on Trump Tower Meeting, Contradicting Past Denials," CNN, June 2, 2108, https://www.cnn.com/2018/06/02/politics/trump-lawyers-statement-trump-tower-russians/index.html.

160    **The best information available**   "Sanders: 'My Credibility Is Probably Higher Than the Media's,'" *Hill*, June 5, 2018, https://thehill.com/homenews/administration/390813-sanders-my-credibility-is-probably-higher-than-the-medias.

160    **"Credibility . . . higher than the media's"**   "Sanders," *Hill*.

162 **Nevertheless extremely serious**   "Who Is Rick Gates, Manafort's Right-Hand Man and Alleged Partner in Crime?" *Guardian*, October 30, 2017, https://www.theguardian .com/us-news/2017/oct/30/rick-gates-paul-manafort-donald-trump.

162 **"Sorry, but this is years ago"**   Donald J. Trump, @realDonaldTrump, Twitter, October 30, 2017, https://twitter.com/realdonaldtrump/status/925005659569041409.

162 **"For a very short period of time"**   "Trump Says Manafort Was on His Team 'for a Very Short Period,'" MSNBC, August 11, 2017, http://www.msnbc.com /rachel-maddow-show/trump-says-manafort-was-his-team-very-short-period.

163 **Rushed in to distance the president**   "Ex-Trump Campaign Adviser: Papadopoulos Was Just a 'Coffee Boy,'" CNN, October 31, 2017, https://www.cnn.com/2017/10/31/politics /caputo-papadopoulos-coffee-boy-cnntv/index.html.

163 **Flynn had accepted a plea deal**   "Flynn Pleads Guilty to Lying to FBI, Is Cooperating with Mueller," CNN, December 1, 2017, https://www.cnn.com/2017/12/01/politics /michael-flynn-charged/index.html.

163 **Many legal experts believed**   "Flynn Has Pleaded Guilty but Signs Are Mueller's Inquiry Has Bigger Fish to Fry," *Guardian*, December 1, 2017, https://www.theguardian .com/us-news/2017/dec/01/michael-flynn-plea-trump-russia-inquiry-analysis.

163 **"Reputation is in tatters"**   Donald J. Trump (@realDonaldTrump), Twitter, December 3, 2017, https://twitter.com/realdonaldtrump/status/937305615218696193.

## Chapter 11: Deep State

165 **"All warfare is based on deception"**   Sun Tzu, *The Art of War*, trans. Lionel Giles, the Internet Classics Archive, http://classics.mit.edu/Tzu/artwar.html.

165 **"The more sensational the better"**   Donald J. Trump with Tony Schwartz, *Trump: The Art of the Deal* (New York: Ballantine, 2015), 56.

166 **"Burrowed into government"**   "Spicer Doesn't Reject Concept of 'Deep State,'" CNN, March 11, 2017, www.cnn.com/2017/03/10/politics/trump-deep-state-sean-spicer /index.html.

166 **Fox News claimed**   "Fox News's FBI Coup Conspiracy Theory, Explained," *Vox*, December 18, 2017, www.vox.com/policy-and-politics/2017/12/18/16790592 /fox-news-coup.

166 **"Don't have time for that"**   Interview with former senior national security official, August 1, 2018.

167 **"This abstract monolithic creature"**   Mark Zaid (national security attorney), in discussion with the author, February 18, 2019.

168 **"Big events must have big causes"**   David Priess (former CIA officer), in discussion with the author, February 13, 2019.

168 **"The last place I want to be"**   Bernstein, discussion.

168 **"The vast majority of intelligence abuses"**   "'Deep State' Myth Won't Fix Wiretapping Mess," CNN, March 17, 2017, https://www.cnn.com/2017/03/17/opinions /wiretapping-deep-state-myth-naftali-opinion/index.html.

169　**"Coming from his own top aides"**　"Five Myths about the Deep State," *Washington Post*, March 10, 2017, https://www.washingtonpost.com/opinions/five-myths-about-the-deep-state/2017/03/10/ddb09b54-04da-11e7-ad5b-d22680e18d10_story.html.

169　**"There is spin"**　"'Deep State' Myth," CNN.

170　**An incoming message from a source**　"Who Cleared Devin Nunes into the White House?" CNN, March 28, 2017, https://www.cnn.com/2017/03/27/politics/devin-nunes-white-house-donald-trump/index.html.

171　**"Incidental collection" during surveillance**　"Monitoring May Have 'Incidentally' Picked Up Trump Aides, House Member Says," *New York Times*, March 22, 2017, https://www.nytimes.com/2017/03/22/us/politics/devin-nunes-wiretapping-trump.html.

172　**"Incidental collection" is what happens**　"FISA Section 702," Senate Republican Policy Committee, December 20, 2017, https://www.rpc.senate.gov/policy-papers/fisa-section-702.

172　**The president's congressional protector**　"In Washington's Daily Trump Wars, Devin Nunes Becomes a Human Shield," *New York Times*, March 24, 2017, https://www.nytimes.com/2017/03/24/us/politics/paul-manafort-russia-house-intelligence.html.

173　**Unmasked or improperly redacted**　"Monitoring," *New York Times*

173　**"What I have read bothers me"**　"Monitoring," *New York Times*

173　**"A whistleblower type"**　"Ryan: Nunes Source a 'Whistleblower Type,'" *Hill*, March 30, 2017, https://thehill.com/homenews/house/326458-ryan-nunes-source-a-whistleblower-type.

173　**Two officials working at the White House**　"2 White House Officials Helped Give Nunes Intelligence Reports," *New York Times*, March 30, 2017, https://www.nytimes.com/2017/03/30/us/politics/devin-nunes-intelligence-reports.html.

173　**The stunt would cost Nunes**　"Rep. Devin Nunes Steps Away from Russia Investigation amid Ethics Complaints," ABC News, April 6, 2017, https://abcnews.go.com/Politics/rep-devin-nunes-steps-russia-probe/story?id=46620555.

174　**He would resume his role**　"Ethics Committee Clears Intelligence Chairman Devin Nunes," CNN, December 7, 2017, https://www.cnn.com/2017/12/07/politics/ethics-committee-devin-nunes/index.html.

174　**"There were times we really wanted"**　Interview with senior FBI official, January 13, 2019.

174　**A parallel investigation**　"House Republicans Quietly Investigate Perceived Corruption at DOJ, FBI," *Politico*, December 20, 2017, https://www.politico.com/story/2017/12/20/house-republicans-quietly-investigate-doj-fbi-310121.

175　**Certain contents of the draft Nunes memo**　"How the House Intelligence Committee Can Make Nunes' FISA Memo Public," CNN, January 20, 2018, https://www.cnn.com/2018/01/20/politics/house-intelligence-nunes-fisa-memo/index.html.

175　**Might make it easier for him**　"Trump Moves toward Releasing Memo He Hopes Will Undermine Russia Probe," CNN, February 2, 2018, https://www.cnn.com/2018/02/01/politics/nunes-memo-donald-trump/index.html.

176 **Compromise classified information** "'Never any Hesitation': Trump Was Quickly Persuaded to Support Memo's Release," *Washington Post*, February 2, 2018, www.washingtonpost.com/politics/never-any-hesitation-trump-was-quickly-convinced-to-support-memos-release/2018/02/01/b67a0246-076d-11e8-8777-2a059f168dd2_story.html.

176 **The bureau's "grave concerns"** "FBI Statement on HPSCI Memo," FBI National Press Office, January 31, 2018, www.fbi.gov/news/pressrel/press-releases/fbi-statement-on-hpsci-memo.

176 **President Trump signed off** "Disputed GOP-Nunes Memo Released with Trump's Approval," CNN, February 2, 2018, https://www.cnn.com/2018/02/02/politics/republican-intelligence-memo/index.html.

178 **The partisan origins of the Steele dossier** "Read the Disputed Memo Here," CNN, February 3, 2018, https://www.cnn.com/2018/02/02/politics/fbi-nunes-memo-full/index.html.

178 **Seeking to discredit Trump** "Republicans Concede Key FBI 'Footnote' in Carter Page Warrant," *Politico*, February 5, 2018, https://www.politico.com/story/2018/02/05/fbi-footnote-carter-page-warrant-390795.

178 **Over one page in length** https://www.lawfareblog.com/what-make-carter-page-fisa-applications.

178 **"This memo totally vindicates 'Trump'"** Donald J. Trump (@realDonaldTrump), Twitter, February 3, 2018, https://twitter.com/realDonaldTrump/status/959798743842349056.

179 **"What went on belowground"** Rep. Eric Swalwell (D-CA), in discussion with the author, November 27, 2018.

181 **"Numerous properly classified . . . passages"** "Trump Blocks Release of Memo Rebutting Republican Claims," *New York Times*, February 9, 2018, https://www.nytimes.com/2018/02/09/us/politics/trump-blocks-release-of-memo-rebutting-republican-claims.html.

182 **"Failed to uncover any evidence"** "Democratic Intelligence Memo Released with Redactions," CNN, February 24, 2018, https://www.cnn.com/2018/02/24/politics/democratic-memo-house-intelligence-released/index.html.

182 **"I know they were in a tough spot"** Swalwell, discussion.

## Chapter 12: Standard Operating Procedure

183 **Seize control of property occupied by Cohen** "Agents Raid Office of Trump Lawyer Michael Cohen in Connection With Stormy Daniels Payments," *Wall Street Journal*, April 9, 2018, https://www.wsj.com/articles/fbi-raids-trump-lawyers-office-1523306297.

184 **"They broke into the office"** "Transcript of Trump's Comments on FBI Raid of Lawyer's Office, Response to Syria Attack," *Wall Street Journal*, April 9, 2018, https://www.wsj.com/articles/transcript-of-trumps-comments-on-fbi-raid-of-lawyers-office-response-to-syria-attack-1523325012.

186 **Close friends with Trump** "Trump: No Cabinet Post for Rudy Giuliani," CNN, December 9, 2016, https://www.cnn.com/2016/12/09/politics/rudy-giuliani-removes-himself-from-consideration-for-trump-cabinet-post/.

186    **Reimbursed Michael Cohen**   "Giuliani Says Trump Repaid Cohen for Stormy
Daniels Hush Money," *New York Times*, May 2, 2018, https://www.nytimes.com/2018
/05/02/us/politics/trump-michael-cohen-stormy-daniels-giuliani.html.

187    **"A mistake"**   "Giuliani on Contradictions about Trump Tower Meeting Letter:
'I Swear to God, It Was a Mistake,'" *Hill*, June 5, 2018, https://thehill.com/homenews
/administration/390698-giuliani-on-contradicting-story-for-trump-tower-meeting-i-
swear-to.

187    **The president could have actually shot Comey**   "Giuliani to HuffPost: Trump
Could Have 'Shot James Comey' and Not Be Prosecuted," CNN, June 4, 2018,
https://www.cnn.com/2018/06/03/politics/rudy-giuliani-trump-shoot-comey-
impeachment/index.html.

187    **"Big storm troopers coming in"**   "Rudy Giuliani's Revealing Interview with
Sean Hannity, Annotated," *Washington Post*, May 3, 2018, https://www.washington
post.com/news/the-fix/wp/2018/05/03/rudy-giulianis-revealing-interview-with-
sean-hannity-annotated/.

187    **"You don't go into a man's house"**   "Giuliani Defends 'Stormtroopers' Comments
about FBI," CNN, May 18, 2018, https://www.cnn.com/2018/05/18/politics/rudy-giuliani-
stormtroopers-cnntv/index.html.

188    **"Aided and abetted that attack"**   Samantha Vinograd (former National Security
Official), in discussion with the author, December 1, 2018.

188    **"We now call it Spygate!"**   "CNN's Zeleny: When Trump Says 'We Now Call
It Spygate,' He Means His Advisers and Fox Newsers," *Mediaite*, May 23, 2018,
https://www.mediaite.com/tv/cnns-zeleny-when-trump-says-we-now-call-it-spygate-
he-means-his-advisers-and-fox-newsers/.

188    **"One of the biggest political scandals in history!"**   Donald J. Trump
(@realDonaldTrump), Twitter, May 23, 2018.

188    **A "confidential human source"**   "Who Is Stefan A. Halper, the FBI Source Who
Assisted the Russia Investigation?" *Washington Post*, May 21, 2018, https://www.washington
post.com/politics/who-is-stefan-a-halper-the-fbi-source-who-assisted-the-russia-
investigation/2018/05/21/22c46caa-5d42-11e8-9ee3-49d6d4814c4c_story.html.

188    **Testimony from Glenn Simpson**   "Who Is the Trump-Linked Source Who
Led the FBI to Treat the Dossier Seriously," *Washington Post*, January 9, 2018,
https://www.washingtonpost.com/news/politics/wp/2018/01/09/who-is-the-trump-
linked-source-who-led-the-fbi-to-treat-the-dossier-seriously/.

188    **"Inside the Trump organization"**   "Read the Full Transcript of Glenn Simpson's
Senate Testimony," *Washington Post*, https://apps.washingtonpost.com/g/documents
/politics/read-the-full-transcript-of-glenn-simpsons-senate-testimony/2700/.

189    **"All documents referring or relating to the individual"**   "Nunes Sought All
Documents on Person Described as Longtime Intelligence Source," *Washington Post*,
May 9, 2018, https://www.washingtonpost.com/world/national-security/nunes-subpoena-
to-justice-dept-requested-all-documents-about-individual-described-as-longtime-
intelligence-source/2018/05/09/93fbc154-53c2-11e8-9c91-7dab596e8252_story.html.

189 **Kelly sided with DOJ**   "Nunes Sought," *Washington Post.*

189 **"It is hugely disconcerting"**   "About That FBI 'Source,'" *Wall Street Journal,* May 10, 2018, www.wsj.com/articles/about-that-fbi-source-1525992611.

189 **"I mean the Obama administration"**   "Obama's FBI Infiltrated the Trump Campaign with a Spy," *The Rush Limbaugh Show,* May 11, 2018, https://www.rushlimbaugh.com /daily/2018/05/11/obamas-fbi-infiltrated-trump-campaign-spy/.

189 **"Not in the United States"**   "'Like the Sickest Spy Novel Ever': Bongino Blasts Report Comey's FBI Had 'Mole' in Trump Campaign," Fox News, May 11, 2018, http://insider.foxnews.com/2018/05/11/fbi-placed-mole-trump-campaign-2016-report-says-bongino-reacts.

190 **A veteran staffer in Republican administrations**   "White House Orders Broader Access to Files About F.B.I. Informant," July 12, 2018, https://www.nytimes.com /2018/07/12/us/politics/white-house-fbi-informant.html.

190 **"I hereby demand"**   Donald J. Trump (@realDonaldTrump), Twitter, May 20, 2018, https://twitter.com/realdonaldtrump/status/998256454590193665.

191 **Would allow Trump to meddle further**   "Inside the DOJ's Struggle with Trump's Demand for a 'Spygate' Investigation," *Vox,* July 3, 2018, https://www.vox.com/policy-and-politics/2018/7/3/17528648/trump-mueller-horowitz-spygate-investigation-fbi-doj.

191 **Might get Rosenstein fired**   "Trump's Demands Escalate Pressure on Rosenstein to Preserve Justice Dept.'s Independence," *New York Times,* May 21, 2018, https://www .nytimes.com/2018/05/21/us/politics/trump-justice-department-rosenstein.html.

191 **Rosenstein chose a third way**   "Everything You Need to Know about the Potential Bombshell DOJ Inspector General Report," CNN, June 7, 2018, https://www.cnn.com /2018/06/07/politics/inspector-general-report-clinton-donald-trump-comey-mccabe /index.html.

191 **"The FBI did exactly"**   "Devin Nunes Reacts to Trey Gowdy Casting Doubt on 'Spygate,'" *Washington Examiner,* June 3, 2018, https://www.washingtonexaminer.com /news/devin-nunes-reacts-to-trey-gowdy-casting-doubt-on-spygate.

191 **"Mr. Gowdy loves the FBI"**   "Devin Nunes Reacts," *Washington Examiner.* "The No. 1 Reason Trump's 'Spygate' Conspiracy Theory Doesn't Make Sense," *Washington Post,* May 23, 2018, https://www.washingtonpost.com/news/the-fix/wp/2018/05/23/the-no-1-reason-trumps-spygate-conspiracy-theory-doesnt-make-sense/5.

## Chapter 13: "Don't Embarrass the Bureau"

193 **Launching a review of the FBI's actions**   "Justice IG to Launch Review into FBI Handling of Clinton Probe," *USA Today,* January 12, 2017, https://www.usatoday.com /story/news/politics/2017/01/12/justice-ig-launch-review-fbi-handling-clinton-probe /96495584/.

194 **MUELLER REMOVED TOP AGENT IN RUSSIA INQUIRY**   "Mueller Removed Top Agent in Russia Inquiry over Possible Anti-Trump Texts," *New York Times,* December 2, 2017, https://www.nytimes.com/2017/12/02/us/politics/mueller-removed-top-fbi-agent-over-possible-anti-trump-texts.html.

194　**"Trump is a loathsome human"**　*A Review of Various Actions by the Federal Bureau of Investigation and Department of Justice in Advance*, Office of the Inspector General, US Department of Justice, June 2018, https://www.justice.gov/file/1071991/download, 399.

194　**"Just has to win now"**　*A Review of Various Actions*, US Department of Justice, 402

195　**"Tainted (no, very dishonest?)"**　Donald J. Trump (@realDonaldTrump), Twitter, December 3, 2017, https://twitter.com/realdonaldtrump/status/937301085156503552.

195　**"Now it all starts to make sense"**　Donald J. Trump (@realDonaldTrump), Twitter, December 3, 2017, https://twitter.com/realdonaldtrump/status/937314665176207360.

195　**"Given $700,000 for wife's campaign"**　Donald J. Trump (@realDonaldTrump), December 23, 2017, https://twitter.com/realdonaldtrump/status/944665687292817415.

195　**"Everything they could to exonerate Hillary Clinton,"**　"'Take Them Out in Cuffs': Pirro Doubles Down on FBI 'Consigliere' McCabe, Agent Strzok," Fox News, December 17, 2017, http://insider.foxnews.com/2017/12/17/judge-jeanine-pirro-opening-statement-fbi-crime-family-mccabe-strzok-ohr-must-be-fired.

196　**Accused of turning a blind eye**　"Rep. Jim Jordan Is Named in New OSU Sexual Abuse Lawsuit," *Rolling Stone*, July 18, 2018, https://www.rollingstone.com/politics/politics-news/jim-jordan-ohio-state-700578/.

196　**No hard evidence**　https://www.nytimes.com/2019/05/17/us/politics/jim-jordan-sexual-abuse-ohio-state.html.

196　**Victim of dark forces**　"GOP Lawmaker: Top FBI Officials Will Be Subpoenaed," *Politico*, December 16, 2017, https://www.politico.com/story/2017/12/16/fbi-subpoenas-bob-goodlatte-jim-jordan-299578.

197　**"Watergate might have turned out differently"**　John Dean, in discussion with the author, January 4, 2019.

198　**No evidence that this bias**　*A Review of Various Actions*, US Department of Justice, 149

199　**A "disgrace"**　"Gohmert Asks Peter Strzok How He Looked into His 'Wife's Eye' during Affair," CNN, July 12, 2018, https://www.cnn.com/2018/07/12/politics/louie-gohmert-peter-strzok-hearing-affair/index.html.

200　**Look into the personal beliefs**　"Acting Attorney General Whitaker Testifies before House Judiciary Committee," CNN, February 8, 2019, http://transcripts.cnn.com/TRANSCRIPTS/1902/08/ip.01.html.

200　**Strzok was fired**　"FBI Agent Peter Strzok Fired over Anti-Trump Texts," *Washington Post*, August 13, 2018, https://www.washingtonpost.com/world/national-security/fbi-agent-peter-strzok-fired-over-anti-trump-texts/2018/08/13/be98f84c-8e8b-11e8-b769-e3fff17f0689_story.html.

201　**Page had quietly resigned**　"2 F.B.I. Officials, Once Key Advisers to Comey, Leave the Bureau," *New York Times*, May 4, 2018, https://www.nytimes.com/2018/05/04/us/politics/james-baker-lisa-page-fbi.html.

201　**McCabe . . . had also been fired**　"Ex-FBI Deputy Director Andrew McCabe Is Fired—and Fires Back," CNN, March 17, 2018, https://www.cnn.com/2018/03/16/politics/andrew-mccabe-fired/index.html.

202    **"Don't embarrass the bureau"**    Ronald Kessler, *The Bureau: The Secret History of the FBI* (New York: St. Martin's, 2002), 187.

## Chapter 14: Felons and Flippers

208    **The word "guilty" a total of eight times**    "Manafort Convicted on 8 Counts; Mistrial Declared on 10 Others," *Washington Post*, August 21, 2018, https://www.washingtonpost.com/world/national-security/manafort-jury-suggests-it-cannot-come-to-a-consensus-on-a-single-count/2018/08/21/a2478ac0-a559-11e8-a656-943eefab5daf_story.html.

208    **Defrauded the government**    "Paul Manafort Found Guilty on Eight Counts," CNN, August 22, 2018, https://www.cnn.com/2018/08/21/politics/paul-manafort-trial-jury/index.html.

208    **The Philippines, Angola, and Zaire**    "Paul Manafort: How Decades of Serving Dictators Led to Role as Trump's Go-To Guy," *Guardian*, October 30, 2017, https://www.theguardian.com/us-news/2017/oct/30/paul-manafort-profile-donald-trump-dictators.

208    **"Paul Manafort's a good man"**    "Trump Decries Manafort Verdict, Says Mueller Investigation a 'Disgrace,'" CNN, August 21, 2018, https://www.cnn.com/2018/08/21/politics/trump-manafort-cohen-mueller/index.html.

208    **"Where is the collusion?"**    "Trump Decries," CNN.

209    **Manafort . . . signed a plea deal**    "Manafort's Deal Reins In a Pardon's Impact," *Politico*, September 14, 2018, https://www.politico.com/story/2018/09/14/manafort-probe-russia-trump-pardon-825751.

209    **Mueller abruptly terminated it**    "Manafort Lied about Business Dealings, Mueller's Team Believes," *Wall Street Journal*, November 28, 2018, https://www.wsj.com/articles/muellers-team-says-manafort-lied-about-business-dealings-ukraine-contact-1543452110.

209    **Had breached his plea agreement**    "Mueller Ended Plea Agreement Because Manafort Allegedly Lied about Business Dealings: Report," *Hill*, November 28, 2018, https://thehill.com/homenews/news/418825-mueller-ended-plea-agreement-because-manafort-allegedly-lied-about-business.

209    **Had also been double-dealing**    "Manafort's Lawyer Said to Brief Trump Attorneys on What He Told Mueller," *New York Times*, November 27, 2018, https://www.nytimes.com/2018/11/27/us/politics/manafort-lawyer-trump-cooperation.html.

209    **Although he'd pleaded guilty**    *United States v. Papadopoulos*, US District Court for the District of Columbia, October 5, 2017, https://www.justice.gov/file/1007346/download.

210    **Working for Western intelligence agencies**    "Papadopoulos: I'm Willing to Testify Before Congress," *Politico*, September 12, 2018, https://www.politico.com/story/2018/09/12/papadopoulos-congress-testify-816830.

210    **He petitioned the court**    "Mueller Opposes Papadopoulos's Push to Delay Prison Time, Notes 'Inconsistent' Tweets," *Hill*, November 21, 2018, https://thehill.com/policy/national-security/417839-mueller-opposes-papadopoulos-push-to-delay-prison-time-cites.

211 **His own lawyer refuted this claim**  "George Papadopoulos' Late Night with the FBI," *Politico*, December 4, 2017, https://www.politico.com/story/2017/12/04/george-papadopoulos-arrest-fbi-277760.

212 **Flynn's lawyers attempted to convince**  "Michael Flynn Asks Judge for Leniency for Lying to F.B.I.," *New York Times*, December 11, 2018, https://www.nytimes.com /2018/12/11/us/politics/michael-flynn-defense-sentencing-memo.html.

213 **"Knows he should not lie to federal agents"**  "Robert Mueller's Team Says Michael Flynn Knew Better Than to Lie to the FBI," *HuffPost*, December 14, 2018, https://www.huffpost.com/entry/robert-mueller-michael-flynn-lies_n_5c140fafe4b0 5d7e5d81eceb.

213 **"I want to be frank with you"**  "We Were FBI Agents. We Want to Know Why Flynn Lied to the Bureau," *Washington Post*, December 19, 2018, https://www.washingtonpost .com/outlook/2018/12/19/we-were-fbi-agents-we-want-know-why-flynn-lied-bureau/.

213 **"No, Your Honor"**  "Former Top-Ranking Security Official in U.S. Admits Under Withering Questioning That He Knew Lying to the FBI Was Bad," *Slate*, December 18, 2018, https://slate.com/news-and-politics/2018/12/michael-flynn-fbi-no-entrapment.html.

214 **The judge wondered why**  *United States v. Flynn*, US District Court for the District of Columbia, December 18, 2018, https://www.justsecurity.org/wp-content/uploads /2018/12/121818am-USA-v-Michael-Flynn-Sentencing.pdf.

214 **Flynn had been "ambushed"**  "Sarah Sanders Touts False Claim That FBI 'Ambushed' Michael Flynn," *HuffPost*, December 18, 2018, https://www.huffingtonpost.com/entry /sarah-sanders-michael-flynn_us_5c191996e4b08db99058198d.

214 **"Reason to walk that back"**  "White House Spokeswoman Sarah Sanders Won't Say Why Trump Bashes 'Rat' Michael Cohen yet Praises Convicted Liar Michael Flynn," CNBC, December 18, 2018, https://www.cnbc.com/2018/12/18/sanders-hedge-on-why-trump-bashes-michael-cohen-yet-praises-flynn.html.

215 **"You have to adhere to the truth"**  Josh Campbell (@joshscampbell), Twitter, December 19, 2018, https://twitter.com/joshscampbell/status/1075360625851691008.

215 **Disseminate the stolen Democratic emails**  "Roger Stone, the 'Trickster' on Trump's Side, Is Under F.B.I. Scrutiny," *New York Times*, March 21, 2017, https://www.nytimes.com /2017/03/21/us/roger-stone-donald-trump-russia.html.

215 **Jerome Corsi**  "Corsi Provided Early Alert to Stone about WikiLeaks Release, According to Draft Special Counsel Document," Washington Post, November 27, 2018, https://www.washingtonpost.com/politics/corsi-provided-early-alert-to-stone-about-wikileaks-release-according-to-draft-special-counsel-document/2018/11/27/9cb68b06-f28e-11e8-80d0-f7e1948d55f4_story.html.

215 **The *Washington Post* later exposed**  "Trump Associate Roger Stone Reveals New Contact with Russian National During 2016 Campaign," *Washington Post*, June 17, 2018, https://www.washingtonpost.com/politics/trump-associate-roger-stone-reveals-new-contact-with-russian-national-during-2016-campaign/2018/06/17/4a8123c8-6fd0-11e8-bd50-b80389a4e569_story.html.

216  **Roger Stone was indicted**   "Mueller Indicts Roger Stone, Says He Was Coordinating with Trump Officials about WikiLeaks' Stolen Emails," CNN, January 25, 2019, https://www.cnn.com/2019/01/25/politics/roger-stone-arrested/index.html.

216  **Trump himself would balk**   "Trump 'Very Disappointed' by FBI Arrest of Roger Stone; Graham Demands Briefing," NBC News, January 31, 2019, https://www.nbcnews.com/politics/donald-trump/trump-says-he-s-very-disappointed-fbi-s-pre-dawn-n965321.

216  **Unusual grand jury activity**   "How CNN Captured Video of the Roger Stone Raid," CNN, January 15, 2019, https://www.cnn.com/2019/01/25/politics/roger-stone-raid/index.html.

216  **Right-wing trolls on social media**   "Debunking Roger Stone's Anti-CNN Conspiracy Theory," CNN, February 13, 2019, www.cnn.com/2019/02/13/media/roger-stone-cnn-conspiracy-theory/index.html.

216  **Huckabee threw gasoline on the situation**   Alex Kaplan (@AlKapDC), Twitter, January 26, 2019, https://twitter.com/AlKapDC/status/1089296318365908994/photo/1.

217  **Huckabee eventually took down his tweet**   Brian Stelter (@brianstelter), Twitter, January 26, 2019, https://twitter.com/brianstelter/status/1089295414254321664.

217  **Hush money in exchange**   "Michael Cohen Says He Arranged Payments to Women at Trump's Direction," *New York Times*, August 21, 2018, https://www.nytimes.com/2018/08/21/nyregion/michael-cohen-plea-deal-trump.html.

217  **[Cohen] pleaded guilty**   "Michael Cohen," *New York Times*.

217  **"If anyone is looking for a good lawyer"**   Donald J. Trump (@realDonaldTrump), Twitter, August 22, 2018, https://twitter.com/realdonaldtrump/status/1032247043992023040.

218  **"It's called 'flipping'"**   "'Trump Says Longstanding Legal Practice of Flipping 'Almost Ought to Be Illegal,'" CNN, August 23, 2018, https://www.cnn.com/2018/08/23/politics/trump-flipping-outlawed/index.html.

218  **"A 'veritable smorgasbord'"**   "Michael Cohen Gets 3 years, Says Trump's 'Dirty Deeds' Led Him to 'Choose Darkness,'" NBC News, December 12, 2018, https://www.nbcnews.com/news/us-news/michael-cohen-gets-3-years-cases-involving-stormy-daniels-lying-n946956.

218  **Trump's company and Russia**   *United States v. Cohen*, US District Court, Southern District of New York, November 29, 2018, https://int.nyt.com/data/documenthelper/501-michael-cohen-court-transcript/ddd84d2b0f5a3425ebc5/optimized/full.pdf#page=1.

218  **Insisted he had no business dealings with Russia**   "Trump Denies Any Links to Russia: 'No Loans, No Nothing,'" CNBC, Mar016 11, 2017, https://www.cnbc.com/2017/05/11/trump-denies-any-links-to-russia-no-loans-no-nothing.html.

218  **Closer relations between the United States and Russia**   "Cohen Pleads Guilty and Details Trump's Involvement in Moscow Tower Project," *New York Times*, November 29, 2018, https://www.nytimes.com/2018/11/29/nyregion/michael-cohen-trump-russia-mueller.html.

219   **Describing Paul Manafort as "brave"**   "Trump Blasts Cohen as 'Weak Person' for
      Guilty Plea," *Hill*, November 29, 2018, https://thehill.com/homenews/administration
      /418881-trump-blasts-cohen-as-weak-person-for-guilty-plea

219   **Everyone knew about**   "The President's Misleading Statements on Trump Tower
      Moscow:
      A Timeline," *Washington Post*, December 3, 2018 https://www.washingtonpost.com
      /politics/2018/12/03/president-trumps-misleading-statements-trump-tower-moscow-
      timeline/.

220   **Indictment of thirteen Russian nationals**   "Mueller Indicts 13 Russian Nationals
      over 2016 Election Interference," CNN, February 17, 2018, https://www.cnn.com
      /2018/02/16/politics/mueller-russia-indictments-election-interference/index.html.

220   **"To sow discord"**   "Mueller Indicts," CNN.

220   **"Any opportunity to criticize Hillary"**   "Mueller Indicts," CNN.

220   **Covert psychological influence operation**   "What Mueller's Indictment Reveals
      About Russia's Internet Research Agency," *New Yorker*, February 16, 2018,
      https://www.newyorker.com/news/news-desk/what-muellers-indictment-reveals-
      about-russias-internet-research-agency.

220   **Twelve GRU officers charged**   "12 Russians Indicted in Mueller Investigation," CNN,
      July 14, 2018, https://www.cnn.com/2018/07/13/politics/russia-investigation-indictments/
      index.html.

221   **"The only Collusion"**   Donald J. Trump (@realDonaldTrump), Twitter, July 7, 2018,
      https://twitter.com/realdonaldtrump/status/1015697664514674689.

221   **Next to Putin on the global stage**   "Donald Trump in Helsinki Was Terrifying.
      Cancel the Washington Sequel," *USA Today*, July 24, 2018, https://www.usatoday
      .com/story/opinion/2018/07/24/cancel-donald-trump-vladimir-putin-helsinki-
      sequel-column/816245002/.

221   **"Putin says it's not Russia"**   "Trump Sides with Russia against FBI at Helsinki
      Summit," BBC News, July 16, 2018, https://www.bbc.com/news/world-europe-44852812.

## Chapter 15: Taken for Granted

226   **"Establish the rule of law"**   Mark Hertling (retired US Army lieutenant general),
      in discussion with the author, August 3, 2018.

228   **"Extremely stable genius"**   https://www.politico.com/story/2019/05/23/trump-
      stable-genius-1342655.

228   **Facing serious allegations**   "F.B.I. Review of Kavanaugh Was Limited from the
      Start," *New York Times*, October 5, 2018, https://www.nytimes.com/2018/10/05/us
      /politics/trump-kavanaugh-fbi.html.

229   **"I must state that, you, sir"**   "Trump Said Kavanaugh Was 'Proven Innocent.'
      He Wasn't," *Washington Post*, October 9, 2018, https://www.washingtonpost.com
      /politics/2018/10/09/trump-said-kavanaugh-was-proven-innocent-he-wasnt/.

230   **"My generals"**   "Trump's Band of 'My Generals' Is Disbanding," Associated Press,
      December 20, 2018, https://www.apnews.com/e10865b9478744b2acf3923985992e11.

230   **Investigate his own political enemies**   "Trump Wanted to Order Justice Dept. to Prosecute Comey and Clinton," *New York Times*, November 20, 2018, https://www.nytimes.com/2018/11/20/us/politics/president-trump-justice-department.html.

230   **"Distinctly different from any other country"**   Hertling, discussion.

## Chapter 16: Hotwash

232   **The term comes from**   *Safe Schools Newsletter*, US Department of Defense Education Activity, https://www.dodea.edu/Offices/Safety/upload/11_7.pdf.

234   **"Extremely careless"**   "Comey Admits 'Mistakes' in Describing Clinton's 'Really Sloppy' Handling of Classified Info," ABC News, April 15, 2018, https://abcnews.go.com/Politics/comey-admits-mistakes-describing-clintons-sloppy-handling-classified/story?id=54487996.

234   **"An act of disloyalty"**   Benjamin Wittes (cofounder of *Lawfare*), in discussion with the author, July 11, 2018.

234   **"I think Comey was wrong"**   Susan Hennessey (executive editor of *Lawfare*), in discussion with the author, July 10, 2018.

235   **"Different words to describe that"**   "Comey Admits 'Mistakes,'" ABC News.

236   **"It was very unusual"**   Chris Swecker (retired FBI agent), in discussion with the author, July 19, 2018.

239   **A money-laundering machine**   "Trump Foundation Agrees to Dissolve under Court Supervision," CNN, December 18, 2018, https://www.cnn.com/2018/12/18/politics/trump-foundation-dissolve/index.html.

239   **Inaugural committee is under criminal investigation**   "Trump Inauguration Spending Under Criminal Investigation by Federal Prosecutors," *Wall Street Journal*, December 13, 2018, https://www.wsj.com/articles/trump-inauguration-spending-under-criminal-investigation-by-federal-prosecutors-11544736455

239   **Nearly every entity**   "Mounting Legal Threats Surround Trump as Nearly Every Organization He Has Led Is Under Investigation," *Washington Post*, December 15, 2018, https://www.washingtonpost.com/politics/mounting-legal-threats-surround-trump-as-nearly-every-organization-he-has-led-is-under-investigation/2018/12/15/4cfb4482-ffbb-11e8-862a-b6a6f3ce8199_story.html.

239   **Called people . . . "rats"**   "What Does Trump Mean When He Calls Cohen a 'Rat'?" ABC News, December 17, 2018, https://abcnews.go.com/Politics/trump-calls-cohen-rat/story?id=59862349.

239   **Go "rough" on criminal suspects**   "DEA Chief to Agents: Disregard Trump Call to Be Rougher with Suspects," *Politico*, August 1, 2017, https://www.politico.com/story/2017/08/01/dea-chief-email-trump-rough-suspects-241207

239   **Has embraced dictators**   "Trump's Embrace of Dictators Is Creating a Climate That Emboldens All Despots," NBC News, October 9, 2018, https://www.nbcnews.com/think/opinion/trump-s-embrace-dictators-creating-climate-emboldens-all-despots-ncna918126.

239    **"Trump is an authoritarian"**    Wittes, discussion.

239    **"Helps to have the referees on your side"**    Steven Levitsky and Daniel Ziblatt,
       *How Democracies Die* (New York: Crown, 2018), 78.

241    **"Member of the FBI senior leadership team"**    Hennessey, discussion.

## Epilogue

243    **Barr memo**    https://www.wsj.com/articles/trumps-attorney-general-pick-criticized-
       an-aspect-of-mueller-probe-in-memo-to-justice-department-11545275973.

243    **Mueller ended his investigation**    https://www.nytimes.com/2019/03/22/us/politics
       /mueller-report.html.

244    **Barr's principal conclusions**    https://www.washingtonpost.com/context/read-
       attorney-general-barr-s-principal-conclusions-of-the-mueller-report/?noteId=9048a12b-
       2332-4645-a1be-d645db216eb5&questionId=218b8095-c5e3-4eab-9135-4170f5b3e87f&utm
       _term=.a96a4d8e6332.

244    **"Complete and Total EXONERATION"**    https://twitter.com/realdonaldtrump
       /status/1109918388133023744.

244    **Special counsel fired off a letter**    https://www.washingtonpost.com/world/national-
       security/mueller-complained-that-barrs-letter-did-not-capture-context-of-trump-
       probe/2019/04/30/d3c8fdb6-6b7b-11e9-a66d-a82d3f3d96d5_story.html?utm_term=
       .404f02e25d19.

245    **Faced the cameras**    https://www.cnn.com/2019/05/29/politics/robert-mueller-special-
       counsel-investigation/index.html.

245    **Possible obstruction of justice**    https://www.apnews.com/e0d125d737be4a21a81bec3d
       9f1dffd8.

246    **"Spying did occur"**    https://www.cnn.com/2019/04/10/politics/barr-doj-investiation-
       fbi-russia/index.html.

246    **"Not the term I would use"**    https://www.politico.com/story/2019/05/07/wray-fbi-
       spying-trump-campaign-1308520.

246    **"Both stunning and scary"**    https://www.cnn.com/2019/04/10/politics/barr-doj-
       investiation-fbi-russia/index.html.

246    **"A serious red line"**    https://www.cbsnews.com/news/william-barr-interview-full-
       transcript-cbs-this-morning-jan-crawford-exclusive-2019-05-31/.